# THE BODY BEAUTIFUL

# THE BODY BEAUTIFUL

Raymond Flynn

Hodder & Stoughton

Copyright © 1998 by Raymond Flynn

First published in Great Britain in 1998
by Hodder and Stoughton
A division of Hodder Headline PLC

10 9 8 7 6 5 4 3 2 1

*British Library Cataloguing in Publication Data*
Flynn, Raymond
The body beautiful
1. Graham, Robert (Fictitious character) – Fiction
2. Eddathorpe (England: Imaginary place) – Fiction
3. Detective and mystery stories
I. Title
823.9'14 [F]

ISBN 0 340 71223 6

Typeset by
Palimpsest Book Production Limited,
Polmont, Stirlingshire
Printed and bound in Great Britain by
Mackays of Chatham PLC, Chatham, Kent

Hodder and Stoughton
A division of Hodder Headline PLC
338 Euston Road
London NW1 3BH

For
Patrick, Naomi,
Michael & Maria Fhé.

# Chapter One

It was cold, it was dark, it was raining; flaming July. Never mind, the scattering of miserable wrinklies, the odd huddled anorak in a doorway, and the occasional family trudging back to an unwelcoming landlady after a night of semi-live entertainment at *Eddathorpe Rocks!* were none of my affair. Me, I was just an innocent dog-walker, a fugitive from the wet beach and the cutting North Sea breezes, an environmental coward hiding in the back streets.

Besides, I'd got troubles of my own to contend with, and all to do with sex. As a Detective Chief Inspector, I had a pregnant subordinate for a start. Nothing, I would hasten to add, to do with me. All perfectly legitimate, but Mrs Paula Spriggs née Baily, the Eddathorpe DI, was in the club. Once the ooohs and ahhs and the congratulations had died down, we were left with questions about maternity leave, and who, pending the big event, was going to take her place. Decisions, decisions: a certain amount of friction among the potential contenders probably lay ahead.

The other problems were routine, at least from a police point of view. Petty even, hardly worth the cost of powder and shot from the CID. Not so if you were the average female member of the public, or even the average Eddathorpe husband, of course.

Somewhere down there among the usual crop of petty burglars and car thieves we'd recently acquired a phantom flasher, and then, on the principle of success breeding success, he'd been joined by an extremely busy Peeping Tom. Not exactly serious crime, you might have thought, and funny in a way; to your cruder, hooting, thick-skinned, callous copper, that is.

The worst summer for years; wind, rain, piercing cold. Enough, according to George Caunt, the borough detective sergeant, to send the most ambitious of brass monkeys on a trip to the welder's shop, and yet we had one idiot leaping out of dark alleys, and presenting his chopper to women amid cries of *Taka looka that, me duck!* while a second was sneaking around the backs of tunnel-back houses, tripping over dustbins, tangling with washing lines, shiking through windows and generally setting himself up as an all-round pest.

Personally, said George, he thought that the flasher's victims would have needed a magnifying glass in weather like this. Not entirely sensitive to public opinion, isn't George.

Beside me, Joe, my not-altogether-cuddly Lakeland terrier, trotted innocently along, exercising one of his newer skills as if the coupling of his name and activities with those of the late, unlamented Soviet dictator was totally undeserved. Freshly obedience-trained, walking sedately at heel, no lead. It was, as my cynical wife had said on more than one occasion recently, a triumph of hope over experience if ever there was one.

Personally, I was inclined to give him the benefit of the doubt. The Wednesday evenings of late winter and early spring had found us trotting briskly around the local Memorial Hall. *Come Joe, sit Joe, stay Joe!* had been the order of the day, and gradually, very gradually, the junior terrorist had begun to emerge as a reasonably well-trained dog.

Ten two-hour sessions of obedience training, and the slightly fixed, glassy grin on the face of the woman in charge of the class on catching sight of an unregenerate Stalin had changed to the kind of welcome that the Christian offers to the sinner that repents. Or so I was beginning to think. About the genuineness of the repentance. More fool me.

There had, I have to admit, already been the occasional cases of backsliding along the way. C-a-t-s were something of a problem, and he still had this tendency to pause by the doorways of over-noisy pubs with the air of a bad-tempered section sergeant intending to rip up the landlord's liquor licence, and kick his recalcitrant clients out into the street. Favours a quiet, well-behaved clientele does Joe, preferably with packets of prawn-flavoured poised generously in the non-drinkholding hand.

I passed Carey's Supermarket; shopping from eight a.m. to eleven p.m. on Thursdays; crazy but true. They'd finally closed, the checkout girls had vanished, and through the locked glass double doors I could see a couple of middle-aged men in dustcoats sweeping up. Every now and again, a man in a suit reluctantly flourished a bunch of keys to release a dilatory member of staff, earning a standard, largely insincere murmur of, 'Good Night!'

The pubs had already turned out; few street corner groups, no yawping, yelling, fighting or other misconduct tonight. No doubt about it, one shower of rain is worth more than an army of coppers on the streets.

Crossing the road beyond the Royal Standard, one of Eddathorpe's older, rougher pubs, I turned right into a maze of side streets. A couple of hundred yards, another right turn, left briefly, another right and I'd eventually find myself back on the Esplanade, a mere fifty yards above home, a nightcap and bed.

Poet's day tomorrow: early start, early finish, and it was this particular Detective Chief Inspector's weekend off. Both Angie and the infant Laura would be pleased.

The last free weekend, as I recalled it, had been ruined by a call out to a major assault nearly twenty miles away in an Aylfleet pub. No real need for the call out; a case of the uniformed divisional commander bleating for a senior CID officer, just because he was there. Aylfleet as well as Eddathorpe was my responsibility CID-wise, and neither it, nor Superintendent Dorothea Spinks, the Boudicca of the east coast, were on my list of deep and abiding loves.

Time for a vague, unfocussed brood on the subject of one of the bulkier human clouds on my horizon, good old Thea and her over-assertive, self-protecting ways. Mind wandering, dog trotting happily, I drifted homewards at a steady pace. Coat collar up, head down against the drizzle, I was only vaguely aware of another figure moving in the same direction, silhouetted occasionally against the inadequate street lights, some twenty or thirty yards in front on the opposite side of the road.

Approaching the turning, I crossed again and entered a dimly-lit side street of late Victorian semi-detached houses with walls, steps and tiny front gardens. Few, if any, had gates. Some lunatic in the Ministry of Supply had made a clean sweep of gates and iron railings, allegedly to build Spitfires, some fifty-odd years before. A futile gesture, of course. The resultant bits and pieces had all been dumped, and the local strays had been peeing gratefully on the unfortunate householders' nasturtiums ever since.

The street was empty apart from the inevitable double row of parked cars, two wheels on the pavement, and a single, suspicious cat which took one look at my companion prior to taking cover under a conveniently situated set of wheels.

Joe continued to trot along amiably, just as though the proverbial butter wouldn't melt.

'No, Joe. Heel!' Practice makes perfect; I managed to inject, I hoped, the exact degree of authority combined with menace into my voice. Unbending as usual, he ignored me, doing his best to give the impression that thoughts of felicide had never entered his head. His tail, however, lost a fraction of its arrogant curl, and his ears definitely drooped.

4

Happy in the possession of a well-behaved dog, I completely failed to react to what happened next.

'That's the one!' Female voice raised in anger, very close at hand.

'Right then, see how the dirty bastard likes a dose of this!' Male voice, and a bulky figure launched itself from behind a hedge and wall from a height advantage of three or four steps. Innocent pedestrian receives fist in face, followed immediately by an explosion of pain in the eyes. Shocked, I drew a breath, only to take a mind-numbing dose of liquid fire into my mouth and nasal passages. Impossible to breathe!

Muggers!

Blind, heaving, choking, I threw one ineffectual punch before I was slammed into the gutter beneath some massive, beery gorilla whose fingers promptly fastened around my throat. Somewhere on the edge of perception, fighting for air, I could hear a cacophony of what sounded like encouraging feminine squeals. The only thing I could think of: a latter-day version of Bonnie and Clyde.

A split second later, seventy-five pounds worth of dog obedience classes went up in smoke as my Lakeland, beside himself with rage, and keening like a runaway electric saw, launched himself into the fight, homing-in on the target the Border lads love best.

A second series of shrieks, this time of terminal pain, traumatised my left ear, and the fingers uncurled, while the weight across my upper chest and diaphragm was abruptly withdrawn.

'Me Balls! Gerrimoff me frigging *Balls*, you bastard! *Araughh! Araughhhhhhhh!*'

Head exploding, with eyes, nose and throat subjected to the fires of hell, and with ninety-five percent of my remaining energies devoted to drawing one, just one more lung-serrating breath, I nevertheless got the message. In the midst of my own agony I refused to sympathise, but I perfectly understood.

For a hundred yards in any direction a sound more terrible than trumpets, more effective than an air-raid siren, rent the night. Sash windows grated; doors were flung open; voices were raised. Suburbia awake! Stalin had reverted to type.

The girl came in the middle of the afternoon, just after I'd woken up from my umpteenth serial snooze; there was nothing else to do. Twentyish by the look of her, blonde, pretty in an anorexic sort of way; skirt too short for her matchstick legs. Expressions of curiosity and delight mixed with envy transfixed the faces of the three elderly men in the six-bed hospital bay. Unashamedly, they settled down to listen: bugger the radio headsets, this was much more fun!

'Hello,' she said. 'Feeling better now?'

Better: an entirely relative term. I peered at her; only vaguely familiar, red cardigan, white blouse and black skirt. My eyes were still sore and she was fuzzy round the edges. Better than what?

'Hello,' I responded cheerlessly. 'Who are you?'

'Beryl. I'm not supposed to be here, I just sneaked in.'

'That's nice.' The nutter's league of uninvited hospital visitors. Just what I needed right now.

'I came to see Bernie, really. He's had to have four stitches, but he's going to be . . . you know, all right.'

'Bernie,' I muttered. 'The crazy bastard who attacked me, Bernard Cork?'

'He means well.'

The brain began to function at last. 'And you're his ruddy girlfriend, right?'

'No-o.' Then, her voice becoming more assured as she went along, 'No, he lives in the ground-floor flat, but he's none too bright. Are you going to send him to prison?'

'Rampton State Hospital, I should think. Anyway, there's no point in talking to me, it's being investigated by somebody else.'

She sounded tearful, 'I just came to apologise, it was all my fault.'

'I've already heard.'

I had: via a steady procession of visitors, some more compassionate than others. Angela, my wife, accompanied by two-year-old Laura had almost wanted to bring back the rope, while George, my detective sergeant, was inclined to be facetious about the whole thing. Detective Inspector Paula Spriggs, accompanied by her bump, was briskly professional as usual; she'd been hurtfully objective about Bernard Cork's mistake. Something about the poor man trying to be a good citizen, or so she'd said.

Never mind, she'd cheered up the nurses no end; scandalous rumours, whispers about dutiful wives being followed by shameless mistresses started circulating, even before she'd left. Hence the current air of excitement among the other patients: randy Detective Chief Inspector scores again.

'A faceful of pepper, and concussion. Damn near a fractured skull. Was that stuff yours?' I lowered my voice; an overactive interest was being displayed in the two beds opposite, not to mention the only other occupied berth on my left-hand side.

She promptly lowered her own volume to a sibilant hiss, and sat down uninvited halfway down the bed.

'The pepper? From Cary's. I bought it early yesterday evening, on the way to work.'

The conversation stalled. A brooding silence: why should I go around encouraging a woman like this?

'I've seen you before,' she offered. 'I work in the Standard, behind the bar.'

Totally fascinating, but hardly the point. I didn't go in there often, I scarcely recognised her, and I certainly hadn't offered that kind of offence. Maybe she just didn't like coppers; maybe she thought she had the right.

'OK,' I said, finally making the necessary effort. 'Why?'

'I thought I was being stalked.'

'Not by me, you weren't.'

Widespread disappointment all around.

'What did he say?' A quavering voice addressing my neighbour from the opposite side of the room.

'Dunno, squire. I wish he'd speak up.'

I pressed the bell, 'Nurse!'

A click of heels and a Staff Nurse appeared.

'Yes, Mr Graham?' Hospital patients, like prisoners in cell blocks, do not make themselves popular by ringing the bell.

'I need somewhere private, please; I want to get up.'

The staff nurse, mid-thirties, agreeably plump, glanced from me to the girl occupying the far side of my bed. She sniffed.

'Police business,' I said hotly. Liar that I am.

'Mr Collins is coming at four.' It sounded as if my request had just been refused.

'Who's Mr Collins?'

'Our ophthalmic consultant.' She made it sound as if I'd belittled an Archangel. Consultants, I gathered, were close to, if not the rightful occupants of, the heavenly throne.

'Ten minutes,' I bargained.

She glanced at the three elderly, expectant faces in the six-bed bay. She sniffed again.

'All right.' Anything to spoil their fun; all three faces fell.

She led Beryl out of the bay while I assumed a blue, well-washed towelling dressing gown over my hospital pyjamas, and made an uncertain grab for the felt slippers in the locker beside my bed. The application of the best part of a drum of pepper, followed by a sinus-wash and subsequent eye baths every couple of hours, hadn't done all that much for my sense of humour, my balance, or my sight.

Three unsympathetic taxpayers watched me suffer. Serve me right. In my dual role as public servant and hospital entertainer, that nurse should certainly have kept me under restraint. Grunts, snorts and other sub-vocal expressions of disapproval thickened the air as they watched me depart.

Mr Collins or no Mr Collins, short of a full set of chains

8

or a straitjacket, I was shortly going home, and bugger my companions. No, on second thoughts, bugger the entire NHS.

'Go on,' said the nurse, 'you can use the office. Ten minutes, mind.'

Beryl perched herself on the edge of a plastic chair; I looked at the slightly more prestigious post behind the desk, but settled for the other visitor's chair opposite. A man in a shabby robe and an old-fashioned pair of stripey pyjamas conducting an interview; a silly sight already, without my having a stab at playing Colonel Blimp.

'OK,' I said, 'so you came to apologise; now you've apologised, what else?'

A hint of amusement lurked behind her eyes, 'I came to see if you were all right. Honest.'

'And?'

'Not very friendly, are you?'

'Friendly,' I said coldly, 'is something I do when I'm feeling fit and well.'

'Not inclined to do a deal, huh?'

'Deal? You were carrying an offensive weapon, and you apparently persuaded this Bernie character to use it on an innocent passer-by. Grievous Bodily Harm reduced to Actual Bodily Harm, perhaps. And that's if they're feeling generous down at the nick.'

'A pinch or two of pepper,' she said scornfully. 'An offensive weapon? How do you make that out?'

'Dangerous stuff,' I replied feelingly. 'If you and your pal Bernie had been a couple of muggers, d'you think you'd have a defence at crown court by saying that?'

There are times when I'm feeling *really* pompous, when, according to Angie, I'm inclined to go the whole hog. Besides, there are ways and means of dealing with offenders, and this wasn't one of them. What about the *Home Office Codes of Practice?* Cautions, a police witness, tapes? I'd already dropped myself well and truly into the cart.

'I was thinking more about a whatsit; a tit for tat.'

'A quid pro quo?' A minimal feeling of unease began to stir, somewhere deep in my gut. This might not be quite so cut and dried as I'd thought.

'Yeah. After all, a girl gotta right to defend herself, huh?'

'Sure,' I said, sarcasm being the lowest form of wit, 'against rampant dog walkers, for example?'

'That's the point, in'it? Dangerous dog: you leave us alone, we leave you alone. Fair enough?'

A slip of a girl, pulling pints in a seaside pub on the edge of the civilised world, and she ought to have been working as the UN Rep for Saddam Hussain.

'The dog,' I said, still on my high horse, 'was defending his master.'

'And Bernie thought he was defending *me*. Look, mate, I was in a panic, so I had me pepper container handy, OK? I've been followed home once or twice; so have the other girls. Bernie was on the doorstep, just going in. I told him about it, he took me pepper off me and Bob's your uncle.'

'And Fanny's your aunt!' It was out before I knew it; a talent for the totally inappropriate. Oh, well.

This time the hint of amusement broadened into an open grin. 'Trust me to score on the only copper for miles. Never seems to be one around when—'

'You want one,' I finished. 'Thanks.'

'It was nothing personal,' she assured me. 'What about it, then?'

'Tell me about these other girls being followed,' I said evasively. 'Are they all going around intending to maim people, too?'

She did, they were, and in the meantime, however eminent the threatened consultant, Robert Graham was definitely planning on going home.

# Chapter Two

Superintendent Edward Baring QPM, having unburdened himself, rested his elbows on his desk, joined the tips of his fingers together, and stared at the three of us with all the warmth of an old-fashioned hanging judge. Monday morning, nine-fifteen, sunlight streaming through the windows of his elaborately furnished office.

Eddathorpe, which once had an independent Borough police, had amalgamated with the county something like fifty years before. That hadn't stopped Teddy from appropriating the office, the furnishings, and, said his enemies, the manner and sheer bloody-mindedness, of the long-departed chief constable. You could define his whole philosophy in one straightforward statement: over God knows how many square miles of farm and fen, he *was* the law.

Personally, I had come round to Paula's way of thinking; to hell with justice, I was all for the quiet life. It wasn't much of a scandal as police scandals went, but a genuine stuff-the-coppers embarrassment factor was present, nevertheless. Noble dog defends master against raving hooligan is one thing, detective chief inspector's mutt savages have-a-go citizen who then gets prosecuted, was a bit like something else.

Paula, demob-happy, one-month-to-maternity-leave Paula, stirred; she didn't like Teddy's tone. 'I don't think anything of the sort, sir,' she said firmly. 'With respect.'

Teddy, crossed, was unable to detect anything remotely resembling the stuff. Nor, from the flat emphasis of her voice and the angle of her uptilted chin, could I. He opened his mouth to distribute another arctic blast, then, attention diverted by the blonde, summer-tented figure before him, he slowly closed his mouth. Chivalry was not, at least so far as the pretty and the pregnant were concerned, entirely dead.

'Go on.'

'It looks,' murmured Paula, 'as if this girl Beryl Matthews has been genuinely followed. So have a couple of her colleagues from the local pubs. They've been frightened to the extent of wanting to protect themselves.'

'Exactly,' Teddy sounded indignant. 'They should have come to the police in the first place. Pepper in handbags, hah!'

'They didn't feel—'

'That we cared?'

'That we had the resources to help them very much; after all—'

'They thought we'd got better things to do?'

She stopped and stared levelly at him across the desk. Tall, thin, almost emaciated, with a head which always looked too small for his body, and with his cold, slightly protuberant grey eyes, Teddy, despite his virtues, was not the most flexible of men. John Calvin, John Knox, Teddy; there were odd occasions when their opponents did well to watch out.

Paula, however, with her over-emphatic make-up, orange linen dress and wide, derisive grin was no soft touch. Not the type to thank anybody for the award of a second prize.

'Look at it this way; this Bernie character tried to help a girl in trouble; what d'you think the press will make of it? *Handicapped Hero Savaged: Police Take Good Samaritan to Court?*'

That, both Derek and I decided, had torn it. We both knew how much Teddy hated the press. Cowardice in the face of the enemy: we both winced.

'Handicapped?'

I looked at Paula with respect: he'd picked up on the buzz word instead. She'd offered him a way out.

'Bernie Cork has learning difficulties,' she said carelessly, 'but he still manages to hold down a regular job.' A nice additional touch that. Just the thing to appeal to the Evangelistic Right.

'Ah.'

Long reflective pause.

'From a personal point of view,' I said, breaking the silence. 'I'm quite prepared to forgive and forget.'

'Especially,' said Teddy nastily, surfacing from a nightmare in which handicapped heroes were interviewed by hoards of tabloid journalists on the steps of Eddathorpe Magistrates Court, 'when you're the one with the savage dog.'

'Joe was being a hero, too.' I protested, 'according to his lights; but let's be realistic, sir, the thought had occurred.' Say it firmly, say it fast; a quick burst of the honesty-is-the-best-policy stuff.

'I suppose,' said Teddy, striving to be fair, 'that your dog can scarcely be blamed. All circumstances considered, huh?' He made it sound as though he's made every effort to find Joe guilty, and, with the utmost reluctance, he'd finally failed.

'Still,' he lifted his eyes and stared directly into my face. 'It's not exactly the first time, is it?'

'The last time,' I stared right back, 'he brought a murder suspect down.'

I was, I knew, putting it a bit high. The truth is that Joe, seeing an anticipated snack disappearing through a barroom door, had pursued the potential donor, and got tangled up in the fleeing suspect's legs. Packets of crisps rather than altruism tend to motivate that dog.

Teddy almost smiled. Contrary bugger; his lips turn downwards whenever he's amused.

'Handicapped, you say?'

Paula nodded.

'All right; official police caution as to future conduct for both of them, Derek, wouldn't you say?'

'Definitely, sir. Yes.' The first and only contribution to the proceedings from the other member of the uniformed branch. Pleasant fellow, Chief Inspector Derek Paget; never rocks the boat. Twenty-nine years' service, one to go, and he devotes most of his remaining energies to drawing his salary and playing golf. Can't even say I blame him at his stage of service; I've known an awful lot of old, battered, pre-grass warhorses who've done exactly the same.

'Arrange it, will you?' Gee, it was only Monday and Derek had got a job.

Thought-reader, is Teddy. He still looked happy, which meant that I wasn't getting off scot-free. 'And Bob,' he fixed me with those cold grey eyes. 'I want you to see the Matthews girl and find out the names of all these other young women. No pepper, no knives, no offensive weapons of any kind, all right? Then, if they're at risk, you can liaise with Derek, and he will arrange some extra police attention. Right?'

Two jobs for the chief inspector, and it was still only Monday, and not yet ten o'clock.

Outside, Derek gave a pretty good impression of a man with a major enquiry on his hands.

'Stirred up a bit of a hornet's nest there, didn't you Bob?'

'Oh, I dunno,' I gave him my disingenuous look. 'Look at it this way, a joint police caution from you, a couple of gentle interviews by me, a bit of attention from the night shift and it's back to the quiet life. After all, prevention is better than cure.'

Derek looked uncertain.

Paula grinned and patted her bump, 'Well done, Alfonso,' she said.

'Three daft girls,' said Detective Sergeant George Caunt disgustedly, turning as if to close the nonexistent garden gate behind him as we left. 'She made it sound as if it was an epidemic of crime.'

Howlett Street in daylight; the place where Robert Graham

had come to grief. Most of the houses looked meaner, smaller, shabbier, and in need of a coat of paint, while the steps from which the figure of Bernie had hurled himself into the fray no longer looked particularly steep. Everything, including Beryl Matthews's story, had been cut down to size.

No more pepper, I'd said. Joint appointment with Bernie for a police caution: see our uniformed chief inspector at six o'clock. She'd tried to look contrite, but she couldn't quite avoid a slightly self-satisfied smirk. Sure, she'd replied, we'll be there; he'll be pleased it's over. Tell him as soon as he gets home from work.

And that's not all she was going to tell him. Beryl the fixer; Beryl the prisoner's friend. I could see it written all over her face. We'd come away with two stalkee's addresses, a slight feeling of anticlimax, and I at least, with a distinct sensation of metaphorical egg adhering to my face. I can swear to it; I've never fancied cheeky, skinny girls.

Our second port of call was less than a hundred yards away, bigger gardens, better painted, that was all. Cranbourne Avenue, another grouping of Victorian houses, huddled in a cul-de-sac this time; lots of separate bells.

She didn't open the door until our third ring, 'Hello,' she said, 'I'm Davinia, I suppose you're from the press?'

George, I suspected, after one glance at the cream lace negligee and its ill-concealed upper contents, was inclined towards an instant change of career. This was not your average puller of the Royal Standard pint. Five foot five or six, violet eyes, spectacular figure and dark, carefully arranged hair. Totally wonderful until she opened her mouth: it was not the West Riding that grated; just the superimposed sound of Thora Hird doing posh.

'No,' I admitted regretfully, 'we're from the police.'

'I suppose you've got some sort of identification?' Then, disappointment tinging her voice, 'They were going to send a cameraman, as well.'

I could well believe it. We both produced warrant cards instead.

'Beryl?' she asked; we nodded. 'You'd better come in.'

Her flat consisted of the whole of the rear of the ground floor; the old dining room was now a bedroom and her sitting room had once been the scene of servant-attended family breakfasts. It was now comfortably, if sparsely, furnished with a long, old-fashioned sofa covered in fading chintz, a single, modern armchair, a drop-leaf dining set, and a three-stage bookshelf made of heavy, polished planks divided by varnished bricks. The sideboard was spindly sixties, with peeling paper-covered handles, and some sort of thin wooden veneer.

She didn't possess more than half a dozen books; a vast collection of dolls, soft toys, rabbits, tigers, giraffes, improbably coloured dogs, and occasional ceramic knick-knacks filled the shelves. A portable television and a music centre occupied the corners on either side of the window overlooking the overgrown garden, while the carpet, an elderly Axminster, was surrounded by a deep margin of floorboard, amateurishly stained.

'We're, er, sorry,' said George, 'that we got you up.'

'Oh, you didn't; I was expecting them to take some pics.'

Two pairs of eyes took in further and better particulars of the negligee, the cleavage, the artfully-teased hair, and finally, the elaborate make-up on display. She had not, we now realised, just got out of bed.

'I'm a quarter-finalist now,' she said.

We both looked dumb.

'*Paulie Parkes' Parade?* You know, *Eddathorpe Rocks?*'

'Oh, the *beauty* contest. Congratulations,' said George.

'So they're going to take—'

'Some glamour shots for the local paper, OK?'

We settled ourselves on the sofa, she occupied the armchair and crossed her legs. The cream negligee parted; legs all the way up. We waited, I hope respectfully, while the necessary rearrangements were made. George looked happier than he had all day; grey-haired, married for thirty years, and slyly promoting the fatherly image, he still fancies himself as a roué.

'Davinia—'

'It's not Davinia, actually. I just thought it sounded better, it's Shirley really, Shirley West.'

'Miss West—'

'But Davinia would be nice,' she admitted wistfully, 'if you don't mind, that is.'

'Oh, no,' George was in there like a flash. 'We don't mind a bit.'

'I was thinking of changing West as well,' she said confidingly. 'What do you think?'

'Well,' said George.

'It's my step-father's name really. Total creep is Gordon; he's not been around for years.'

'In that case,' said George, taking his cue, 'change it; something more striking, perhaps.'

'I went to a foster home,' she leaned forward earnestly, 'after me mother died and Gordon buggered off.' The negligee, we both noticed, wasn't all that secure. 'Mr and Mrs Vernwey; what do you think?'

George looked doubtful, 'Sounds like the Welsh lake.'

I could see it coming, hours of aimless chat; confidences being exchanged between the next Miss United Kingdom, and the cuddly, grey-haired gent.

'Your friend Beryl,' I said firmly, 'that's why we came.'

'Friend? I suppose so; we work together. I've not known her long; three or four months, maybe. Since early April when I arrived.'

'She tells me she's been followed home from time to time; you too.'

'Twice.'

'That's all? I got the impression—'

'I've had the tapping at the window, though. I told 'em to fuck off.'

George stirred uncomfortably: a goddess with feet of clay.

'It started about a fortnight ago; I was a bit later than usual leaving work, about twenty to twelve. Footsteps, you know in the street. Whenever I stopped, they stopped; and he sort of huddled into the side. Two nights on the trot, it happened.'

'Description?'

'A man.' She hesitated momentarily, 'Didn't hang around to take photos, or anything.'

'Young, old; short, tall?'

'He was just an outline against the streetlamps, and they're pretty rotten around here. Bulky, I suppose; he never got closer than twenty or thirty yards.'

'Did he follow you all the way from work?'

'Couldn't really tell the first time; I only cottoned-on for the last two or three hundred yards. Second time probably, yes.'

'How can you be sure it wasn't coincidence, or even that it was the same man?'

'Believe me, I *know*.'

Just like Beryl Matthews; one drum of pepper, one detective chief inspector in hospital. She knew too.

'Tell me about the window tapping.'

'Couple of nights later; a week last Friday, I think. Got home, got undressed, and there was this big fat face squashed up against the window.' She gave a perfunctory nod in the direction of the heavy, half-drawn drapes.

'Big and fat?'

'I can't be all that certain, can I? It was all squashed up against the glass. Silly sod.'

'You got undressed in here? Why not in the bedroom?' George sounded surprised.

'The long arctic summers,' she said sarcastically. 'There's a gas fire in here.'

'Then what?'

'I rushed over to the window and bashed my fist against the glass; he shot back like a rocket, I can tell you.'

'Did you call anyone?'

'Nope. Front ground floor's unoccupied, and the upstairs tenants are like the three wise monkeys, believe me.'

'I see. But he came back?'

'Yes.'

'And that's when he tapped?'

'Right: I've kept the curtains drawn, but he's only tapped once since. I rushed over to the window, but he was too quick.'

'Too quick for what?' George again.

'This!' She came smoothly to her feet, walked over to the window and reached behind the right hand curtain. 'Me big bottle of squeegee bleach: up with the sash, an' then he was going to get the special offer, mate!'

Not at all funny. I winced. What is it they say about that stuff: kills ninety-nine percent of all household germs? Pepper, I decided, paled into insignificance beside this.

'This following business,' said George. 'You been carrying anything else?'

'I was,' she said primly refastening her belt before resuming her seat, 'until Beryl made a prat of herself. I've stopped now; seems a bit silly, anyway, looking back.'

'And what were you carrying prior to that?'

'A sort of knife,' she admitted shamefacedly. 'Silly to panic. I realise that now.'

'A sort of knife, eh?'

'Boyfriend gave it to me, back in Barnsley, ages ago. Top right-hand drawer.'

George did the honours; sideboard, top right-hand drawer. Closed, it was long and curved like an old-fashioned cut-throat razor. Pretty, and evil; steel and mother-of-pearl. Just what the well dressed yob would like to be wearing: a genuine six-inch vendetta knife; single edged, with a wicked point and a wavy, meticulously sharpened blade.

'Don't you think . . . ?'

'OK.' Davinia sounded resigned to losing it. 'Silly, just like I said.'

George closed the knife and slipped it into his pocket, 'Want a receipt?'

Instead of replying, she gave him a crooked grin.

George looked from me to the bleach bottle on the windowsill. Household bleach, and in her own home come to that. I shrugged.

'Kitchen's the place for bleach,' I said. 'Or the bathroom. And your door should be locked, and your windows should stay shut. Never mind the Rambo stuff in future; you ought to have reported your prowler to the police.'

'Oh yeah?' She kept the grin. 'And what would you do about it; send a bobby round t'gleg through the window hisself?'

Grossly defamatory: totally unfair. But casting an entirely new light, I suppose, on the activities of your average uniform patrol.

# Chapter Three

'Pykett,' said George, 'Maureen Pykett, now that's more like.'
I knew exactly what he meant. Skinny Beryl was smart and
chippy, the sort to answer back, while Shirley, alias Davinia,
was upmarket stuff. In Royal Standard terms, however, Maureen
definitely belonged.

She was, or had been, a natural blonde, but her hair was
streaking already, and she possessed what can only be described
as a lived-in face. Not ugly, not haggard, but lining, thickening a
bit. The sort of face that inspires a spot of maudlin confidence,
or a saddish chat-up around closing time, after the fourth, or
possibly the fifth, pint. Not unattractive; still a good, even
abundant figure.

The lounge was nearly empty; it wasn't the kind of place
that usually attracted a lot of lunchtime trade. By craning my
neck I could see her serving a small group of overalled men in
the bar, but the green-carpeted, Dralon-seated best room, with
its small, shiny tables was empty apart from ourselves and a
cheaply-dressed elderly couple tucking into a basket meal in the
far corner of the room.

'I remember her now,' I said. 'Didn't recognise the name, but
I've seen her before.'

'Not like the old days,' said George with a glint. 'Before your
time. Topless, every Friday and Saturday night.'

I took a second look through the barroom gap, 'Must have been quite a long time ago.'

George looked almost offended, 'Don't be like that. Advertised in the local paper they did. Topless barmaids and strippers, every Friday night, Saturday night and Sunday lunch. Then they went too far.'

'Got raided?'

'Yep, indecent show. Two of the strippers got fined, but not before they claimed to have done it in front of half the County Council, and most of the CID.'

'My, my,' I said admiringly, 'this thriving metropolis. The sights you've seen.'

'Jealousy gets you nowhere, boss.' He tapped smartly on the bar-top with a fifty-pence piece, 'When you're ready, my love!'

She took a long time coming, but she greeted George effusively when she finally arrived.

'Hello, an' how's me darling Georgie? Long time since you were in this neck of the woods.'

Precisely how long, I wondered. Especially when this particular glade was something less than half a mile from Eddathorpe nick.

''Lo, Maureen. Know Mr Graham, eh?'

'Chief inspector; hasn't visited us more than three or four times since he's been here,' she said. 'Doesn't fancy the low company, perhaps.' Not unfriendly; marginally critical, all the same. She'd marked me down as unsociable, anti-Standard; not intending to fall over herself with enthusiasm for mere rank, I gathered. A long time away from home, but still a trace of an Irish accent somewhere along the line.

I gave her a moderate hello, and ordered two pints of the guest bitter of the month; a high gravity brew with some outlandish name.

'Real ale; filtered through used nappies and genuine army socks,' she said. 'I wouldn't if I were you.'

'Two pints of the local chemicals and E numbers, then,'

amended George hastily. 'You know where you are with those. Got anything to eat?'

'Haman'salad, turkey'an'salad, cheese'an'salad, hot meat pies.'

'I don't suppose—'

She shook her head, 'Don't even think it, but the sandwiches are alright.'

'Round of turkey, round of ham. The landlord isn't going to get rich on you.'

'Old misery-guts? He's hardly shown his face this morning, and a fat chance I care. Wouldn't do this for everybody, mind you,' she said as she served the beer. George paid, and included half of shandy for herself.

'I take it I'm only a witness, then?' She handed over two plates of sandwiches and took an infinitestimal sip of her drink.

'Witness?'

'Sure, I thought at first you might have come to arrest me for carrying a bazooka in me handbag, after what Beryl done.'

'Ah,' I said. 'You've heard.'

'Heard?' A smile flickered somewhere behind her eyes. 'Believe me, mister, there's hardly anybody around here who hasn't heard. And there are some,' she added, 'that want to buy her free drinks.'

'Bernie, too?'

'Not Bernie,' she dropped her voice, 'he's not the sort to provide with drink, poor lamb.'

I raised my eyebrows.

'Harmless, but it's likely to upset the poor creature, so it is.'

'Right. And are you?'

'Am I what?'

'Carrying a bazooka in your handbag?'

'I am not. I'm a big girl now, and I can look after meself.'

George awarded her his big appreciative grin. Girls, women, grandmothers; he loved 'em all. And there weren't many who didn't like George.

She leaned confidentially across the bar; she was wearing a

frilly, low-cut blouse in something that might have been mistaken for pale green silk. We both devoted a polite moment to the chi-rho pendant dangling provocatively between her breasts before we looked away. Better than any advertising campaign to attract clientele to the Royal Standard on those long-lost Friday and Saturday nights.

Her shoulders shifted fractionally, but only for the benefit of George, I would have thought. 'They're a pair of silly young girls,' she said. 'Beryl and that Davinia, or whatever she likes to call herself from time to time.'

'Ah.'

'Her real name's Shirley, you know. Battering her eyelashes, wriggling her backside at the men.'

'Batting,' I said automatically.

'Drink your drink, mister, and listen. I know very well what I mean.'

'Sorry.'

'It was that Davinia's boyfriend's idea, y' know, at the start.'

I was startled, 'The one in Barnsley? Carrying a knife?'

She smiled pityingly at George, 'Are you sure he's a chief inspector?' she asked. 'He doesn't half get things muddled up.'

George, enjoying the moment, loyal to the last, grinned. Then he took a long swig of beer. 'You're even ahead of me, love,' he admitted in the end.

'The Aylfleet boyfriend,' she said. 'The one who persuaded her to join the Paul Pry contest.' She pulled a face, 'The one in the marina with the boat.'

If he was *in* the marina already, what need did he have of a boat? Leave it; just stick to the facts ma'am, such as they were.

'The Paulie Parkes contest,' I said incautiously. 'He used to be on TV.'

'So did *Muffin the Mule*.' Unfair; unless this was intended solely as a criticism of Paulie, the man I'd once loved to switch off. If she was getting personal, however, she'd missed the mark; I wasn't anywhere near as old as that.

'For the benefit of us thickos,' I pleaded, 'just run that past me again.'

She sighed heavily, a very worthwhile exercise, according to George. 'Davinia started in April; just before what you might call the season got underway.'

I liked that. *What you might call the season*, a phrase to make the Eddathorpe Chamber of Commerce cringe.

'She's a great believer in the big bucks, right? Not to worry if they're not in the first flush of their manhood, but fair field to her, anyway; I wouldn't call her a whore.'

How generous: poetic too, in its way.

'Anyway, she had at least two boyfriends in the first five weeks, and now she's met this feller and she thinks she's doing well. Fortyish, as smooth as you like; he lives on this motorboat and spreads his cash.'

'But not the sort of motorboat you'd drive around the ornamental pond,' suggested George.

'Are you going to let me finish, now? This character tells her that there's a big shining future for her out there. Start small with the *Eddathorpe Rocks!* and after that it's onwards and upwards, me dear.'

'Vile seducer meets country maiden; read about that. Think I might have seen the film as well.' Light irony isn't his strong point, not when you're dealing with George.

Maureen Pykett tapped the counter with the flat of her hand, 'Just put your money where your mouth is. Tenners in a pile, right here on the bar, my man!'

'This, er, beauty contest; it's a fix, you reckon?'

'I'm saying nothing, mind you: nothing at all.'

'What's this character's name?'

'Sheppard; Ralph Sheppard.'

'Pronounced Raffe?' Loves small town gossip; fond of taking the Mickey too, is George.

'Not when you come from where I come from, it's not.'

'Ralph,' I said soothingly, joining the non-u pronunciation

team. 'I take it he's got some sort of connection with *Eddathorpe Rocks?*'

Once again she shrugged, 'I wouldn't know.'

No point in shrugging if you're my shape, so I tried my world-weary sigh. 'OK I'll bear it in mind. In the meantime, what about this following business; did you know that Beryl was carrying pepper, and that Davinia had a knife?'

'That's what I said; between them they're a pair of very silly girls.'

'So you didn't feel the need?'

'No.'

'But you've been followed yourself?'

'Not for the first time, it might not even be the last.' She glistened at George. There's no fool like an old fool: he preened.

'Can you, er . . .'

'I live on Alma Street; alone, if you want to know. I usually work lunchtimes, but I sometimes swap with Davinia, right? I've heard footsteps, not too close, mind you, a couple of times. I stopped; he stopped. I went on, and he started again.'

'When was this?'

She treated George to an action replay of the shrug. 'Some-time last week; Tuesday, maybe? An' then I can't exactly say, 'cause I was after replacing her for three or four nights the week before.'

'No description?'

'Too far back, it was just a shape. Some poor damn loser, if you like; no woman, no guts and no sense. Totally harmless; that's what I told 'em. Never hurt a fly.'

'You really believe that?' George looked at her sharply; incredulity tinged his voice.

'Take it or leave it.' Two out of three, now, playing it down. Still, Maureen hadn't purchased pepper; Maureen, hopefully, kept her squeegee bottle in the kitchen, and she had recently given up carrying a knife.

'I'm not saying it's Jack the Ripper, love, but this man could be a nasty piece of work.'

'Ah, come on, now. You're just like them two daft girls; you mean well, but you're putting it far too high. You're peelers; you're supposed to have been around. You want to stand on this side of the bar, watching them fantasising while they're clutching their sticky little pints.

'Two thirds of 'em would like a grope, and darsen't, and now and again you're bound to find one who'll follow a barmaid home. Strictly amateurs, boys; no big deal.'

'I wish I had your confidence,' I said gloomily. 'Potentially—'

'Potentially,' she mocked. 'And in the long run, we're all dead. If you think like that, it surprises me how you ever manage to sleep at night.'

I liked Maureen; stress counsellor to the constabulary; guide, philosopher and friend to passing police. Her version of the message was clear enough; relax, eat your nice sandwich, sup your pint.

The trouble was, she wasn't altogether soothing, not when you took on board the truth and accuracy of part, at least, of what she'd just said.

Sixteen-and-a-half stone of detective chief superintendent was occupying my office chair when I got back. Peter Fairfield, the only man I know with horizontal creases in the legs of his suits. It makes him look like an aging, untidy elephant in need of a quick dry clean.

I wasn't too happy about the fate of my chair, either. A swivel affair with a central, gas-loaded spring pillar for comfort, I doubted if it had been built to accommodate people of his weight. One fidget too many, one fractured gas seal, and boom! the contents of the central tube could soon be climbing skywards at a NASA rate of knots. Not the happiest of post-prandial thoughts.

'Just passing,' he said.

A very old chestnut, and I greeted it with the usual statutory smile. Eddathorpe: nobody ever passed. One road in; one road out: you either intended to come here, or not. And many of those who'd come on purpose regretted it; wind, rain, tatty amusements, terminal boredom, not to mention the rapacious locals, long before their overpriced holiday fortnight was up.

'We-ll,' he smiled in return, deploying his slow, innocent-bumpkin grin. Overdone, I've always thought, but more than a few idiots, inside and outside the force, had taken Peter Fairfield at face value, immediately prior to coming horribly unstuck. 'Thought I'd do the rounds, Robert. Anything to get away from the madhouse for a couple of hours. Paper and meetings; meetings and pushing paper, that's all I ever seem to do. Came out to see the real coppering being done.'

The good, practical policeman unwillingly trapped in the headquarters' administrative maze. My heart bled.

'Nice to see you, sir.'

A touch too much of Uriah Heep? Practical politics, more like. Be nice to the brass, and you might have a chance of sending it smiling on its way; the sooner the better, though. The less welcome it felt, the more likely it was to stick around, dig for the occasional cock-up, and otherwise interfere. Peter Fairfield, when inclined, could interfere at something approaching nine on the Richter scale.

'Hear you've had a bit of a problem, Bob.' Doing the serious voice, I noted. The ribald amusement, the callous disregard for other people's suffering, was being kept decently under wraps.

'It could have been worse.'

'You've sorted out these women and their offensive weapons, huh?'

'In the process, sir; now.'

'Fine, fine; it wouldn't look too good, though, if one of them ended up getting attacked. Any lines of enquiry, so far?'

'Very little, sir. No descriptions worth circulating, but all three victims work at the same pub. Chief Inspector Paget has promised some uniformed attention, and I'm arranging for visits by a couple of DCs.'

'Are these connected to the other incidents?'

'I don't know yet.'

'You don't know a lot, do you?' Dangerously, he shifted in my chair. 'Try one or two of these for size.'

He opened the pink manila folder he'd placed prominently in the centre of my desk, and handed over a sheaf of CRO 74s: the details of conviction and photographs of something more than a dozen men.

'Sir?'

'The buggers have lost 'em.' It was today's cryptic clue. 'Wouldn't pay the idle bastards in brass washers, meself.'

I shuffled through the Criminal Record office forms; rape, attempted rape, grievous bodily harm on female, serious indecent assault ... We were, I gathered, talking sex offenders here. I didn't need to be much of a detective to work that one out. The question of wages due to idle buggers would probably be answered in due course.

'It's a new initiative,' he said with deliberate distaste. 'Liaison between the Probation and After Care Service, and us.'

It figured, Admiral Fairfield was flying signals: enemy in sight! Priests, pastors, ministers, social workers, community workers, probation officers, hostel wardens, and for all I knew, cats' home managers and RSPCA officials, could all fall under his arbitrary ban.

'These can't all be local,' I said, distracting him, carefully keeping any suggestion of panic out of my voice. If this was a selection of home-grown talent, why didn't I know them? Where had I been living for the past two-and-a-half years?

Fairfield sighed, 'They don't necessarily live around the corner,' he said. 'And this is just a selection; all convicted within the Force area, and released within the past five years. Offences involving kids.

'This is just the beginning, Bob. Project Recap, they call it:

trace the present whereabouts of the worst of 'em, then go for the rest. The legislation isn't retrospective, but anybody convicted after the first of September last year has to register their whereabouts, and they go on to a Sexual Offenders' Register.

'The Courts now order it on conviction, and they're all supposed to do it; they're notified on release and given a form, but it's a total disaster at the moment. About fifty percent of the bastards have gone to ground, anyway, and the older offenders don't have to register at all if they were released before the effective date.'

'Oh.'

'Most of these beauties came out of prison,' he indicated the sheaf of photographs and forms, 'before the new legislation came in. They got their dose of tea and sympathy, and buggered off to parts unknown. In the present political climate,' he added grimly, 'if one of 'em reoffends while he's on the loose, we'll still get most of the bad publicity and all of the blame.'

'You mean,' I translated, 'the Probation and After Care Service dealt with them so long as they were on parole. Then they lost touch, and anyway, this initiative is a strictly unofficial thing?'

He looked at me reproachfully; he'd practically been bitten by one of his own. The sound of a CID man being moderate; playing counsel for the defence.

'Depends how you want to put it,' he said.

'Did any of them,' I asked, 'fail to notify a change of address, or clear off while they were actually under supervision?'

'Him,' he said, twitching one of the forms out of my fingers, 'and him'. He snatched at number two.

Two natural-born killers if ever I saw them, both with unshaven faces and mad, light-reflecting eyes. Dramatic, I had to admit; not that police photography counts for much.

Stick a bishop in the cells for twelve hours, feed him the standard microwaved pap, question him, and then put him up before the studio lights next morning, and flash! you've captured an axe murderer staring hopelessly into his prospects of twenty years inside. Especially when you've taken away his shoelaces, and he's trying to keep his trousers up without benefit of belt.

'So,' I said, 'this isn't official, is it? Other than the ones still on parole, the rest are entitled to do what they like?'

'Not if I have anything to do with it.' He bared his teeth suggestively.

It had, I realised, been an unfortunate turn of phrase. Besides, I didn't even disagree with him on the whole; it was just that the redneck presentation was inclined to get my goat. Or, putting it another way, if you're being paid to be a reactionary oppressor, you ought at least to give the impression of being subtle, sensitive and urbane. The *Guardian* would probably have loved Torquemada, if only he'd smiled occasionally and worn a smart blue suit.

'OK,' I said, 'we could come across them locally, but they could be anywhere in the county, right?'

'Anywhere in the country, you mean. But they started off by being our problem, and I'd like to keep track. Everybody sees the pictures, and the uniform inspectors can brief their shifts.'

I stared at the sheaf of forms without enthusiasm; needle in a haystack stuff. Troublesome; unexciting, like eighty-five percent of police routine.

Fairfield rose heavily to his feet, 'Just one more thing, Bob.'

I knew it: the Parthian shot. Not just passing, not routine; he'd come here for something else. Detective chief superintendents do not come chasing half way across the county for the sheer pleasure of playing the man from the Pony Express.

'Yessir?'

'No complaint at this stage; a word to the wise, that's all.'

Like that, was it? The messenger bearing ill tidings, but not the official despatch. I nodded.

'Malcolm Cartwright, he's one of your lads?'

Detective Constable Malcolm Cartwright; Big Malc, and no need for the question, he knew bloody well. A quiet, conscientious man; domestic troubles, and he was never going to climb.

I nodded again; not the moment for the fulsome remark. Time for the name, rank and number only, I decided. I might be a chief inspector, but these were my people, this was my patch. And until further notice there was still only one game in town so far as Headquarters was concerned: them against us.

'A little bird's been telling me,' said Fairfield succinctly. 'Bank loans; debts. Sort him out before he comes a cropper, OK?'

If there was one thing I hated, it was the hole-in-the-corner, sneaking Eddathorpe bird. It twittered, it insinuated, and sometimes it downright lied. Now it had reached as far as the County's laughing factory, penetrating the upper echelons of the CID with its nasty little voice.

For four months out of the twelve, the Eddathorpe locals bowed and scraped, banked their cash and merrily rang their tills. For the remaining eight they had far too little to do, so the culture of gossip flourished. It was their idea of fun, and now they'd extended the season: slander and backbiting all the year round.

Nevertheless, I was relieved; bad news, but it could have been considerably worse. Constable in debt: potential disciplinary offence, but unlikely to go that far in this day and age. Nothing criminal, thank God.

Briefly, I gave a thought to Fairfield's little bird: some local business wheel, or was it strutting around wearing shiny silver buttons on a black barathea suit? Peter was highly unlikely to say.

Assurances, platitudes, my best semi-sincere smile, and he was off. I resumed the vacated seat of power behind my desk and worked out the best way of tackling Malc. Malcolm the overtime hunter, the guy with the kid at boarding school, and the sad, unstable wife. Doing his best, I knew, to keep the child away from the domestic flak. Gloomily, I fiddled with Fairfield's stack of forms; how far was he in debt? Had he, indeed, already gone too far?

Speculation ceased; my eyes focused with a snap. One particular descriptive form, one of the brace of parole-breakers he'd flourished in my face. Never mind the picture: several years old and unfamiliar to me, anyway; never seen him before in my life. Stare instead at the name on the form, and the explanatory note.

Alan Alfred Pykett, CRO, convicted rapist, released nearly twelve months ago from a ten-year sentence. Wanted on warrant for breach of parole conditions, and no current address ...

# Chapter Four

'Don't worry about it,' said Angie dismissively. 'You can't expect to do everything all at once. There are only twenty-four hours in a day.'

She leaned back comfortably, baby in bed, her cup of after-dinner coffee in hand, and smiled. She was right of course. Relax, forget it, sufficient unto the day is the evil thereof, to adopt the well-known Teddy Baring biblical phrase.

I felt uneasy, nevertheless; nobody at home at Alma Street, and, unusually, I hadn't retrieved much of the Maureeen Pykett story from George. Normally a bottomless mine of local information, accurate, semi-accurate, and downright slanderous, this time he'd failed.

Sure, Maureen was something of a local fixture, comparing her with Eddathorpe's usual shifting population of hotel, restaurant and bar workers, that is. She'd been around for years; well, three or four, at least, and no, he'd not meant to give me the impression that their relationship went back far into the mists of time.

The stripper and topless-barmaid scandal had taken place a mere twelve months before I'd arrived in town. So far as George was concerned, he'd always thought she was a single woman; no wedding ring, no form.

She'd originally come from County Mayo, Maureen had told him, twenty-odd years before, aged about eighteen. No contact with her relations for years, he'd gathered: sad life. She might, he added helpfully, following her arrival in England, have had to arrange for somebody to adopt a kid. No husband, no Alan Pykett; not so far as he knew.

I was still, however, uneasy; not many Pyketts, not many parole-breaking rapists either, around. I'd telephoned Head-quarters CID; somebody had dug out Alan Alfred's file, read over the antecedents prepared for crown court; they were nearly eight years old. No wife's name listed: one stark entry; divorced.

It would have been nice to have gone round to the Alma Street address, found her at home, and had this quiet, confidential chat. Did she, had she ever, had a husband named Alan? Had he been to prison? Had he been hanging around lately, and was she as unconcerned about the possibility of her being stalked by a man as she seemed?

'Probably coincidence,' said Angie comfortingly when I told her. 'Deal with it tomorrow; nothing in it; let it wait.' And the more she soothed, the more it niggled. The wifely things I wanted to hear only seemed to make it worse.

Finally, unable to settle down for the evening, I rang the nick. Detective Constables Malcolm Cartwright and Roy Lamb were on the late shift. A reminder of a forthcoming supervisory chat, but first things first.

'Oh,' pause, 'her,' said big Malc when I asked him to visit. 'Lively lass.' Even over the phone I could hear a distinct leer in his voice.

'Know her, do you?'

'Not, er, intimately, boss.' I was relieved to hear it; Malcolm was already subject to enough problems of his own.

'But her reputation has gone before?'

'Naw, not really, I suppose. Puts everything in the shop window though, eh?'

'Take Roy with you,' I said, doing my best to ensure that one detective constable in particular was not going to be in any position to buy, 'and when you ask her, try to deploy some tact.

And by the way, show your faces at the Royal Standard, reassure the female staff and see who's hanging around there, later on.'

'OK.'

Already, I was beginning to regret my impatience, this itch that wouldn't let me put off until tomorrow that which I could do tonight.

'Never satisfied,' said Angie from the depths of her armchair when I put down the phone.

'Better safe than sorry.'

'Ha! Got two minutes for boring old domesticity now, perhaps? I received a letter today.'

'Sorry,' I said absently. 'Who from?'

'The chairman of Governors, Sandridge Junior School; the interview's next week.'

'Well, congratulations: great.' Not entirely sincere, but it sounded all right. At least I had the wit for that.

Once Laura had started to toddle, Angie too had acquired this professional itch. A full-time teacher in a junior school throughout the first phase of our marriage, she'd continued for a while after our bust-up, then, pregnant with Laura, she'd given up her job and followed me to Eddathorpe when I swapped Forces and joined the Eddathorpe elite. That, at least, was the official, slightly sanitised version of events.

The past being another country, or so they say, I was beginning to believe this version myself. Not that it was entirely untrue; just a touch mendacious in the bits it conveniently missed out, especially the GBH I'd committed on her ex-boyfriend, Superintendent Clive Jones, and the exact paternity of our infant, now aged two.

Besides, we'd both, I hoped, come to terms with our troubles. I still loved Angie; I loved Laura too. She was, to all intents and purposes, ours, and nosy, gossiping Eddathorpe, particularly its nosy gossiping coppers, could go and mind their own ...

'I suppose,' I said hesitantly, 'you're sure about all this?'

'Sure about all what?' Angie was reserving her fire.

'Going, er, back to work like this? What about looking after Laura, for example?'

'Come on, Rob; it's a part-time job in a junior school, not the chairmanship of ICI. Job-share; five afternoons a week, and I haven't even got it yet.'

'I know, but—'

'Worried about the child care? OK, so I'm using Val, but she's your ex-girlfriend's relation, not mine.'

Time for an indignant choke: ex-girlfriend, indeed! Straight from Angie's department of dirty tricks, and absolutely untrue. Valerie Todd, child minder, five doors down the road. She was the second (and childless) wife of Richard Todd, Esquire, alias Tricky Dicky, garage owner and local entrepreneur; a largish, but ever-so-slightly-wobbly Eddathorpe wheel.

On my arrival in Eddathorpe, I had become embroiled with the clan Todd. To be strictly accurate, I'd become embroiled in the investigation of the ancient, undetected Alice Draper murder, which involved, among a cast of thousands, Dicky, his brother, their distant connections, and one or two of their hangers-on.

Early in the resurrected enquiry, and living alone in a short-lease wooden shack, I'd met Junoesque Mary, my age, a local councillor and Tricky Dickey's ex-spouse. Pleasant woman, widely admired; except by my wife, that is.

Once Angie arrived in town, the female population had lost no time in recruiting her to their ranks, and serving up the usual Eddathorpe mixture of coffee mornings and malicious feminine tales. And Angie ... Well, Angie was human, and maybe she seized upon my nonexistent affair with Mary as a cobbled-up excuse for her own bit of extramarital fun.

'Mary,' I said, 'was never—'

'OK.' No niggles, no apparent jealousy; she positively beamed.

'Then why on earth did you say that?'

'Thought I'd change the subject, darling. I didn't want to hold another discussion about the pros and cons of working wives.'

'I love you, too.'

'Smashing; does that mean you're going to treat me to an early night?'

There are, I reflected, some contests that men were never meant to win.

The early bird, I collected the usual curling pile of faxes, memos, crime bulletins and CID mail from the pigeonhole in the general office before I climbed the stairs to my office. Playing postie to my juniors; but I wasn't proud.

Eric Forster, the civilian clerk, fat, barely thirty, but acting middle-aged, smiled slyly as I passed him. Nominally photo-copying, I noticed, but always awaiting the opportunity to chat. Well, gossip really, and usually at somebody else's expense.

'Heard about all the excitement last night?' he said.

Having just walked in, it was pretty obvious that I hadn't. Yet another little Eddathorpe birdie dying to be first with the news.

I shook my head; it doesn't do to look too eager when the natives go around wearing that particular knowing look; it boded ill for somebody, somewhere along the line.

'Domestos ended up in casualty; a fist in the face, and a bad ankle, or so they say.'

'Domestos?'

Police Constable Clifford Appleby, big, slow, country-bred and barely twenty-three. I knew him all right, but news of the injury in conjunction with the use of the less-than comp-limentary nickname didn't incline me towards membership of any chattering civvy fan clubs at this particular moment in time.

'Y'must know him.' The sly smile broadened into a conspira-torial grin, 'That new lad, Appleby: they call him Domestos 'cos he's supposed to be thick and strong.'

I stared at him blankly; the old, old stand-by: idle and foolish remarks will be ignored.

'Casualty, you say?'

I watched the grin fade; only practising, but there are times when there's a certain mean pleasure to be derived from doing that. I believe in spreading a little sunshine wherever I can.

'Er, yes; that's right.'

I raised my eyebrows, and waited for the rest of the news.

'Lost a shiker; somewhere down the backs in Howlett Street,' he said, 'apparently.' He paused to ensure that he was getting my undivided attention at last, 'He'd seen this man hanging about, and he didn't like his looks, so pretended to ignore him, and disappeared round the corner to give him a chance, like.' Five out of ten for trying, anyway: making a bid for devious, rather than thick.

'Then, when he came back a couple of minutes later, this feller had disappeared. Dom – Appleby – went round the backs of the houses to check, and he caught this creep at somebody's kitchen window, looking in.

'Anyway, he sneaks up on him in 'is Commando sole size tens, ready to make an arrest, and then just for a joke, he decides to put the shits up this character by leaning over his shoulder and saying, "'Ello, 'ello, 'ello!" before he makes his grab. So he did.'

'And?'

'This bastard whips round, gives him a belt in the mouth, and scrambles over the nearest fence. Clifford Appleby follows, the fence collapses and he sprains an ankle. Tenant reckons we owe her a new fence. It's just like the Keystone Kops.'

'Description?'

'Young; slim, sweater and jeans, collar-length hair. Maybe twenty, he said. It was dark.'

One head, two arms and two legs, but he didn't sound much like Davinia's possessor of the big fat face. On Howlett Street, though, with another policeman entertaining the neighbours, and for the second time in four days.

'I suppose,' said Malc bitterly, 'there's no point in asking you who started all this?'

'Mr Fairfield asked me to talk to you; it's for your own good.'

'That's not what I meant: I'm talking about the grassing bastards who won't keep their noses out of my affairs.'

Me, for example? I tried to put myself in his shoes – head down, peering belligerently at me from under lowered lids, and with his jaw and lower lip thrust forward; the body language said it all. Angry, stubborn, resentful: all the same, domestically and financially he was in a mess. But would I want unsolicited help in similar circumstances? Would I welcome interference from a higher ranking, if well-meaning prat?

'Malc,' I said, trying for friendly, striving ineffectually for a touch of camaraderie, and knowing perfectly well that I was three pips too late, 'we've got to do something; you can't go on like this. From what you've told me so far, you owe nearly nine thousand pounds, plus the mortgage, and what about the cost of keeping Sally at school?'

Sally: for an instant I felt almost like the caring, sharing senior executive. I'd actually remembered his daughter's name.

'Susan,' he said.

Oh God.

'And, if you absolutely have to know, taking into account the mortgage arrears, it's nearer ten.' A supplementary put-down rather than an admission, I gathered.

'How the hell did you manage to get in a mess like this?'

'I didn't exactly *manage* anything, did I? Well, Ginnie had these credit cards, for a start.'

'I take it she doesn't have them now?'

'No; the companies saw to that! Then I took out some loans to cover the debts, and somehow it seemed easier to get another one after that. You know how it is, they just mounted up ...'

I didn't know, but it didn't take a genius to work it out. Virginia, his wife, psychologically unstable; backwards and forwards to hospital whenever her devils struck, and big Malc, clinging desperately to the wreckage of their marriage for several years.

However active the canteen gossip, we only got to hear about the more public events: the rows with the neighbours, her occasional phone calls and visits to the front office counter; the newspaper-filled sandwiches she packed him for lunch when she was feeling particularly cross . . .

'Er, Malc,' I said hesitantly, there was no easy way to put this. 'These additional loans; they're, ah, OK, huh?'

Even as I said it, I felt a certain self-contempt. Oblique to the point of total incomprehensibility. Spit it out you mug!

'OK?' No help there, and serve me right.

'You did declare all your previous debts when you took the new loans out?'

You did not, in other words, commit a criminal deception on the finance houses or the banks by suppressing the existing liabilities? He didn't react: he had another target in mind, and, thankfully, that particular shaft went completely over his head, for the time being, at least.

'They don't care,' his voice was laced with bitter irony. 'They work on a points system: so many points for years of employment, so many for owning the house, and about ten million additional brownies, if you're in the Force. It doesn't matter to them, boss, providing you're not actually bankrupt at the time.'

Again, I could imagine; private enterprise at its best. All the same, we were, thank heavens, only discussing multiple cases of civil debt.

'You've really got to sort it; get everything together and see the Welfare Officer, huh?'

'And what's he going to do, then? Wave a magic wand?'

'He can probably arrange to consolidate the loan at the lowest possible rate of interest for a start, and make sure the repayments are well spread out.'

'Yeah?'

'And,' I said, raising some enthusiasm myself, 'the Force has funds to help out in cases like this. The Police Federation and one of the ACCs have a committee—'

'Charity?'

'Stuff charity,' I said, hoping for the best. 'The funds are there, and you're one of us.'

The lowered eyes slid away from me at last, and the muscles of his face twisted into something that wasn't a grin.

'You'll ring him for me, boss?'

'Yes.'

Silence.

Done and dusted: embarrassment all round, and one of the scummier things you get paid to do.

He rose to go; one of those occasions when people have to shuffle out somehow, and others, with less than armour-plated skin have to stay and watch.

'That woman,' he said, making some sort of exit. 'The one we went to see last night. No answer; we tried the neighbours too. Still nobody at home.'

# Chapter Five

'I don't particularly like this pub,' said George. And that was before we'd even managed to ease ourselves through the brown-stained double doors.

'I thought you liked at least one of the barmaids,' I replied. He rewarded me with what is technically known as an old fashioned look.

Personally, I would have preferred to spend my lunch hour at a better class of watering hole, myself. Cigarette-scarred tables, nicotine-yellow ceilings, and the occasional artistic slash to the chair seats of the hostelry in question does nothing to enhance the flavour of my pint. Still, business before pleasure, if only from time to time.

A lot more people in the bar today; still a bit chilly for the second week in July but a promise, nevertheless, of reluctant sunshine; a change in the weather had brought them out. A squat, thirty-something figure with curly brown hair, dressed in a silky, half-unbuttoned shirt, and wearing some sort of gold medallion amidst the jungle proudly displayed on his chest, was busy serving the unexpected spate of customers with a sullen, man-being-put-upon air.

'She ain't here,' he said to George, unsmiling, when he finally got around to serving us.

George beamed, 'Always thought you were called Danny-boy, Danny; not Psychic Smith.'

'Not funny, Sergeant Caunt,' the landlord grumbled, shoving two pints of bitter ungraciously across the bar. 'It's all right for some, swanning around all day at public expense, but she's not turned in this mornin' and I've been badly let down.'

'Maureen?'

'Yeah, Maureen. Makes a change from that other fly-by-night, I suppose. Haven't set eyes on *her* since before she won her round in the arse-waggling contest last Saturday night.'

'Where is she then?'

'Don't know, and I don't bloody care.'

'Maureen, not Davinia,' explained George.

'Oh, her! That Beryl phoned me; reckons the idle cow is sick.'

'Well then, she probably is.'

'Sick of work, more like. I phoned back, an' she isn't at home, is she?'

'Beryl?' George was spreading confusion.

'Maureen, you duff.'

The landlord took the proffered fiver, and ostentatiously held it up to the light prior to ringing it into the till. Still morose, he slapped down the change with an air of finality before moving quickly away to serve two teenies flaunting rings in their navels below short, turquoise tank tops and hardly-worth-bothering skirts. Two lagers with blackcurrant, and a spot of bosom thrusting in a blatant attempt to make the landlord's day. I shuddered, and George stared thoughtfully down the bar.

'Reckon they're under age?'

'What for?'

'Anything.' He grinned. That, at least, was something; knowing George, I'd almost expected a counterstrike in the form of an immediate police purge on Danny-boy Smith for allowing teenage boozing. Caunt's revenge.

We both took a long, satisfying pull at our pints. A mutual decision; not popular, nothing worthwhile for us here, drink up and get out. I was within an inch and a half of an empty glass when the doors were flung back, and a familiar, vibrant, matchstick figure made its way over to the bar.

Another tank top, another skirt that could easily have passed as a scarf, and a pair of hoops in her ears of a type that might once have belonged to Captain Kidd.

'Never fear, Beryl's here!' she carolled cheerfully. Then, as Smith turned, scowling, 'Come on, love, nice smile; the Indians aren't going to get ya, after all; the Cavalry's arrived.'

She didn't get the smile, but she was certainly worth half a dozen of him. Beryl bustled about, serving three customers to his one, a joke here, a smart remark there, wrestling with the drawer of the battered till, and banging down change.

The crowd of thirsty customers diminished, and within minutes, the landlord, still chuntering under his breath, was able to stump sourly off, leaving her in sole charge of both the connected bars. She was, I noticed, already one large gin and tonic, and the price of another, ahead. Grateful drinkers; popular girl.

'That's the last we'll see of him until three o'clock,' she said with satisfaction, scarcely bothering to lower her voice as she leaned confidentially across the bar. 'MCP.'

'Male chauvinist pig,' translated George unnecessarily.

'But only until you can't think of something worse,' she agreed.

'How did you get on last night?'

She stared.

'You and Bernie Cork,' I added. For a moment there, she looked as if she'd had something else in mind.

'Oh, the caution, you mean. No problems; pure pussycat, that Mr Paget of yours. Pity he's not a few years younger, and it's a shame about the lack of hair.'

George, with a head like a grey Norfolk thatch, preened. This did not go unremarked.

'I've always fancied the experienced older man.'

'Down, boy,' I muttered. 'She's only taking the mick.'

47

'Okay,' said George amiably, giving her a wink. 'But I've already noticed how she managed to sweet-talk you!'

'We came to an arrangement,' I said.

'Yeah,' she said wickedly, 'something foreign called a quid pro quo.'

'Apart from the police caution, Beryl, what else happened last night?' Get in quick; find out what you'd like to know.

'Hey! Aren't your lot supposed to know everything about everything around here? One-thirty in the morning, and another copper gets thumped, practically under me bedroom window, this time, and *you're* the one who's asking *me?*'

'You saw it?'

'Heard it, more like. Sounded like an elephant in collision with a goods train, but it was nearly all over by the time we got out of bed. Next door he was, when your man almost caught him, but by the time we got to the window your peeper was just a backside hefting over the top of their fence.'

'Who's we?'

She ignored me. 'Can't half swear, that mate of yours. Didn't expect a policeman to use such words.'

'You would,' said George, 'if you'd just broken an ankle like that.'

'It's not broken. That bloody civvy clerk and his rumours,' I said impatiently. 'It's just a sprain.' Nothing if not persistent, I kept on plugging, 'Who's *we?*'

'Me and my big mouth.' This time she did lower her voice, and leaned even further across the bar. 'Look,' she said. 'I rang misery-guts this morning, and told him she'd got a woman's thinggummy, just to put him off. But she's not sick, OK? She just wants a few days to herself.'

'Maureen?'

'Right.'

'So she's staying with you?'

'Well, she was there when I left, but she thinks that whoever it was went to the wrong house last night, geddit? This stalking

48

thing is really getting on her nerves; she's scared that it's somebody specially after her, y'know.'

I didn't know anything of the sort. Maureen had been the only happy one, apparently, the day before. So what, then, had suddenly changed her mind?

Bernie Cork by daylight looked something like the human version of an unmade bed. Big and flobberley, a word which George mendaciously claimed to have coined on the spot. His pale hair stuck out at all angles, while his face was soft, unshaven and round; he had something of a stomach at twenty-five and his whole body gave the impression of bulk without strength. Humiliating, to say the least, to have been successfully ambushed by a man like that. He moved, I noticed, with a rolling gait, his legs kept carefully apart.

'Still off work?' I asked as he let us into the Howlett Street house. His injuries, obviously, were longer-lasting than mine.

'Week's holiday; good job an' all.' From the way he was moving, I could see his point. I felt a twinge of sympathy, but I forbore to ask why he was wasting his precious time off, instead of cancelling his holiday and reporting sick.

'Not going away then?' George, making conversation as we went along, and being rewarded by a look of utter disgust.

'Live at the seaside, doan I? Where's to go?'

He indicated the stairway, 'Top o' the landing, turn right.'

Feet firmly planted apart, he watched us mount the stairs, and waited until we'd almost reached the top.

'She's out, y'know.'

'We've just met Beryl, thanks.'

'The other one, Maureen. She's gone.'

'Gone out?'

'Gone, gone. Suitcase an' everything, almost as soon as Beryl went to work.'

'I don't suppose,' said George, leaning over the bannisters, 'that you've any idea where she went?'

'No.' Still walking carefully, he made his way towards the back of the house. 'Wouldn't tell you lot if I did.' A door slammed. Not the policeman's friend, and no longer a shining example of civic responsibility, Mr Bernard Cork.

Forget the two-bedroomed terraced house on Alma Street, it still bore that empty and deserted look. We knocked, we checked the doors and windows, the neighbours still knew nothing; we walked away.

'Backwards and forwards,' muttered George. 'Why don't we use the car?'

'The exercise will do you good.'

'Why so worried anyway, boss?'

'Not worried, careful. Maureen Pykett the potential victim versus Alan Pykett the rapist on the loose,' I said.

'Could still be coincidence,' offered George.

'And if the idle bugger who took his antecedents in the first place had done his job properly, we'd know.'

'Even assuming you're right, she must have divorced Pykett ages before he went to court. So why would he want to come after her after all this time?'

'Why do nutters ever do anything?' I moaned. 'Fancy another stroll?'

'Who else is there?'

'Davinia, alias Shirley,' I said encouragingly. 'Good looker; she'll bring a touch of glamour to your life.'

Not, as it happened, true.

No answer to the bell when we got there, and an unlocked outside door. Inside, there was still no reply to our knocking, and contrary to the advice I'd given, her door was on the latch.

In the smashed-up living room we found one of the dolls from her collection suspended from the central lamp shade with a kitchen skewer through its gut. A blonde-haired, beribboned milkmaid swinging; a yoke across her shoulders, a piece of string around her neck.

The bedroom was in chaos; wardrobe partially emptied, its contents scattered, the dressing table drawers ripped out. Davinia was there too, of course. Nothing but a madman's afterthought now; lying naked on her back with her knees drawn up, face hidden by a pillow, and discarded on top of her own churned-up bed like a second, vandalised doll.

Her black brassiere and knickers, her dress and tights lay cut and scattered contemptuously across and around her. Sickening sight, and, complementing the visual horror, an equally sickening smell.

Thinking about it now, I can still evoke that stink. A stomach-churning combination of dank, airless room, urine-soaked mattress, and the sickly-sweet contents of a scattered drawerful of half-used make-up, mingling with the aroma from a broken bottle which had once held an ounce or two of none-too-expensive scent.

George paused for a moment beside the bed, taking reluctant, sideways glances at the corpse. One of the reasons I like him; he's not a man for the macho image, the strut and the knowing bluster when it comes to the crunch. He looked it, I felt it: not so much pale as green. Slowly, almost guiltily, his eyes slid from floor to bed and back again while he sucked in his cheeks.

'For God's sake, George, this is neither the time nor the place. Get out of here if you're going to be sick!'

Another gross misunderstanding: he didn't even bother to reply. My eyes followed him as he stooped, finger and thumb delicately poised, and then in the very act of reaching forward to grasp his prize, he stopped, leaving the scrap of crumpled foil severely alone.

'Rule number one,' he muttered in self-admonition, stretching back to his full height, 'do not bugger up the scene.' Cautiously, almost as if he was stepping in his own indented footprints, he moved back.

'Calculating sort of bastard,' I muttered.

He nodded understandingly while we both stared at the discarded contraceptive wrapper on the floor beside the bed.

Having made one such mistake already, I was not, of course, referring to George.

# Chapter Six

'*Another* murder enquiry? How the hell do you manage it? God on a donkey, Bob!' Not new, not especially funny, and just a trifle forced. Trying to sound like one of the boys again, Superintendent Dorothea Spinks.

I shrugged my shoulders, and stared levelly at the big, bold, uniformed figure across the desk. A handsome woman, a more than imposing presence at fifty-plus, but I had no intention of being treated like a beggar, or being bullied by her. Aylfleet was part of my area, and I had every right to call upon the resources of its CID.

Unlike Teddy Baring, who lived his official life in the Edwardian splendour of the long-departed Eddathorpe Chief Constable's pad, Thea's office was vaguely scruffy, distinctly cramped; this had its advantages in some ways, she dominated the place, a beacon of excellence in a less than perfect world.

'The Force,' I said, opening mildly, 'deals with a dozen murders or more, every year.'

'And most of them are domestics.' She sat up very straight, as crisp as her uniform blouse, and looked at me with a distinctly unfriendly eye. 'They hardly take any detecting, do they? Man and wife, lover on lover; sometimes it's relation versus relation, perhaps even father and son. You're the only feller I know who makes a career out of complications, my lad.'

53

Headmistress speaking to the newly-joined member of the mixed infants; *my lad.*

'It's almost two years since your last one,' I said.

'Seventeen months since *your* last one, you mean. I was lumbered with it, or perhaps you don't remember,' she replied.

Tactical error: a lady with a precise, mathematical mind. Far from conciliating her, I'd got her looking really cross. I remembered all right, and I'd have done far better to keep the Graham mouth firmly shut. Foisted with an Eddathorpe murder by devious Teddy Baring, and all on the strength of a very dubious technicality, that had been Dorothea's line, and she'd stuck to it all the way through the enquiry. Detected or not, Dorothea was hardly the forgiving and forgetting type.

Not the moment to refight ancient battles, though; much better to stick to the current point.

'Superintendent,' I said, 'Ma'am. I need six bodies from Aylfleet divisional CID. I know it's inconvenient; I know you're understaffed, but since the reorganisation Eddathorpe and Aylfleet are a single entity from a Criminal Investigation point of view.'

'I'm still the divisional commander here, and the CID is not an independent fief.'

I glanced surreptitiously at my watch; three and a half hours into a murder enquiry, and I was stroking egos some twenty miles from the scene of the real action, instead of getting on with the job. Time for an oblique threat.

'It's your decision at this stage, of course, but the head of CID will want a divisional breakdown of personnel we've drafted to the teams.'

Not entirely subtle, and I wasn't happy with the technique. Can't win by myself, so I'm going to threaten to tell my big brother about you! Besides, somewhere round about the dawn of time, Chief Superintendent Fairfield and Thea had been lovers, or so I'd been told. The subsequent bust-up had apparently left some rawish feelings on both sides, and Mr Fairfield, I had already noticed, was not entirely happy about tangling with Miss Spinks.

'You are not,' said Thea aggressively, 'taking Detective Inspector Wake.'

That was better: a retreat to prepared positions, I think it's called. In any case, her attitude at least indicated that she liked her current detective inspector a lot more than she'd liked the last. Another bone of contention between us, until her old DI, Derek Rodway, had found himself a rich window, and resigned under what Thea liked to describe as a bit of a cloud.

'DS Prentice, and five.' Not my favourite CID personality, the Aylfleet detective sergeant, but he was experienced, and a very good cop.

'Four, it's the leave season.' She watched my face, and threw in her final offer. 'And one Aide to CID.'

I nodded, always try to look friendly and cooperative, especially when you're on the way out.

'I suppose we have to make the effort,' she conceded reluctantly as I left. 'It's murder, after all. But personally, Bob, I don't care how many bimbos get strangled so long as you refrain from stealing my people, and you keep your convoluted ruddy enquiries well away from me.'

Unbelievably callous, and widely-known as a sore loser, is Dorothea Spinks.

I had that tense, knotted feeling in my stomach, and despite the mints in my mouth, a touch of acid kept trying to force its way back up. The lights, the steel tables, the busy whirl of the extractor fan, the background taste of chemicals and canned air, were only too familiar. The entire room, in fact, with its air of chill, clinical depression, plus the sight of Malc Cartwright in his role as exhibits officer, the photographer from Scenes of Crime and the five-foot-nothing mortuary attendant in his trailing white coat, all contributed to an almost nightmarish feeling of *déjà vu*.

Twenty years experience of bodies and highly qualified ghouls with sharp, shining knives, and I'd never got over the sights, sounds and smells associated with a post mortem. Not that I'd been doing murder enquiries for all that time, but a long, unhappy trail of heart attacks, carcinomas, fatal road accidents, suicides and even accidental drownings and electrocutions, bedevilled my early uniformed, acting-coroner's-officer, past.

Sometimes, combined with the touch of dread, I experience a marginal sense of smugness, almost of pride, in the way I react. The feeling that the guy who finds himself getting used to mortuaries must be at least one step nearer to the funny farm than the rest. I wonder how many other coppers pause from time to time and get it too: *look, folks, in spite of everything, I can still be sensitive, therefore I'm still sane!*

Not the sort of thing to admit to your colleagues, and if, as a fellow member of the cloth, you're ever tempted, choose a stranger in a distant Force area and give him a false name and address afterwards. I was just suffering from a touch of self-pity combined with a spot of irrational guilt, if the truth be told.

I reserved the remainder of my attention for Professor Andrew Lawrence, the Senior Home Office pathologist, rather than the corpse. I envied him, almost. A tall, thin, almost cadaverous man, pleasant enough in his way, and always so objective, so dedicated to the task in hand. Looking first, then swabbing delicately, taking samples; searching for traces of the enemy, combing pubic hair.

Slit, examine, snip, weigh and lay aside. Putting things on metal trays while the mortuary attendant hovered; removing oesophagus, trachea, heart and lungs in one fell swoop, and murmuring into the miniature tape recorder slung around his neck. *And by the way, the liver goes on a separate tray, over there.*

Apart, of course, from his air of effortless superiority, the scientific detachment, his vast professional experience and the string of letters after his name, he had another even more important advantage over humble, subjective me. He'd not been chatting to this extremely pretty girl, and casually handing out random chunks of policemanly advice while he took a series of sneaky looks at a pair of half-concealed, living, bouncing breasts, less than thirty-six hours before.

Big Malc, in his familiar role as Exhibits Officer, had no such qualms. One thing about him, he could take the occasional postmortem examination in his stride. A damn sight steadier than me, I noticed. He did not, however, take matters to extremes. None of that overactive ghoul performance which some coppers go in for, just to show they're on top of the job.

Malc Cartwright kept well back; he simply observed and listed, helping out with the neatly written self-adhesive labels, leaving the mortuary attendant to play with the contents of the little, and not so little, plastic bags.

'You're very quiet, Chief Inspector.' Eventually, Lawrence looked up from his final, macabre task, and gave me the ghost of a thin-lipped smile.

I was not only quiet, I was trying not to watch him stitching up what was now little more than an empty sack.

'I was thinking about the time of death.'

'Oh yes? Of course.' Not the most sympathetic of men. 'Ten to twelve hours before I first saw her. Rigor was well established, and with the consistent temperature within the room, I would say it was almost certainly between one and three.'

'A.m.?'

Silly remark. By this time he knew he'd got me rattled, and he gave me an ironic, scientist-to-queasy-layman look. 'Asphyxiated, but she wasn't strangled,' he volunteered.

'No?' I'd been guessing when I spoke to Thea, and I'd obviously guessed wrong. A little knowledge, as they say, is a dangerous thing. I'd noticed the congested face, and the pinpricks of blood below the skin when Lawrence had first peeled back her lips during his preliminary examination at the scene. Petechia: he'd told me about it before.

'No marks on her neck,' he continued, 'no signs of internal

bruising; hyoid intact. That pillow wasn't there just for fun, you know. Smothered, not strangled, wouldn't you say?'

I said nothing: do not trespass on other people's professional territory. Keep the medical opinions to yourself in future, and the big mouth firmly shut.

'No signs of struggle?'

'Some bruising to the right shoulder and both upper arms, more bruising, fingermarks on her inner thighs, but not as many external injuries as one would have thought. No real signs of a lengthy, sustained defence.'

Inspiration struck; another unconsidered opinion. There are times when I can never take my own advice.

'What about an accident, then?' I said, 'One of those, er, silly sexual games, where they increase their pleasure by—'

A spot of verbal flatulence, I'm sorry to say. Mortuary fever, not really thinking it through, and taking no account whatsoever of the dangling, violated doll.

'No.'

'So it was rape?'

'Internal damage, certainly; not what *I* would call a game.' He stared at me in a way which made me believe he thought Bluebeard had come alive. 'But there's no evidence of normal sexual penetration; absolutely not.' Delicacy from a pathologist? I think he meant no sperm. 'This, ah, contraceptive device—'

'Foil packet,' I said. 'A cheapish brand called *Glees*; franchised and sold via machines, mostly.'

'Er, lubricated?'

'No.'

He sighed gently. Policemen aren't there to play Mr Sensitive, nor are pathologists, but for a moment it shut us both up.

'There is,' he said finally, 'one other significant thing. You say she wasn't robbed?'

'Bit of a problem there,' I admitted. 'You saw it, the place was wrecked. Nevertheless, her handbag and purse were intact; she had something less than thirty pounds, and there was a gold bracelet and one or two other bits and pieces in one of those musical jewellery boxes on her dressing table. Worth taking, had it been your average burglar, I'd have thought.'

'Interesting, then; step a little closer, Mr Graham, and look at this!' He splayed the fingers of his right hand and took a firm grip of the skull, tilting her head to the right while I took a single reluctant pace forward.

'Well?' He pointed.

'She's had her ears pierced,' I said.

'And here,' this time he used both hands, rigor was still present and he had some difficulty tilting the head the other way. 'What do you see now?' Gently, he inserted a gloved forefinger beneath the lobe of her right ear. Pierced again; brilliant! these operations, just like ears, usually came in twos ... And then I saw what he meant; an almost infinitesimal bead of dried blood left in the cavity of the pierced lobe.

'Nothing spectacular,' he said smugly, 'but I think we may safely say that somebody has been a trifle rough.'

A wrapper, but no contraceptive: no semen, therefore no DNA ... Little or nothing below her fingernails, and up to a moment before, no suggestion of robbery or theft.

Now we had at least the possibility of the killer having taken a pair of earrings from the body. A possibility rising to a probability, to be fair; I could forgive him for sounding smug.

One problem, however; maybe two. First, I would have to get Forensic to check the remaining earrings in her box. No point in chasing around for stolen property if she'd damaged her ear herself. Secondly, we'd no idea of what kind of earrings we might be looking for, or who we were dealing with.

A rapist, almost certainly; an inept thief, perhaps; a souvenir hunter, possibly; or a brutal boyfriend with sense enough to remove some useful evidence by recovering his gift?

Malc stirred uneasily; only speculating, but I'd stared for a few moments too long, too hard at Professor Andrew Lawrence, job completed, stepping back.

✳   ✳   ✳

'Violent nutters; they oughta hang the lot!' The voice of Detective Constable Patrick Goodall, middle England's answer to the wit and wisdom of Ian Paisley; everything the *Guardian* had ever said about the police. Keen, blond, muscular, mid-twenties, probably well-meaning too; there were times when I could almost stand him, apart from his addiction to the loud, unconsidered opinion. No GBH intended nevertheless; just a Rottweiler puppy at play.

This was not, however, the moment for a stirring reiteration of the mindless canteen code. I had thirty-eight detectives milling about in an Incident Room awaiting a full briefing, and I was already going to have to struggle with the formed opinions of thirty-plus. Collectively, they'd already decided that Alan Pykett, the well-known rapist had dunnit. Find him; get him to cough; wrap it up.

'Alright, settle down!' Paula Baily's voice rose above the ruck. Then, failing to achieve an immediate result, she paused for a couple of seconds, filled her lungs, and yelled a blunt, 'Hey, you lot! Shuddup!'

Reluctantly, they settled, while George, practising his self-appointed role as acting-detective-inspector-designate, looked across the room and grinned at Roger Prentice's carefully composed, neutral face. A man who hadn't passed his police promotion examination indulging in a spot of premature triumphalism over a man who had. Probably an injustice from the Prentice point of view, but I could rely on George, and George knew the town. I simply wished he could bear to keep his obvious satisfaction to himself.

'Right, ladies and gents, this is what we've got so far ...' Thirty-odd pairs of eyes settled on my face as I started the routine; name, age, occupation of the deceased; the circumstances and the cause of death, the lines of enquiry we were going to pursue. A straight performance; no attention-grabbing funnies, and absolutely no inclination towards the graveyard jokes.

Listening, the house-to-house enquiry teams looked slightly less than chuffed. The main briefing, thanks to Thea, was late and some of the teams had had to be dragged back to the station after making a start. Most of them had already found out that going from door to door with a clipboard is only one degree less boring and unproductive than chasing double-glazing sales.

Lumbered, their expressions told me, with the unexciting bits, so I did my moderate, slightly over-emphatic best to psych 'em up. I wanted details of the whereabouts and movements of all males, I told them, in all the surrounding streets; complaints, suspicions, rumours about Peeping Toms, male oddities, the lot.

Pump everybody for information; gossip and tales of neighbourly Eddathorpe malice gratefully received. Age limits? If they were big enough they were old enough on the one hand, and if they were still getting around without benefit of crutches or an electric wheelchair on the other, I wanted a questionnaire and a descriptive form completed: not terribly likely, but granddads were still in the frame.

'But we've got a suspect, haven't we?' piped an impatient, marginally-aggressive voice the moment I paused for breath. Windy bosses indulging in useless enquiries just to protect their own career prospects, that's what he meant. There's at least one of 'em at every briefing, and you can always rely on Pat. Briefly, I almost regretted seconding him from sleepy Retton, the Eddathorpe sub-station, for the duration of the enquiry.

Only in a sense, Patrick,' I said patiently. 'We've got a number of possibilities. There's probably a couple of sexual offenders active around here, as well as some question of Alan Pykett visiting the town to see his ex-wife. We've also that old theatrical has-been Pauline Parkes and got a couple of the victim's boyfriends and ex-boyfriends to look at, too.'

Briefly, I ploughed through the Pykett story for the benefit of the rest of the assembled troops. 'It's an urgent line of enquiry,' I concluded, 'but it's all a bit speculative, so

far, and we're not going to put all our eggs in one basket, OK?'

A rumble of assent, the scraping of chairs signalled the end
of the meeting. Until, that is, the Retton wrecker made his
final bid for fame. 'It's all very well looking for this character's
ex-ruddy-wife to help us,' he muttered. 'She might not have
buggered off at all. Maybe he's found her, and we're already
looking at a double event.'

Covering all the eventualities they call it, and there's absolutely
nothing like a few words of cheerful optimism from a junior
colleague to lighten the mood when things are looking tough.

# Chapter Seven

'Don't think I can help,' said Davinia's caring employer and our favourite landlord, Danny-boy Smith. 'Haven't seen hide nor hair, have we, Mary, since closing time, Friday night?'

His wife nodded carefully, afraid, perhaps, of disturbing her elaborately coiffured, piled-up chestnut hair. Too much lipstick, too much make-up altogether, and she had this talent for letting the sound trickle through the narrowest of slits in her scarcely-moving, over-enamelled mouth.

'No,' she said. 'Not since Friday night.'

'What time was that?'

'Around half-eleven. Same time as you got thumped.' She remained impassive, but I thought I detected a hint of pleasure behind her husband's eyes.

'Oh yes; the Beryl and Bernie show.' I kept my voice even, 'I take it, then, that Beryl left here first?'

'That's right,' Danny resumed command. He crossed his legs comfortably, and leaned back in one of a pair of shabby armchairs which graced the living room of the pub manager's flat.

'Any special reason for that?'

'Equality of labour, Squire. Shirley, or Davinia, or whatever you like to call her, was still washing glasses. Mary made her, and serve her right; busy night Friday, and she'd turned up nearly half an hour late.'

George, careless of consequences, grimaced. Danny telling it how it was; but not a lot of sympathy for the dead.

'And was there any particular reason for that?' he asked.

'No, mate; just being her usual lackadaisical self.'

'You don't sound particularly impressed with her; but despite that, you'd kept her on here for something like three months, nevertheless?'

'Three and a bit. She was nothing special, but staff are hard to find.'

'Wages?'

'Same as everybody else around here; four quid an hour.'

'She was pretty, though; I suppose that must have pulled 'em in?'

'I suppose.'

'You don't sound too sure?'

'In my opinion,' said Mary Smith flatly, 'she was more trouble than she was worth.'

'In what way?'

'Men.'

'Aw, come on now, me darling.' Danny-boy shuffled uncomfortably. 'It wasn't as bad as all that.'

'You would say that; you are one, a man I mean. Pub managers were too poor for her, thank God, and I suppose you've got a bit more sense than most; that's why I married you.' She flashed him a look that might have been approval, but it would have chilled me.

'Meaning you knew some men that hadn't got any?' I jumped in quickly, 'No sense?'

'She had a couple of boyfriends,' muttered the landlord placatingly, shaking his head at his wife, trying to calm things down. 'Bound to have had in the time she was here; that's all. Mary was upset because of the beauty contest, and the time she took off 'cos she wanted to go on holiday abroad with some man.'

'Inconveniencing people,' spat the woman. 'Swapping backwards and forwards with Maureen, and being absent for five days on the trot.'

'This, er, man . . .' I started.

'Don't know, don't care, didn't ask.' This with the air of a Duchess who wouldn't demean herself by chattering with the staff.

'Of course we knew,' contradicted Danny, still in conciliatory mode, but receiving an icy glitter for his pains. 'She reckoned that the first one was a rock star.' His mouth twisted cynically, 'She met him here in the bar, or so she said. And the second one was called Ralph, we knew that much; he had a boat down at Aylthorpe dock.'

'Marina, not dock,' snapped his wife, plunging back into the working class. 'And to hear her talk you'd think she'd captured a multi-millionaire.'

'And apart from that?'

The landlord shrugged, and Mary gave us both a vacant, unfriendly stare.

'So, she, er, had the night off for the beauty contest on Saturday; what about Sunday?'

'Her proper night off.'

'I see.'

'And on Monday afternoon she called in sick,' said the woman tartly. 'Taking advantage again, if you ask me.'

'She called at the pub?'

'Of course not; wouldn't chance showing her face, would she? She spoke to me on the phone.'

'And not the first time, eh?'

'Well,' once again Danny stepped in, 'she'd been off a couple of times before, but as for her swinging it, you couldn't really tell.' Cautious, embarrassed on his wife's behalf, perhaps, he was still trying to deflect the female wrath.

'Any trouble while she was here?' asked George.

'No, why?'

'Surely you knew about the stalker; the Peeping Tom?'

'Oh, yes. Him.'

'Him,' George mimicked, 'and now the poor kid's dead; don't you think there might possibly be some significance in that?'

'I suppose,' he repeated. 'The girls chattered about it a bit, but to be honest I didn't take too much notice at the time. Peepers are hardly the Royal Standard type.'

'Really?' George was playing it straight.

'I tell you, Sergeant.' Danny sat up and his voice achieved an almost-convincing snap of authority at last. 'Perverts wouldn't last long on my premises, I can tell you that. My customers know the score, one false move, and they're out.'

We both kept quiet, but we took the statement; two statements, in fact, for what they were worth. Then we declined a drink and edged our way out politely; it was a matter of principle, something along the lines of not fraternising with the enemy, I suppose.


Councillor Albert Flaxman stirred uneasily in the visitor's chair. New blue suit in honour of the Labour Party victory in the Borough Council elections to go with his old red tie, I noticed. Co-op, naturally, being Albert, and none too expensive at that.

Albert was one of the two local politicians about whom I cared a damn. Conservative Mary Todd, the ex-spouse of Richard and a former mayor, who was rapidly achieving the status of an old friend, and Albert, Labour, from the other side of the tracks. How's that for police impartiality in the midst of Eddathorpe's grubby political games?

'It's not very nice,' said Albert. 'I don't know how to tell you this.'

A small, almost gnome-like figure in his sixties, with a creased face and a shrewd, not to say cynical sense of humour, he was, nevertheless, something of a puritan, another member of Teddy Baring's straight-laced nonconformist gang. Trouble, I assumed. He wasn't usually the reticent type, nor was he normally well known for beating about the bush.

'You probably know this already, I'm the Chairman of Governors of Sandridge school.'

My turn to feel uneasy; this simply wasn't his style. With Angie making a job application, the last place I expected him to mention was Sandridge junior school. No contracts, no canvassing, no favours, no jobs; no nods and winks, and positively no deals. A scrupulous man. Whatever some of his more disreputable council colleagues did, Albert Flaxman played it straight.

'Yes,' I said cautiously, 'I know.'

'Where your wife has made an application for a part-time post.' A precise, almost prim little speech. Stating the obvious, too. He eyed me with such a palpable air of embarrassment; whatever I had coming he was having more than ordinary difficulty in getting it out.

'I want to show you a letter.'

'Yes?'

'Addressed to me: anonymous, of course.'

'Hmmm.'

Finally, he took the plunge. Say it, say it straight, and get it over with: no frills. I could practically hear the wheels grinding; it wasn't hard to read Albert's mind.

'The person who wrote it tells me that your wife is an adulteress, practically a prostitute, and totally unfit to be placed in charge of innocent young kids. That's my cleaned-up version; I wouldn't put my tongue to the original, it's obscene.'

You go to see complainants day after day: burglaries, thefts, assaults, indecency, the lot. You sympathise, of course, but you'd be mad to get too emotionally involved, so it all becomes part of the job. Remain objective: do what you have to do, and pass along to do the next. Profitless to become a crusader; in that direction temptation, malpractice, trouble, lies.

Then, once in a lifetime, perhaps, it happens to you: something above and beyond a car taken, or a house screwed: your child assaulted, missing even, your own wife attacked. Something that really hits home. And instantly, ninety percent of the professionalism goes flying out of the window, and all you feel is raw red rage and the desire to rip some bastard's arm out of its socket prior to beating him over the head with the sticky end until he drops.

For a few seconds, at least, you know exactly how a criminal feels; no foresight of consequences. Just get out there and do exactly what you want. It scares you a bit, afterwards, and even when reason reasserts itself you feel a bit inadequate. Cowardly even, for letting such a feeble excuse as respect (or is it fear?) of the laws, or civilised behaviour stand in your way.

'Can I see it?'

Delicately, Albert reached into the inside pocket of his coat, and removed two objects, each enclosed in a plastic freezer bag. He placed them flat on the desk in front of me, side by side, and with this operation completed, he sank back into his chair and looked at them with an air of absolute disgust. One envelope, stamped, addressed and franked, and a single, crudely-typed page.

I eyed them too, but I didn't attempt to read the letter immediately, and I didn't touch.

'Nobody else has seen 'em; I came straight to you.'

'I see, and what else do you propose to do about this?' Pretty sure about Albert Flaxman, but not absolutely. A prick of shame for doing it, but I had to ask.

'Nothing.' Slowly, he raised his eyes and stared unflinchingly into my face. 'Not unless you want me to give you a statement and a set of fingerprints for elimination purposes, lad. Then again, we might both be better off burning the buggers and forgetting about it,' he said.

'Wonderful to see you, my dear fellow; call me Paulie,' said Paulie Parkes, leading us into the living room of his flat. 'And you're, ah, Sergeant Caunt, hmm?'

Half past eleven in the morning, and we'd dragged him

out of bed, so somehow I doubted his sentiments, just a bit.

It wasn't so much the cerise dressing gown worn over a pair of silk pyjamas patterned in a particularly virulent shade of green and blue, or even the baring of the teeth to display a dazzling assembly of bridgework that put me off. The handshake had something to do with it. Left hand around the shoulder, drawing the victim close to Paulie's slipping chest, while the right squeezed hard, either in pseudo-sincerity, or in an attempt to bring tears to his opponent's eyes.

Silly, but I was provoked into squeezing back; smiling equally insincerely, while keeping an eye out for evidence of pain, or at least discomfort, on his smoothly-tanned, scarcely-wrinkled face. Sunny Spain or a health farm sunbed; he hadn't acquired that expensive scorching among the sandcastles, drizzle and deckchairs of scintillating Eddathorpe on Sea.

'I should think,' he said merrily, having fought the handshake to a slightly embarrassing draw, 'that the good sergeant has to be pretty careful with his pronunciation with a name like that, ha, ha.'

George, swallowing the insult, celebrating the instant recognition of a brand-new enemy of the State, stretched his face into a mirthless grin, and placed both hands firmly behind his back. He needn't have bothered; the hand of friendship wasn't extended to underlings in this particular neck of the woods.

'Drinks, eh?' A novel sort of breakfast, I would have thought.

'Not at the moment, thanks.'

'Oh, come on now; do I detect a touch of the Agatha Christies, here? *Not while we're on duty, madam!* Spare me that, please; I know exactly what it's like. Double whiskies for any CID man worth his salt!'

Turning his back, he made for a lavishly stocked brick and mahogany bar in one corner of his lounge. Practically groaning with a huge selection of multi-coloured bottles, it certainly went with the furiously promoted showbiz image on display throughout the whole of his first-floor, bay-windowed seaward-facing apartment. A fair amount of money here, at least in Eddathorpe terms.

A plethora of signed, framed photographs of celebrities smothered every available surface, and a prominently displayed, vaguely humanoid figure lurked among a collection of heavily engraved invitation cards on the mantelpiece of his Adamish fireplace. Some sort of variety award. Almost involuntarily, my eyes, as they were meant to, were drawn to one, gloriously isolated item bearing the italicised inscription, *In the Presence of HRH* ... The pasteboard was, however, curving slightly against the wall where it was propped. Far from being a current invite, then; well-thumbed.

We both sank into a matching pair of green and white pigskin armchairs, and we were each rewarded with nearly three quarters of a tumbler of very good malt.

'The Macallan,' he said unnecessarily, taking a hefty sample from his own brimming glass. 'Won't insult it with water; this has been maturing in sherry casks for fully eighteen years.'

Fully: maybe he'd done the commercial; maybe he got lots of freebies. Perhaps he was worth cultivating, after all. Unworthy thought.

'Cheers!' I sipped. George, always a bad sign, balanced an untouched glass.

'Now then, what can I do for you, boys?'

I looked firmly at George: reluctantly, as if he was breaking some sort of code of the Caunts, he took a minimal sample of malt.

Unscrupulously, having tested, I gulped; it wasn't every day you met a ham like this, and from a strictly personal point of view, I thought we were both going to deserve a pretty substantial slug.

'I understand you run the beauty contest at *Eddathorpe Rocks!*'

'My dear fellow, I am *Eddathorpe Rocks!* A couple of tickets, eh? No problem; no problems whatsoever.' He probably even meant it. His smile said it all; why should the police be different? He dealt with scroungers and freeloaders every day.

'Haven't you heard about the trouble, er, Paulie?' George trundled into life.

'Heard what?' A diminution of the over-amiable beam. Progress at last. Then, after staring into George's blank, marginally hostile face for a fraction of a second, he completely changed tack. Official business; thou shalt not patronise the filth. Message received and understood.

'Oh, about those bloody women, you mean? I never thought the CID would interest themselves in *them*.'

'What bloody women?' Sometimes I don't know why I bother; my sergeant was in there like a knife.

'You know, Adele Simpson and her gang; moustaches, grunt-grunt voices and comfortable shoes.' He wasn't kidding, either; a genuine gleam of evangelistic fervour shone in his eyes.

'Feminists,' said George encouragingly.

'Among other things, yes.'

Memory stirred; the local paper. Paulie and his beauty contest were a target: angry women on the march. Parading girls in bikinis diminished the value of womanhood, fostered an insulting, stereotypical image of females as objects of chauvinist sexual innuendo, and encouraged male abuse.

A bit of a mouthful, perhaps, but in the light of recent events and in some quarters at least, Paulie, as a promoter of pulchritude, probably had a new career in front of him as Eddathorpe's most unpopular man.

'Lesbians?' asked George, his voice like silk.

'OK!' The beam was back.

'For your information, Paulie,' oh, God! I knew that expression, 'I know her husband; Adele Simpson is a member of the Townswomen's Guild, and she's the mother of two.'

'Another havering, right-on liberal, huh?' Their eyes locked, this was definitely war.

Liberal? Not George. Not normally, not on your life; but

there's an exception to every rule. So far as Paulie Parkes was concerned, George had joined up for the duration now, and by this time he was wearing his nasty, newly-commissioned, hostilities-only, look. There are times when I realise, too late, that I ought to have discouraged George.

'We are here,' I said hastily in my best cardboard-copper voice, 'to make enquiries in connection with the death of Shirley West.'

'Who?' Parkes sounded puzzled; George had the grace to look slightly abashed.

'Haven't you read the papers, Mr Parkes; seen the TV news last night?'

'Should I have? No.'

'Does the name Davinia ring a bell?'

'Davinia? You can't possibly mean Davinia? She's a quarter-finalist. That could bugger up the whole caboodle; terrible publicity. Oh Christ!'

Abandoning the beginnings of a very promising feud, he sank into the matching pigskin sofa, imbibed a substantial amount of his malt, and brooded. 'Colin's going to be very upset,' he muttered after a very long pause.

'Colin?'

'Colin Critchley; *Immortal Sins*,' he made it sound as if I should have known. Then, peering into my uncomprehending face, he sighed heavily. 'Ex-boyfriend. It's a band.'

The other ex-boyfriend. And naturally, a band.

'Overdose?'

'What makes you say that?'

'Well, you're here,' he said vaguely, 'and you never know with these young tarts. So it wasn't drugs? That's something, I suppose.' He was obviously talking himself into feeling happier as he went along. 'Tracing relatives, are you?'

'No, there's only a stepfather, and he's been informed. He's back in his hometown, thanks.'

'An accident, then?'

72

'Try murder,' suggested George.

Silence; it sank in.

'Good God!' Another pause. 'You realise what this means, don't you? They'll crucify me; shred me up and spit me out, the bloody cows!'

'I don't quite follow,' I said.

'Look,' he leaned forward earnestly, not forgetting to take another substantial swig, 'I've got the Pavilion Theatre; it's *my* Summer show, Monday to Saturday, every evening at eight and a Wednesday matinee.

'It's leased from the council, and every Saturday for the last three years, we've brought on the girls. New punters in the guesthouses every weekend, and a new crop of contestants on the stage, OK?'

'Gotcha,' said George. A light, a malicious light of understanding was dawning in his eyes.

'And every bloody year,' said Paulie feelingly, 'it gets harder. The council likes it, it's good publicity, and the winner goes forward to the National finals, hm? The punters like it too, but there's a lot of opposition to a touch of wriggle and wobble these days, and it's getting worse.'

'Degrading to women,' I said.

'You've joined them, have you? You one of 'em and all?'

Nothing spectacular, but the fruity thespian accent was beginning to slip. Executive stress, not to mention the whisky, was beginning to show.

'I was just helping you along.'

'Oh! Well, imagine the screams of outrage after this; They're going to screw me and my show to the deck, my dear fellow.'

'Yes,' said George with totally unnecessary relish, 'I suppose they—'

For once I managed to silence him with a scowl.

'How did you come across, er, Davinia?' I asked.

His eyes slid away from George, the rabbit gladly abandoning a staring match with a stoat. 'Oh, the usual way, she came in response to the publicity. Won her heat, and now she's in the final eight.'

'Not now, she's not.'

He flicked the briefest of glances back at George, 'Quite!'

'This ex-boyfriend of hers . . .'

'Well, I'm only assuming he's ex.' For the first time Paulie Parkes looked uneasy, he shuffled in his chair, biting his lower lip, and swirling the remaining whisky around in his glass. 'I ought to tell you, I suppose.'

You ought, and please get on with it. No help here.

'Colin is in my show.'

'Yes.' I'd already managed to guess.

'He's doing the season with me.' Paulie playing uneasy by this time, looking down at his glass. 'A very talented boy; group, even. Nearly had a single in the top forty, y'know, last year: cutting their first album soon.'

I could imagine: the Pavilion Theatre, Eddathorpe, followed by Vegas, instant stardom, and the conquest of the showbiz world.

'He, er, met Davinia a couple of months ago.'

'Before or after she entered your contest?'

'Well,' he tried the confiding smile, 'as a matter of fact, before. But she won fair and square,' he added hastily. I looked him straight in the eye; something to make him wriggle. Worth bearing in mind, but I wasn't investigating yet another shabby Eddathorpe scam. Still, things weren't quite adding up; the contents of another conversation stirred.

'If Colin is her ex-boyfriend, who's Ralph?'

He looked blank.

'Or Raffe; Raffe Sheppard, huh?'

'Don't know what you're talking about; you tell me.'

'Introduced Davinia to your contest; owns a boat.'

'Colin *lives* on a boat for the time being, down at Aylfleet. He rents it, and as it happens it's my boat. He was supposed to be living there by himself, and now without so much as a by-your-leave, he's invited one of his mates.'

'Raffe?'

'Never heard of him, and you obviously don't know Colin. Bit of a rough diamond; he wouldn't be seen dead going around with anybody called Ralph, or Raffe.'

'So it was definitely Colin who introduced her to your contest?'

'Well, yes, in a way. I suppose so.'

A touch of confusion: two boats? two separate men? Maureen Pykett, in her brief role as our informant, was obviously none too hot.

'Not quite true then, what you were saying about the way she entered your contest?'

'Anyway,' he said reluctantly, ignoring the point. 'A misunderstanding with Colin, that's all. Nothing heavy; only having a bit of fun.'

'Oh, yes?'

'Colin was out of order; went completely over the top. There was nothing very much to it at all.'

Two rude, crude coppers exchanged a slightly lascivious, totally understanding look. No doubt about it; neither of us would ever starve. We could, if times turned bad, always open a fortune-telling cabin down by Paulie's theatre, on our stub of a pier.

George, happy at last, placed his scarcely-touched drink on the floor beside him, and rummaged in his briefcase for his clipboard, a descriptive form and an enquiry questionnaire.

'Bit of fun, you say? Ah, well, I suppose you have to expect it,' he added smugly, 'the appeal of the older man!' And while Paulie Parkes was still trying to formulate a suitable reply, he shuffled his papers briskly and pulled the cap off his pen.

# Chapter Eight

'I have been talking,' said Teddy Baring with mild distaste, 'to the egregious Paulie Parkes.'

'Phone call?'

'Yes.'

'Complaints already? He didn't waste much time.'

Teddy treated me to a hint of his sour, down-turned smile. Egregious, as in sharp, notorious, remarkable; not exactly complimentary, I gathered: something along the lines of remarkably bad.

I was pretty sure that Teddy, as considered in his opinions as he was precise and old-fashioned in his language, hadn't reached his conclusions on the basis of a single telephone call. Revelations were on the cards.

'Nothing serious, Bob, just a lot of moaning and groaning, and a hint of how important he is; or used to be, once. Stuck his head above the parapet, nevertheless, and from your point of view, he's an interesting man.'

'Malt whisky for breakfast,' I agreed hypocritically. There's something about Eddathorpe; treachery in the very air. Fortunately, for the health of my own ego, he didn't ask.

'It would be nice,' sniffed Teddy, 'if he paid for his expensive pleasures from time to time.' An almost unique attitude for a copper, very much agin' the drink. 'He's rapidly becoming a professional debtor. Checked up on him locally, yet?'

'Not yet.'

'You know his background, of course? A so-called personality, once. He ran this TV game show: greedy people running about and shouting and screaming while he egged 'em on. Humiliation with prizes, that sort of thing.'

Teddy, as if looking for an ally, stared at me through his slightly protuberant grey eyes for signs of approval. Paulie Parkes, for reasons still known only to himself, was not exactly Teddy's favourite TV man.

'A couple of ex-wives,' I said provocatively, waiting to see where this was going to lead.

'Three: hence, no doubt, the debts.'

This wasn't Teddy at all: a puritan, yes. Pretty straight-laced, but what about the edge of malice in his voice? More to it than an unnatural desire to gossip; somewhere, somehow, Paulie Parkes had managed to rattle the Baring cage.

'You don't know, then?' He looked at me intently, narrow head cocked to one side. 'He was found not guilty, of course.'

'Sorry, boss; I've no idea what you're on about at all.'

'Rape; back in the eighties. No publicity, strict anonymity in those days, unless a guilty verdict was brought in.'

I remembered: a dodgy, relatively short-lived experiment, when our legislators decreed the keeping the names of defendants as well as female victims under wraps. A kind of spurious equality between the complainant and the accused. One or two of the tabloids, whose editors had once screamed for abolition, now wanted it back. Somebody, somewhere had been holding an exciting office party, perhaps.

'Not locally?' Surely, George and his almost perfect intelligence system hadn't let me down?

'No, down in the Met.'

'Then how——?'

'A course at the Staff College; I met this Metropolitan DCI. Amazing what you get to know about the rich and the would-be famous while you're there.'

Bramshill, frequently criticised, derided even, by vast numbers of lowly, jealous plods who affected to hold the entire institution in contempt. A useful snippet of knowledge, but not part of the official college curriculum, all the same.

'One of those date-rape things,' continued Teddy, acid etching his voice. 'He was lucky to walk away. Took this girl researcher out, and wined and dined her. Spent a couple of hundred pounds, and wanted a return on his capital. She said no.'

'Insufficient evidence, sir?'

'It looked good at the time; she complained the same night, she had the usual signs of penetration and she was marked. They'd even got a neighbour who'd heard her screaming from the next flat.'

'But?'

Teddy shrugged. 'The usual load of rubbish; he claimed consent and squeals of ecstasy; he also had an excellent QC. The DCI who dealt with him reckoned it cost him close on thirty-five thousand pounds by the time he was through.

'No publicity, as I say, but it was the end of the game show. It was all downhill after that, and a few years later he ends up running a tacky little show at the end of the Eddathorpe pier.'

I raised my eyebrows, 'And all we've got left is a stubby little platform; it's not even a proper pier!'

'Exactly.' Vengefully, Teddy Baring grinned. The Eddathorpe pier, like that at Wigan, was something of a joke. Not that we hadn't had a proper, full-length Victorian affair, once. But the storm of 1987 had put paid to that. All that now remained was a truncated stub shored-up with girders and surrounded by a frill of concrete blocks. The theatre, once near the entrance, now found itself situated uneasily at the end of the negotiable bit.

Not for the first time, I found myself facing both ways at once. Parkes, a bad bugger, apparently; but it was a difficult one all the same. After all, he'd only been found guilty after the second or third tomato juice in the Staff College bar.

Gloomily, I counted the current score; one dead, one missing, the possibility of two serious sex offenders on the loose, and the potential for at least a couple of enthusiastic amateurs on top of that. And all in the middle of the season, in one small seaside town. I was sitting on a powder keg: time, more than time, for the proverbial early arrest.

'Well,' said Teddy, 'is he fit?'

Has he done it? Will he do? And that from a man who normally used words as bloodlessly, as precisely as the voice on the speaking clock. My turn to give a bit of a grin; it wasn't exactly in character, our greying, balding, uniformed superintendent laying on a touch of slangy Jack-the-lad from the rougher element within the CID.

'We took a statement, and completed the usual descriptive form. He reckons he was at the theatre until around half-past-ten, twenty to eleven, maybe, on Monday night. Then he went for a drink and a meal with one or two of the cast. Got home at roughly quarter-to-one.'

'Alone?'

'No; he says he had one of the junior wannabes in for a nightca – sorry, member of the chorus,' I added hastily, noting his expression. Today, apparently, was one of those occasions when only superintendents did the trendy chat. 'But she didn't stay all night. Got the girl a late-night taxi a few minutes before two.'

'Couldn't stand him, huh?' The Baring imagination was obviously at work. 'He must be sixty, if he's a day.'

'Fifty-eight, but he's got one of these miniature multi-gyms fitted up in his bathroom, boss.'

His face muscles moved fractionally. Subtle innuendo; it was Teddy's kind of dig. 'I won't even ask you how you discovered that.'

'This telephone call, boss. Did he have something in mind, if it wasn't a specific complaint?'

'Putting down poison, I suspect.' Briefly, he consulted the note pad at his elbow. 'Colin,' he said.

'What about him?'

'Owns a boat?'

'No. sir. It's Paulie Parkes's boat. He keeps it at Aylfleet, but Colin Critchley's living on it with a mate. Colin's the lead guitarist with a group called *Immortal Sins.*'

'Remind me,' murmured Teddy, 'not to go within two hundred yards of that theatre until they close the show.' I remained unsurprised; not an aficionado, then. Not what you might call a popular music fan.

'Colin's got a very nasty temper, or so Parkes says. Parkes also says he told you that this Colin person knew Davinia, but he got the impression that you didn't take too much notice at the time. Thought a more senior officer ought to be put in the picture, so to speak.'

'Helpful bastard,' I said.

Teddy looked down his nose. Bad language: however mild the expression, he disapproved. Not for the first time, I wondered how and why he'd ever stuck to this crude, blasphemous, irreligious mob.

'Something else; he doesn't want to give a false impression. He wants to be fair, and he's speaking against his own interests as well.'

'Oh, yes?' It wouldn't have taken a genius to detect a tone of heavy irony in either voice.

'He's had to think long and hard before telling us this; bad publicity and ammunition for some women's group that's persecuting his show, he says. But men hang around his theatre; hoping to meet women, you know.'

'Gee whiz!'

'Especially last Saturday night.' Teddy abandoned the act. 'The night our victim won her quarter-final heat, a man got as far as the beauty contestants' dressing room; they had to throw him out. He says you'll understand why he had to think it over before he volunteered.'

'Did he provide a description?'

'Fattish, scruffy, middle-aged. They didn't take a lot of notice, apparently. It's not exactly unknown.'

'And was this intruder looking specifically for Davinia West?'

'He never bothered asking; Parkes just got the house manager and one of the backstage labourers to give him the Big E. His words, not mine,' Teddy thrust a forefinger against the entry on his pad.

'He doesn't know, does he, that you're aware of his, er, exciting past?'

Teddy simply looked.

'Thank you, sir.'

You, I promised myself, are very likely to experience another short, sharp visit, Paulie Parkes.

Angie's shoulder-length blonde hair fell across her face like a curtain, hiding her expression. Toddler in bed, me with the dog curled at my feet, we should have been all set for one of those gentle, evening-together domestic scenes between husband and wife. Instead, Angie sat brooding over her coffee cup at the table, while I stirred uneasily in my armchair, wondering whether I should have kept this particular problem firmly to myself.

'Do you think I ought to withdraw my application?' she said sombrely, barely touching the edge of the plastic-shrouded sheet of paper with the tip of one finger.

'No.'

Another silence. Then, 'Man or woman?' she asked.

'Woman,' I said. 'Not a man's style, I think.'

'Standing up for the male sex, are you?' She managed the ghost of a smile.

'Not exactly,' I said, a touch of bitterness intruding; it had been a long day. 'There are some crimes that're exclusively a male preserve. Believe me, they make shoving a bit of paper through a letterbox pale beside them.'

'I didn't think anybody really hated me that much.'

'Perhaps it's me; maybe they're just having a go through you.'

Perversely, I wished that I could have stirred her up. Get the adrenaline pumping in the way I'd reacted on first seeing the poison-pen letter: up in the air, and really good and mad. Instead, she'd wilted a bit; the victim, but it was all her fault.

'I'm sorry, Rob.' Little or nothing to do with the letter itself; she was brooding over a nasty little game of consequences, and I knew exactly what she meant.

Nevertheless, I was shocked; not like flaming-tempered Angie at all. I wouldn't have put me down as the placid type, but Angie usually struck the sparks. Seventy percent of the emotional fireworks were usually lit by her.

'What did Albert Flaxman say?'

'He suggested burning it, but I took a statement, instead.'

She nodded, 'They can always send another, can't they? Or a flood of them, any time they like. For all we know, they probably already have. What are you going to do next?'

'Nothing, yet.'

'But what about,' she touched the plastic again, 'fingerprints, or something.'

'It's a possibility,' I conceded, 'but think about it, love; what happens if I go to Scenes of Crime? One, we haven't got a suspect, so they'd have to do a full-system search in the hope of matching a single set of prints, even if there are any, and two, they're bound to gossip. The police force is a village; these things always get out.'

'It's out already, by the look of this.'

True: I lived with it, but the people who saw my personal file, and knew my reasons for abandoning my old force, had seen a lot worse in their time. Headquarters Personnel department was discreet; Peter Fairfield, on the subject of bruised, floored, uniformed whiz kids was quietly amused, and Superintendent Edward Baring had only ever broached the subject once, and then obliquely; he was far too polite.

As for the rest, the rumours that might well have percolated across force boundaries came under the heading of old, unsubstantiated gossip: it would be a different matter if the tale-bearers had fresh tidings of an enquiry, complete with news of the purple-stained letters and envelopes which follow a fingerprint examination, to salivate over in the police canteen.

'Have you said anything to anybody at all?'

'No.' Teddy: almost, but not quite. I'd teetered on the edge during the course of the afternoon, but the opportunity never seemed to arise.

'And is that it, then? Do nothing, and hope they go away? Surely, once they realise that Councillor Flaxman won't play, they'll try again?'

'A bit of passing bile,' I said hopefully. 'Maybe they've got it out of their system by now.'

She sat upright; the curtain of hair flicked back.

'I doubt it.'

So did I.

'I had a look around some of the offices,' I confessed reluctantly, 'before I came home. Took samples from some of the typewriters; it doesn't take an expert to tell me that I haven't got a match.'

'I thought you said you'd done nothing,' she accused. I ignored that.

'Tomorrow,' I muttered, 'given the opportunity, empty offices and so on, I'll do the rest.'

'Don't you trust your colleagues?' Suddenly, in the absence of another target, a hint of hostility entered her voice. 'And I thought you said it was a woman, not a man?'

'Just covering the possibilities; besides, there are two uni-formed policewomen as well as any number of female civilians knocking around.'

'You obviously think a lot about them, doing that.' Niggling, sarcastic now; a hint of how much she disliked the police force, still barely managing to put up with it, on the quiet.

'It's got to be somebody,' I said foolishly, a remark worthy of genius, on the whole. 'And anyway, what about you and your coffee-sipping circles? Who have you managed to offend?'

It was a wonderful evening, and we did it all by ourselves. No open warfare, something short of a mutual nuclear strike. Absolutely profitless, all the same.

Ostensibly, we were discussing the letter; in reality, we stupidly chipped our way around the edges of the past-and-hopefully-done-with, and gnawed away at old hurts that neither of us could do anything about.

The poison-pen writer would have been delighted: two supposedly grown-up people without a useful idea between them. And neither with a scrap of common sense.

# Chapter Nine

'Got 'im!' Detective Constable Patrick Goodall at the top of his voice and form. The incident room echoed to what can only be described as his vulgar triumphalism. 'Nothing like a bit of local knowledge to start you off.'

Neither the assembled DCs nor the select band of civvy clerks looked all that impressed. Pat, running his own one-man public relations outfit as usual, pressed on. 'Just waiting for fatty Forster to get us a print-out of his previous, downstairs, an' we're going to interview the little scumbag,' he said.

'You mean you haven't actually stitched him up for murder, yet?' One of the other DCs was having a bit of fun.

'Don't be so daft!' Wrapped up in his own sense of self-importance, Pat failed to see the trap. 'I'm only saying we've managed to eliminate one possibility, that's all. Weary Willie's harmless, apart from his bein' a flasher, he wouldn't hurt a fly.'

'If he's armless, how does he manage to get—' the DC paused, seeing Paula come into the room.

'It out of his trousers,' she finished smartly. 'Don't mind me, I've heard it all before.'

Young, a stranger to Eddathorpe and unused to pregnant females in charge of incident rooms, he blushed.

She walked over to the briefing board, awarding me a reproachful look en route. Her incident room being turned into a cabaret in her absence; the boss present, and failing to run a sufficiently-tight ship.

'I hear you've arrested Weary Willie Fraser,' she said severely to Pat. 'You ought to have thought about him long ago, hadn't you? He's a Retton lad.'

Pat, seconded from Retton for the duration of the enquiry, failed to look contrite. 'We thought he'd packed it in,' he muttered. 'How was I to know he'd started up again, five miles down the road?'

'Probably comes in on the bus,' suggested someone.

'Using his old age pensioner's pass.'

'Specially to expose himself on our seafront; shame!'

'He's not all that old,' snapped Pat, incensed, 'and he's bought himself a Reliant Robin, if you must know.'

A howl of derision went up.

'OK, OK,' said Paula. 'Playtime over, settle down; and Pat, Malc is waiting for you in the custody suite; best get your skates on, eh?'

Marginally deflated, Pat Goodall made for the door.

'And Pat.'

'Yes, boss?' He turned towards her with something approaching a sheepish grin.

'He might, as you say, be harmless,' somehow she managed the tiniest stress on the aitch, 'but when you do the interview, make absolutely sure you get a complete picture of his recent movements, especially over Monday night. Any doubts, any discrepancies whatsoever, and you terminate the interview and notify me or Mr Graham; right?'

'Bet he bought it from Schumacher,' said one of the civvies, pushing his luck. Then, his voice trailing away, 'The Reliant Robin, I mean.'

Paula awarded him the Glare. He ducked; suddenly, unexpectedly, the flickering screen of his VDU assumed an immense importance in his life.

Paula, lips pursed, pinned the name-card and photograph up

next to the briefing board; Charles Plantagenet Fraser, 48 years, CRO, and a back street Retton address. Heavy-shouldered, beer-bellied, scruffy; not exactly the kingly type.

'*Plantagenet?*' I asked.

'You never know,' said Paula wisely. 'Anyway, it's nothing to do with me.'

'I'll believe you; what about Weary Willie, then?'

She looked disparagingly around the room, 'Police humour,' she said. 'Him being a flasher, and all. He's not what you might call over-virile, if you see what I mean. I don't suppose I need to expl—'

'No; that's more than sufficient, thanks.'

She stared pensively at the card, 'They were just driving past; bit of luck, I suppose, Pat and Malcolm picking him up like that.' She sounded almost depressed, her whole attitude less than enthusiastic today. 'He's in the system, though. We'd have got around to interviewing him, in the end.'

'Along with a couple of dozen others.'

'Yeah.' Long pause. 'Can I have a word in private, boss?'

'Sure.'

She picked up her handbag from the side of her desk, and with a nod to Roger Prentice, she followed me out of the room, her progress followed by half a dozen curious, probably slightly resentful, pairs of eyes. Not at all like Paula; she'd spoiled their fun.

Settled in the visitor's chair in my office she unclasped the top of her bag. 'You might have noticed, boss; I'm not in a jokey mood today. I'd like to have a word with the funny bugger who did this!'

My heart sank as she withdrew the inevitable plastic-sheathed envelope and single sheet of paper, and placed them flat on my desk. An illustrated message this time, but I knew, more or less what to expect.

The envelope, cheap brown manila, foolscap size, was addressed to her husband, Detective Constable Andrew N

Spriggs at their home, and once again the note itself was poorly typed.

Below a crudely pasted photograph of a baby, obviously clipped from a newspaper, was the simple message:

'IT COULD BELONG TO A PASSING MILKMAN.
THEN AGAIN IT COULD BE YOURS.
ME, I THINK IT BELONGS TO THE RANDY DCI
WHO'S BEEN FUCKING HER.
I THINK WE OUGHT TO BE TOLD DON'T YOU?'

'First post this morning,' said Paula. 'It's a crummy old type-writer; they've had to double-strike on the Bs and Os.

'Andy wants you to institute a disciplinary enquiry to trace whoever did it; he was far from chuffed.'

I touched the edge of the plastic covering the envelope; Andrew N Spriggs. It was jumping to conclusions; nevertheless, there was that second initial: how very precise.

I searched in my pockets for my keys, unlocked, removed Albert's missive from my top right-hand drawer and passed it across the desk.

Paula read it in silence.

'So Andy reckons it's definitely a copper, huh?'

*Britannia* it was not, and it was hardly going to cause a stir of envy among the millionaire yachtsmen of Monte Carlo and Cannes. It looked, however, like a sound, if somewhat scruffy and neglected seagoing boat. About thirty feet long, relatively low in the water, with what looked to me like a top-heavy covered bridge, a well in the stern, and broad in comparison with its length. And that's as far as I went; one visit to *HMS Victory* as a kid, and a few early games of Pooh-sticks, covers the extent of my technical knowledge of things that float.

'Could do with a clean up,' said George judiciously, wearing his nautical head. 'Do we shout ahoy! or what?'

I glanced briefly along the double line of craft moored to Aylfleet Marina's central wooden jetty, some with safe and stable gangplanks, others without. Just my luck. *Seasprite*, moored stern-on, with an uncertain little gap between vessel and shore guarded by a couple of old car tyres to prevent damage to the hull, was without. I looked down: I could just, if I tried, manage to fall into the yard or so of oily water between jetty and boat and create a vacancy for an Eddathorpe DCI.

A hop, skip and a jump, and I was over the stern with a passing thought as to how I was going to make my way back in due course. Boats, even tied-up boats, move uncomfortably; they do not provide a stable platform from which to jump. As a non-subscriber to the seagoing traditions of our island race, I wondered how I would ever get home.

I watched with interest as George, older, heavier, inappropriately dressed for the occasion in a three-piece suit, scrambled aboard. He was worse than me. Our clumsy arrival appeared to have gone unnoticed; the door to the cabin remained firmly shut, and the sounds of something suspiciously like Radio One could be heard echoing tinnily from inside.

'Knock,' I said to George, 'and don't forget to wipe your feet.'

A literal-minded fellow, he knocked.

'Just a minute.'

The sound of the radio ceased, to be followed by indistinct scrapings and a thumping noise. Finally, after a struggle with the sliding hatch, the top half of Colin Critchley appeared, peering up at us, leaning unsteadily across three or four companion-way steps.

'Police?'

'Mr Critchley? Detective Chief Inspector Graham; Detective Sergeant Caunt.'

He waved aside the proffered warrant cards. 'I was expecting you as soon as I heard.' A definite criticism. 'Watch your heads as you step down.' Politely, he reached upwards and thrust back a pair of hinged flaps above his head to allow us inside.

He was not, at first sight, a prepossessing young man. Broad-shouldered, slim-hipped, OK; dressed in the prototypical orange open-necked shirt and black leather waistcoat; but his face was sallow, washed-out, and his eyes, with tiny creases around the outer corners, looked old.

His stare, and the twist to the lips, not so much cynical as weary, gave him a peculiar, twenty-five rising fifty, look, which might have had its appeal to the kids hopefully hanging around the stage door. To my jealous, if inexperienced eye, a lifetime of late nights and groupies were etched in the slashes on either side of his mouth. He was, as it turned out, twenty-three.

'Scumbag told me las' night,' he said, waving us on to one of the oak benches covered in long, leatherette cushions which ran the length of the saloon-cum-galley on either side, with a fold-down table in between. 'Take the weight off your feet.'

The accent was definitely Midlands, with an entirely incongruous touch of the Southern States. The rhinestone-cowboy bit. The tight jeans, the heels on his yellow boots, and the big-buckle belt around his waist did nothing to mitigate the image. Country and Western, I would have guessed, rather than Rock.

Like Teddy, however, I've never got much further than the Last Night of the Proms, myself. Tone-deaf, written-off as a fuddy-duddy by my own wife, I'm hardly in a position to judge.

'Well,' he sat himself down opposite and leaned forward. 'First, I'm sorry, dead sorry about her, right? Second, has that snivelling cocksucker told you I done it, yet?'

'What?'

'Aw, cummon; you oughta have seen the way he was behavin' last night. Columbo just wasn't in it, man. He practically told me I'd done it to stuff him personally, along with his ratty little show.'

'And did you?' Good old George. 'Do it?' he said. Against

the rules; he wasn't supposed to say that. Only one member of the party was allowed to play at being disarmingly blunt.

'No, course I didn't.' Challenged, bounced in his turn, Critchley looked genuinely shocked.

'That's all right then,' said George.

We both looked as amiable as possible, and we allowed ourselves a ten-second pause.

'You mean that's it?'

'Well, no, er, Colin, it isn't it.' Looking as cuddly and unthreatening as possible, I smiled. Puts the wind up people if you do it properly all the same. 'We were hoping you were going to fill in some background, and tell us all about her. You were one of her boyfriends, after all.'

'She was gorgeous, she came from Barnsley, she was stupid and I was screwing her for about three weeks.'

'Some people,' I said mildly, 'might think that was a smartarse way of putting it. A particularly callous thing to say.'

'Are coppers allowed to talk to you like that?'

'This copper's going to. He'd have bought a ticket if he'd wanted to see you putting on an act.'

'You're lying, aren't you?' Critchley straightened up and stared fearfully at George. 'It's not all right. You're playing with me, then you're gonna pounce.'

'Pounce?'

'I don't know how to talk to you; I dunno what to say. Paulie says you've already made up your minds.' Suddenly, he sounded about fourteen, and he was scared. I'd been right about one thing at least, the macho stuff had peeled away. Somebody, presumably Paulie Parkes, had stretched him almost to breaking point. He'd not been able to sustain much of a front.

'Why don't you just tell us how you met her,' said George. 'Then we'll get around to friend Paulie in due course.' He peeled back his lips in what was meant to be a reassuring, anti-Paulie demonstration. Critchley simply stared; he'd failed entirely to catch the tone of voice. Instead, he appeared to have fixated solely on the threatening grin.

'Oh my God,' he muttered. 'He showed me the newspapers, you know, last night. Horrible; nothing more than a silly kid, and all.'

That made two of them, and for a man who'd expressed total disinterest in the media and all its works, by evening it sounded as though Paulie had become a very busy boy. Still, keep him going, we hadn't come for the tea-and-sympathy stuff.

'You sound just like Paulie,' I said. 'He tried to tell us he never reads the papers or watches TV news.'

'I don't have a telly.'

'No, but you've got a radio, old son. It was blasting out when we knocked. Local radio was putting it out every hour, on the hour, all day.'

'I knew nothing, I tell ya, not until he jumped me last night. Look, I get up; I have a meal, and I usually just hang around. Whenever we have a rehearsal, I go and meet the lads.

'Maybe we hang around again; maybe we go out for a drink. One show in the evenings, six days a week, and on Wednesday's there's another in the afternoon.

'As I say; up, meals, show, bit of a laugh, bed and that's it. I'm trying to save money, if you must know. When it gets to the end of the season it's going to be sod off Paulie Parkes, and the others feel the same.'

'Fine,' I said. 'So where did you find time to meet Davinia, in this busy jet-set life?'

'At the Standard; I was in there with Nigel 'bout eight, nine weeks ago.'

I looked ignorant.

'One of the band; Nigel Laud. The others are Matthew Priestly and Jason McNaught, OK?' Three more enquiries for the computer; George scrawled, looking cross.

'We might as well have the name of this other mate of yours while we're at it, I suppose.'

'What mate?'

'The one you invited to live here without so much as a by-your-leave.' George made a fair stab at imitating Parkes.

'Paulie again, eh?' Critchley sneered. 'God, that man's a snide: Nigel, OK? Nigel stays here, on and off. Sometimes he's here; sometimes he has a night with his parents; sometimes he stays with a girl.'

'Then why didn't Parkes simply say he was a member of the band?'

'Look, you might as well know; Paulie financed us in the first place, partially, anyway. Gear, van; got us a few gigs when we started out. He thought he owned us, after that.'

'We had a keyboard player who went AWOL as soon as the season started, an' I replaced him with Nigel. That old bastard just can't stand not bein' consulted an' having his finger in every pie, so he makes the odd inu – inuwhatsit, OK?'

'Innuendo?'

'Yeah.'

'About what?'

'Nigel, well, Nigel's sorta pretty, right. Paulie likes to pretend he's queer.'

'But he's not?'

'No; not that it matters to anybody but a creep.' He stared challengingly at what he obviously regarded as a pair of homophobic cops, paused, and added sarcastically, 'I could probably get ya some signed testimonials, if you like.'

'So, that first time in the pub, both you and Nigel chatted her up?' George plodded on; he'd been insulted by experts in his time.

'S'right; nothing wrong with that, is there? She's got a fantastic body – what am I saying? Oh, Christ!'

Body: an evocative word at the best of times. Not so hard-boiled, after all; a more sensitive figure than I'd thought at first.

'I wouldn't have thought,' said George, 'that the Royal Standard was your kind of pub.'

For the first time Colin Critchley's face relaxed into something approaching a grin. 'You've been hearing things, huh?'

'A thousand a week, according to Paulie,' agreed George.

'Yeah, yeah; with me living on a luxury yacht an' all?' He looked around disparagingly and sniffed; the stained folding table, the shabby fittings, and the slight but all-pervasive background smell of damp.

'He tells everybody that. Big-hearted bastard, giving the young talent a thousand a week. True, sometimes. When he remembers to pay us; when Santa Claus drives his reindeer down the prom! An' it's a thousand a week divided between four. Bet he never told you that?'

'About Davinia ...' Time for me to put a stopper on the professional revelations, fascinating though they were.

'Like I said, lovely kid.' This, with an age gap of all of eighteen months. 'Chatted her up, went out with her; willing and able, if you see what I mean.'

'And then?'

'Thought I might give her a leg-up as well as a leg-over, all right?' He just couldn't resist it; backwards and forwards between vulnerable youngster and brittle-voiced prat.

'Paulie Parkes and his Saturday night parade?'

'Yeah, that was Colin's little mistake, I guess. I even encouraged her.'

'Is the contest a fix?'

'She must have been hoping so. I figure that's what Paulie told her, anyway. *One session on mah casting-couch, honey, an' you're gonna be jest fine.*' It sounded nothing like Paulie; a talent for self-parody was creeping in.

'And you found out?'

'Found out? I walked in on him, pal. We all knew about the little girls and the sofa in his office; ah just didn't expect to find mah woman with him, all tangled up!'

'How long ago was this?'

'Weeks ago. Long before,' he added slyly, 'she reached the quarter-finals, anyway.'

'Fight with him?' enquired George hopefully.

'No,' regret tinged his voice. 'One good belt, but I ain't stupid. I left it at that; he's about as old as God.'

'What happened afterwards?'

'With Davinia?' He blew out his cheeks. 'Nothin', absolutely nothin'; the way I see it, we all gotta earn a living, and I'm still part of the show. Look at me.'

'You didn't pack her up?'

'You think I kept her after that? In your dreams, man! I mean I didn't specially blame her; that's all. If she figured she could get anything out of a lying creep like Paulie, good luck! That's what I mean about her being a stupid kid.'

'It finished, just like that? Did she try to say anything, to explain?'

'What's to explain? Another Miss Roundheels; end of story. Happens all the time; a bit of a slag.'

'So, you never saw or spoke to her after that?'

'I saw her, sure. She won the quarter-final last Saturday night.'

'Oh, yes,' I said. 'A bit of trouble, eh?'

'Trouble?'

'Man hanging about the dressing rooms; security slung 'im out?'

'Oh, the purse, you mean?'

'What purse?'

'They caught this middle-aged idiot hanging about. Paulie thought he was looking for a bit of tit, so they hassled him a bit, then they just got rid. Should have searched him before they did it, right? One of the girls lost a purse with twenty quid in it.'

'Why wasn't it reported?'

'It wasn't Paulie's twenty quid, I suppose.' He gave us something approaching a mirthless grin.

'And Davinia; you're sure you never saw her again after the bust-up; apart from at the show?'

He paused, uneasy again. What was left of the grin disappeared; then he said reluctantly, 'Saw her one more time, I suppose. In the pub.'

'You went back to the Royal Standard?' George wasn't the only one who pricked up his ears.

'Nope; she came here to Aylfleet one lunchtime; three, four weeks ago.'

'Your local?'

'Yep, the Lion.'

'And?'

'I walked out. Nothing to say; I didn't want his leavings.'

'What about her?'

'Aw, cummon; more bullshit, man. Some crap about her struggling, and Paulie being the bad guy. She never said a word about it at the time.'

'Tell me,' I said, trying for the bounce, 'did she ever give you your present back?'

'What present?'

'Earrings, maybe?'

'Oh, sure, anything like that.' No hesitation, and a straight sarcastic grin. 'Not even one of those cuddly rabbits she was so fond of; no.' Looking back on it, there might have been the merest trace of a sneer in his voice, but I didn't bother to pick him up on it at the time.

A spot of reiteration now. Going over the boring bits, or taking further and better particulars, as the lawyers say.

'Fancy telling us all about your movements on Monday night?' suggested George.

# Chapter Ten

'He's gone off to the continong,' said the bearded labourer, scarcely pausing with his paintbrush on the rails at the edge of the main Marina dock. Then, with heavy humour, 'Better weather over there!'

We stared gloomily at the empty berth. No signs of Ralph Sheppard, nor *The Blue Marlin*, which was, according to our informant, a pretty up-market boat. Personally, I could have done with a spot of luxury living after our visit to Colin Critchley and all that depressing smell of damp.

'When will he be back?'

'No idea, mate: weekend, next week, who knows?' Then, mockingly, to our retreating backs, 'Shall I let him know you called?'

'There's always at least one ruddy comedian,' muttered George.

'Never mind,' I said.

'Does that mean we can go and arrest Paulie Parkes?'

'Whatever,' I asked innocently, 'would make you want to go and do a thing like that?'

'Well, for one thing he's a complete and utter wanker,' said George.

I pretended to consider the options, 'Good, but not quite good enough.'

'He right up there, boss. Just for starters, what about that old case of rape?'

'It hardly got off the ground.'

'Our victim told Colin that he'd had a go at her.'

'And he didn't believe her, remember? He wouldn't accept what she told him, and he was there.'

'Insufficient evidence?'

'Not yet.'

'All the same, he's got a very funny attitude to sex. Tacky; he can't seem to leave the subject alone. All this rubbish about lesbians and queers and stuff.'

'Not to mention priapism.'

'Eh?'

'It's when you're old and past it,' I informed him rudely, 'and you've still got this unnatural interest in bedding birds.'

'Sometimes,' he replied sadly, 'I feel quite sorry for you, boss. There's nothing unnatural about it at all.'

He was a very young, very new DC; younger than Patrick Goodall at a guess. A virtual stranger to me, and behaving like a pup with two tails.

'We've got him, sir,' he said.

Not so far as I could see; all we had was a longish strip of green-printed paper completed in blue biro, dated 23 September, 1979, together with a fax. He'd set both of them carefully side by side on my desk.

The marriage certificate drew my attention first. In the Registration District of Salford, Lancs (Sub-district of Regent Road), a marriage had been solemnised between Alan Alfred Pykett, bachelor, 32 years, described as a labourer, and Maureen Sullivan, 19 years, spinster and hotel employee. The name of the groom's father was blank, and his occupation listed as unknown, while the bride's parent, Francis Xavier Sullivan, was a farmer. No address shown, but in the light of what she'd said to George, County Mayo, Ireland, seemed a fairish bet.

'Yes? How do we tie this up?'

'Greater Manchester, boss. Fax of the details from a Local Intelligence card; 1980, 1981, and 1982: Salford address, it's Pykett all right, his date of birth matches with the subsequent rape conviction in our county, and she's the right age. No prosecutions, but there's a series of domestic violence complaints, and visits from his local police.'

No prosecutions, and somebody, somewhere in the depths of a Local Intelligence office had kept an unweeded record relating to a local troublemaker in a filing cabinet for damn nearly twenty years. I liked it: the civil liberties mob would probably have a fit.

'Well done; so our Alan was definitely married to our Maureen at one stage. Great! How did you find this out?'

'Prison records, boss; I backtracked from them. They had a bloody sight more information on Pykett than our antecedents and CRO 74.'

'What about the divorce?'

The youngest DC sucked his teeth, 'Not yet; the courts are trying to turn up the decree absolute for me, but the records aren't centralised, and there's no saying whether it was in the Manchester court.'

'I don't suppose,' I said ungratefully, shuffling both the copy certificate and the fax into a file, 'that you've got any signs of a body to go with all this?'

'I hope not, boss.'

'Eh? Oh, yes; see what you mean.' Depressing, when you get pulled-up short, your attention jerked in the general direction of the nastier possibilities, by some inexperienced kid. The body I wanted was Pykett, and preferably alive. I did not, under any circumstances, want news of his deceased and for-mer spouse.

'Nothing on her at all?'

'We've got a driver who says he might have seen a woman answering her description at the bus station, talking to a man the afternoon she disappeared. Rusty-coloured coat, small suitcase; pretty much the same as her.'

'They showed him Pykett's picture?'

'He's not even sure about the woman; he hardly glanced at the man.'

'And he's got no idea what bus, if any, that he, she or they might have caught?' Selfishly, I wanted everything, and the touch of bitterness showed in my voice.

''Fraid not.' The youngest DC sounded guilty, as if he, personally, had let me down.

'But we are trying all the buses?' My voice had been sharper than I'd intended. 'Sorry; hardly your fault.'

'Something else, boss.'

'Hmmm?'

'DS Prentice and Detective Inspector Spriggs; they told me to tell you they've had a bit of trouble with a bloke called Gordon West who says he's Davinia's dad.'

'It's her stepdad, if he's anything at all. In any case he buggered off years ago, somewhere in South Yorks; where the hell did they manage to turn him up?'

'He found us; he came to complain about a TV news crew. He reckons he heard about the murder from the South Yorkshire police. They took a bit of a statement, and once they'd stirred him up he went and phoned the TV news. They got him to come to Eddathorpe under false pretences by promising him two hundred quid, or so he says.'

'Let me guess; some sort of amateur vulture doing an interview for cash?'

'S'right; he reckons he came all the way from South Yorkshire because they'd promised, and once he'd done the interview outside her house, they welshed. He wants his money, as well as the bus fare and all.'

'What about the statement; have we got it yet?'

'On its way, but it's nothing worthwhile; mother dead, stepdaughter in care. Just as you say, he hadn't even seen her for two or three years. And the TV boys say his trip was expenses only, chum.

'Anyway, once he came in we grabbed him, showed him the corpse, and took another statement off him for the Coroner. He's fit to be tied, 'cos he's now the witness for the ID.'

'So what happened?'

'He turned nasty; reckoned we owed him for the statement. He wouldn't accept that we weren't taking sides in a civil dispute with the boys from the Telly. Roger Prentice had to escort him out.'

'Tough luck,' I said absently, my mind still occupied elsewhere. 'So long as we've got a statement and an address.'

The police are not responsible for everything that happens, particularly to your strictly temporary, entirely mercenary, estranged and only-acting dad. Not part of my murder enquiry, either: not on my personal list for tea and sympathy. Full stop.

How was I supposed to know that he was some sort of uncertified nutter with a degree in mayhem and a talent for anti-police revenge? Or that thanks, in part at least, to him and his grievance, a typical Eddathorpe thunderstorm was about to break?

Peter Fairfield was back, from which I deduced that he either loved the seaside, or he hadn't got anything better to do. Unfair really, if I was overseeing an undetected murder enquiry, I'd probably want to keep my eye on the investigating DCI.

'Seen this?' He tossed across the early afternoon edition of the *Eastern Free Press* across my desk.

### 'CRIME PREVENTION CHAIR RESIGNS
Police Defend Criminals Instead of Public,
Says Disgusted Ex-chief.'

I glanced at the headline, 'Oh, good.'

'And what's that supposed to mean?'

'If Ian Buchanan is now the ex-chairman of the Crime Prevention Panel, boss, it's the best news I've had all day.'

Fairfield scowled; I showed no signs of moving, so he settled himself reluctantly in the visitor's chair. 'Read the rest of it before you say that.'

'Buchanan,' I persisted, 'is nothing but a pest. Minor business-man, and total pain. He thinks he owns the place because he's got a Ford Granada, and more than one blue suit.'

No answering smile, no lightening of the atmosphere; the scowl intensified by roughly twenty-five percent.

'He says he's going to become a vigilante now.'

I read on:

*'In the course of a hastily convened emergency meeting of the Eddathorpe and District Crime Prevention Panel at the Chamber of Commerce last night, local businessman, Ian Buchanan, 63, the chair of the committee, launched a full-scale attack on police attitudes towards local crime.*

*'Questioned regarding rumours that a recently paroled rapist was being sought in connection with the Cranbourne Avenue death of model-girl Davinia West, 21, Superintendent Edward Baring, the Eddathorpe police commander, refused to be drawn.*

*'It would be premature and inimical to our enquiries,' he said, 'to discuss the identity of any possible suspects at this stage.''*

'Eddathorpe and its ruddy rumours,' I muttered irritably, 'I wonder where he managed to dredge that one up.'

I paused for a moment while I chewed over an old feud; nothing serious from my point of view, but I disliked Buchanan. Old man Buchanan hated me. Something to do with a row in a pub during the course of a former enquiry, Joe showing his teeth, and an elderly, overweight loudmouth beating a precipitate retreat.

*'"That is entirely typical," claimed Mr Buchanan, "of the spineless attitude of the local police. They would much sooner hide behind a bureaucratic smoke*

*screen than warn vulnerable women and children of the dreadful truth. A*
*murderous sex maniac is stalking our streets; the police know his identity,*
*and they're refusing to release his name.""*

'Windbag,' I offered.

'According to the *Free Press*,' said Fairfield grimly, 'that
windbag went on to resign from the Crime Prevention Panel;
then he claimed he was going to hold a public meeting tonight
to drum up public support for citizen street patrols. He reckons
he's hired the ballroom at Eddathorpe Town Hall, and he hopes
all concerned citizens will turn up.'

'Anybody with seventy-five quid,' I agreed morosely, 'can hire
the ballroom. But he probably won't get much of an audience,'
I added hopefully, 'with a bit of luck.'

'The Chief won't care,' said Fairfield in his gentle, striving-to-
be-reasonable voice, 'whether the audience is confined to three
one-legged men and a solitary mongrel dog. Any suggestion of
people other than the police patrolling the streets, and he'll go
absolutely apeshit, Bob.'

'Have you spoken to Mr Baring, sir?' No doubt about it,
Buchanan was right. Bureaucracy: nothing, absolutely nothing
like passing the buck.

'He's out.'

'Well, he obviously knows all about it, sir, and I'm sure he'll
have everything in hand.'

'And he's the divisional commander, eh?' Peter Fairfield
looked positively benign. 'I'm sure he's got everything under
control. He'll probably take Derek Paget with him, and everything will be fine from a uniform point of view.'

I nodded, relieved, but not for long.

'You're my eyes and ears, Bob, and I want *you* there as well.
Firstly, if there's any shit flying, I want a full report, and
secondly, I don't want to see any of it splattering all over the
CID. You take my point?'

Politics: a spot of interdepartmental nose wiping, at best,

and if things turn nasty, make sure it's at uniform branch expense.

'Oh, yes,' I said.

Having auditioned me for the role of Judas Iscariot, Fairfield, in his capacity as Director of the production had given me the part. That was the real point at issue, and I definitely understood.

# Chapter Eleven

The meeting started at half past seven, and I collected samples from the remaining office typewriters, finally searching cupboards for old, unused machines, well before I left. *The quick brown fox*, I typed repeatedly, *jumped over the lazy dog;* then I reproduced both of the poisonous little messages underneath.

The result, frustration mingled with relief. Even to my untrained eye the remaining typescripts didn't match. Nothing to submit to the experts; no embarrassing gossip from that source, at least. That still left the problem posed by the possibility of latent fingerprints, especially if we now had a police suspect in our sights.

On joining the Force every recruit, like the majority of criminals, has his fingerprints taken as a matter of routine. Elimination prints; a permanent record in the Headquarters' files. It's amazing how often the new, enthusiastic PC Plod visits a burglary, only to find himself on the receiving end of sarcastic memos for having smeared his dabs over every polished surface in sight.

So, if Andy Sprigg's hypothesis held good, all I had to do was submit the letters and envelopes for fingerprint examination, and I'd stand a fighting chance of identifying the guilty woman, or man, thereby introducing another spicy subject for merry canteen tales.

*Heard the latest about Bob Graham, the Eddathorpe DCI? His wife used to put it about a bit in his old Force, that's probably why he moved, and now he's got this female DI in the pudding club.*

*Bet he won't get into any trouble, either; big bosses' whitewash job, all round. Bloody chief inspectors, it's all right for some . . .*

Somewhat wearily, preparing at last to share the tale, I made my way along the corridor to Teddy's office and knocked.

'Come!'

He was using the old chief constable's dressing room for its original purpose; he'd changed out of uniform in preparation for the town hall meeting, and he was just knotting his tie.

'Hello, Bob, I've heard Fairfield wants you to come to meet Ian Buchanan and his pals, and look after the interests of the poor, persecuted CID.'

First things first: no chance to talk about anonymous letters, after all. It was said evenly enough, but was it my imagination, or was there just a touch of hostility in his voice?

That's the trouble with having two masters; the divisional commander expects your undivided loyalty, while the head of CID expects exactly the same, and deep down, there's always that underlying tension between the uniform branch and those unreliable buggers in plain clothes.

To the tidy mind of the ambitious uniformed officer, the CID presents a slightly anarchical, certainly boozy, distinctly cowboy image. An outfit upon which the man with a field marshal's baton in his knapsack keeps a distinctly wary eye. And all this in spite of the fact that a year or two among the savages may provide a useful stepping-stone to ACC and Chief Constable rank.

To the dyed in the wool thief-taker, however, it's his whole career. There's a tendency for him to harbour a touch of resentment against would-be command level wooden-tops who deal in buzz words, working-parties and the latest politically inspired fashion in policing concepts.

A degree of tension, they say, is creative, but I've been in places where gentle games of interdepartmental bat and ball have degenerated into blood-feuds and outright guerilla warfare. So I'm yet to be convinced.

'Mr Fairfield only wants—'

'To protect his own back, I know.' Teddy gave a final hitch to his tie and put on his jacket before leaving his executive cubbyhole and walking over to his desk.

'I don't know what he's making such a fuss about; I was dealing with people like Buchanan before he was born.'

Teddy was certainly the elder, but this comment was so patently absurd that I grinned. He looked blank for a moment, then he relented, 'Well, perhaps not quite.'

For somebody who was about to go out and calm an enraged citizenry, however, he looked far too relaxed. Teddy, usually so austere, unwilling to show his feelings, wore an air of bravado; he looked positively smug.

Seating himself behind his magnificent, leather-tooled desk he picked up his phone, 'Plenty of time before we go; coffee for two, I think?'

The hostility, if it had ever existed, was gone. A quarter of an hour with the coffee cups; a suitable moment, then, to break the news and engage in a tactical chat.

It was obvious that Superintendent Edward Baring had been busy, and without going into sordid details he wanted me to know. He had about him this studied air of the general psyched-up for battle, or a possible echo of carefree Sir Francis Drake. Never mind the ruddy coffee; I ought to have brought a set of carpet bowls to work.

The Town Hall ballroom was designed and built for a more luxurious, certainly more leisured age. It was constructed, like the Grand Esplanade, the now-abandoned railway station and the Pavilion Theatre itself, for a seaside boom which never quite took off.

Some late Victorian optimist had persuaded the council of the day to build something more appropriate to Blackpool in terms of size, and, to be honest, a Parisian brothel in terms of taste. Tricked out in scarlet, ivory and gilt, with naked cherubs and half-draped plaster ladies peeping coyly from balcony, pillar and door lintel here and there, the whole place was a kind of late nineteenth-century grocer's dream of opulence and lust.

Potentially, too, it was one of the most expensive white elephants on the east coast. Someday, somebody was going to have to dig deep into the public purse to restore this abortion to its original state. So unpleasant was the whole architectural and decorative effect that English Heritage was almost bound to scream for a preservation order and astronomical sums in restoration money, in the end.

In the meantime, dust gathered in all the kinks and crannies, and under the attentions of generations of dancers, boppers, jivers, rockers, cigarette smokers and ticket-toting vandals, the gilt darkened, and the plaster mouldings cracked, crumbled and chipped.

The crimson velvet curtains were still drawn across the stage when we arrived, but four or five dozen spindly, gold-painted chairs had been set out in rows at the front. Two thirds of the room remained empty and echoed with the footsteps of every new arrival as he made his way to his seat.

Less than half the seats were occupied, and the overwhelming majority of the audience was male. A mixture of blazers and ties, jeans and tee shirts; the short-haired and shaven, the tattooed and tough. Heads turned as we made our way across the bare, sprung floor and took our places at the back. Teddy received one or two nods and a single smile, but the majority looked indifferent, blank.

Teddy sat down, took a poll of the audience and glanced surreptitiously at his watch. I didn't comment, but he appeared to be disappointed, almost as if he was expecting a better attended house.

At twenty-eight minutes past seven, a contingent of women arrived. Suits and shiny handbags for the most part, among whom

I recognised the ex-mayoral figure of my old friend Mary Todd. She waved, and grateful for the sight of one possible ally in the midst of an apparently hostile world, I waved back.

Teddy leaned towards me and whispered, 'D'you know the woman next to her, Bob?'

I shook my head.

'Adele Simpson?'

I took another look at the row of women, at the splendidly-groomed, square-shouldered figure settling into her seat beside Mary, and inwardly shuddered.

'No.'

The whole idea of an ally was obviously illusory: the suits, the handbags, the expressions, the whole air of efficiency and mutual support. Vigilante material to a woman: ladies who lunch. Teddy, apparently undismayed, kept peeking over his shoulder, still flicking back his cuff occasionally to examine his watch.

At the last moment, another clatter of footsteps; this time it was clogs, interspersed with the flop of sandals and and the dull thud of Doc Marten boots. Females all right, but from what might be politely described as a different socio-economic class. Not more than eight, but led by a squat, bosomy, unfortunately familiar figure, this group posed a threat entirely disproportionate to its size.

Bernice. I didn't remember her surname, but I recalled her all right. She lived in a campervan on the estuary, Aylfleet way, amidst a commune of like-minded pals. Feminism, New-ageism, and Animal Rights: demonstrations and campaigns a speciality, dragons slain. It wasn't that I didn't like Bernice; she was cheerful, she was always busy at something, she was even fun, but anarchy was her middle name.

The last time we'd met I'd been making early-morning enquiries on her semi-permanent New Age site. She was not, as I recalled it, a great admirer of men. Dressed only in her knickers, and a T-shirt proclaiming marriage as legalised rape, she'd thrown out the source of her all-night entertainment within a couple of minutes of my first knock. She had also described him as a worm, while she tossed him, tealess and shivering, out of her bed and into a chill, February dawn. Violent campaigns against stalkers, rapists and sex criminals in general were definitely right up her street.

The curtains eventually parted to a smattering of polite applause to reveal a platform party of three, with the belligerent, cuboid figure of Ian Buchanan in the chair, flaunting his inevitable tribal tie. The red, orange, green and yellow of a particularly virulent tartan clashed somehow with the unhealthy crimson of his face.

The man on his left looked fairly unexceptionable, blue suit, glasses, early middle age; businessman, probably a drinking crony, I thought. The man on his right, however, splendidly blazered and badged, was, as I might have expected, the statutory military gent. Long retired, obviously; slightly nervous, but pleased to be invited at all. It was not, I was pleased to note, a well-supported platform, nor was it exactly bulging with Eddathorpe's *crème de la crème*.

'Good evening Ladies and Gentlemen,' Buchanan rose. 'It is good to see you here in such numbers. It is a reflection, I think, of the concern, no, the disquiet felt by the overwhelming majority of the citizens of this town over the recent terrible events, and to the inadequate, may I say derisory, police response to them, that has brought you from your homes tonight.'

He paused, and stared challengingly in our direction over the serried ranks of the fifty one representatives of the moral majority present. Teddy countered with a look of terminal boredom. He would have to do better than that; I sighed.

'Over recent weeks, in my role as chairman of your Crime Prevention Panel,' he tried to make it sound like the Committee of Public Safety, Paris, circa 1789, 'I have become increasingly alarmed by the spate of disgusting sexual offences which have been taking place in the midst of our previously peaceful community.

'Perverts have been stalking our streets and frightening our women. Disgusting, filthy old men have been peering into our homes at night, and the police appear to be unable or unwilling to take the appropriate action.'

News to me: other than Weary Willie, we'd so far drawn a blank, so why not target the foul-minded young, or the equally revolting middle-aged?

'The result could have been predicted. A young woman has now been slain in our midst, and the local forces of law and order are not only helpless, they are actively protecting the identity of a convicted rapist, who, I am reliably informed, is a prime suspect in this case.'

I had to admit it, clichés or not, Ian Buchanan had a nicely rounded turn of phrase. The touch of rolling Lowland Scots in his voice helped the message along. Teddy, no mean exponent of Old Testament-style cadences himself, had a rival on his hands.

'Not only that,' he held up a dramatic, admonitory hand, 'the police, in their arrogance, in their callous indifference to the sufferings of the relatives of the victims of crime, have displayed total indifference to the grief of the victim's own father, Mr Gordon West!'

Third row, right-hand side; a broad, middle-aged, slightly disreputable figure struggled to its feet, turned to face the meeting and awarded us an awkward wave, before resuming its seat. From a small section of the audience, he received a sympathetic, if desultory round of applause.

'The police have ignored Mr West's legitimate concerns; his enquiries have met with a wall of silence,' thundered Buchanan. 'When he persisted in his quest for justice, what happened? I'll tell you what happened, ladies and gentlemen; he was ejected from the police station for his pains!'

'Shame!' A solitary skinhead trying to stir things up.

'Is any of this true?' muttered Teddy out of one corner of his mouth.

'A travesty,' I whispered, adopting the speaker's style. 'An absolute travesty, boss.'

Buchanan droned on; he made his points, he illustrated them with anecdotes and examples, then he rolled them out all over again. Some of his audience, I was pleased to note, began to play shuffle-bottom and murmur amongst themselves. Teddy took no notice whatsoever of the openings being offered, he stayed absolutely dumb.

Eventually, Buchanan reluctantly yielded to the military gent, whose elaborate, gold-wired blazer badge appeared to be that of some defunct, and strictly noncombatant Corps. It was time, he claimed, for parties of vigorous, civic-minded men to come forward and reclaim their proud heritage as Englishmen, by taking law enforcement back into their own hands as they had done so effectively in centuries past.

'Charlies,' announced some know-all at the front.

'I *beg* your pardon?'

'Charlies,' reiterated the voice obligingly. 'Decrepit old men who used to patrol the streets in the days before there were proper police. Always getting beaten up: silly old jossers, just like you!'

One or two inadequately suppressed titters came from the body of the hall.

'We already have,' announced the speaker grandly, 'a small group of young and responsible men upon whom we can rely. They will form the nucleus around which we will build our street patrols.'

'Yeah,' this time the voice was female, 'and what guarantee do we have that you haven't recruited an absolute gang of tossers?'

'Skinheads,' called somebody else.

'Fascist perverts!' yelled another supporter of Bernice.

The presence of the half-dozen sets of haircuts, tattoos and industrial toecaps began to make sense.

'Only neo-fascists enjoy strutting around doin' things like that.' And this from an elderly, mousey figure in whose mouth you'd have bet that butter wouldn't melt.

'Why,' shouted Bernice, in tones in which conspiracies are denounced, 'are you only going on about MEN all the time? How d'yer know they're safe?'

Buchanan sprang indignantly to his feet, only to be upstaged by Adele Simpson, who rose with impressive dignity and announced, 'The young lady over there has a point.'

Simmering, he sat down, while Mrs Simpson told 'em how it was.

'I came here tonight,' she said, 'in the hope of hearing some common sense. Women are being exploited in this town, their dignity as human beings is being undermined.

'The murder victim herself was unfortunately involved in a so-called beauty contest at our local theatre, whose sole purpose was to expose women to degradation and lust. Is it any wonder that women are devalued into objects, even attacked, when men are encouraged to think of us as sexual toys?'

'Right on, me darlin!' This from another supporter of Bernice.

'I had some hopes that an effort would be made to understand the basis of the problem and attack the disease, rather than the symptoms.'

'Hear, hear!' A steady, supportive thud of Doc-Marten-shod feet, and a couple of catcalls and counter-shouts, while the cut-glass voice rose above the fray.

'What do I find instead? Yet another group of males are proposing to stroke their own egos by putting some sort of uncontrollable tinpot army on the streets to supplement the police. How, for a start, do they propose to check upon and guarantee the good character of their recruits?'

'Notice!' Bernice was on the air again, 'They only want MEN!'

'How do we know they're not shikers, themselves?'

'Gropers?'

'All men together, stalking girls!'

'Joined by this guy supposed to be convicted of the rape!'

'And the police wouldn't vet 'em for convictions on behalf of these idiots, so they'd never know!'

A couple of the potential volunteers, braver than the rest, were on their feet, 'We're trying to protect yer! Siddown yer silly cows!'

'Shut up! Shut up! Shut up!' Ian Buchanan, having neglected to provide himself with a chairman's gavel, was on his feet, puce with excitement and rage.

'Superintendent, this is disgraceful; it's an organised claque. I demand that you throw these troublemakers out!'

Teddy, called upon at last, rose majestically to his feet. Relative silence fell.

'I was rather afraid this would happen,' he said. Another version of *I told you so*. Hardly designed to conciliate; something along the lines of a red rag to a bull.

'I demand,' yelled Buchanan, 'that you stop—'

'You are the chairman of the meeting,' enunciated Teddy clearly, 'you control it. It is no part of police duty to secure an uninterrupted hearing for speakers, nor to prevent members of your audience from exercising free speech.'

More catcalls, drowned in a ragged cheer.

'If,' continued Teddy remorselessly, 'the meeting does become disruptive, you can always ask me to ask the offenders for their names and addresses. Of course,' he added, deadpan, 'I will have to be the judge of whether it has become disruptive, or not.'

'These people are disruptive already, and I want them to leave!'

'Very well.' Councillor Mrs Mary Todd, was up and running, doing her Lady Bracknell, and gesturing with a regal hand. 'We have no wish to remain when you so obviously wish to exclude us. So much for protecting women; I think we've heard quite enough!'

The respectable, middle-class element, strategically settled, as I now belatedly noticed, over two or three rows of seats, came smartly to its feet, and with numerous cries of 'Excuse me, please!' prepared to depart. The men at the end of the rows, instead of merely standing to let them file past, joined the exodus too, and a good third of the audience began to shuffle out.

Bernice, no mean tactician herself, seized the day.

'Silly old sod!' She stood.

'Makes yer puke!' The sisterhood, following her example, rose to its collective feet and stomped out. The fun having terminated, a considerable proportion of the remaining male contingent did the same, leaving the platform party, a scattered group of the old and infirm, half a dozen would-be vigilantes, Davinia's dad and two policemen in their seats.

Teddy surveyed his stricken battlefield, eyed the remnant and shook his head. 'Time to go, Bob,' he murmured sadly. 'Who are we to intrude on private grief?'

# Chapter Twelve

———————————◆———————————

'Teddy made his excuses,' said Paula, 'he says he won't be joining us for lunch.'

One eye on the road, the other on the provider of this not entirely unexpected news, I grinned. 'Go on, tell me his excuse.'

'Appointment at headquarters, or so he says.'

'Really?'

She shook her head, 'It's not that he's unsociable, you know,' she said charitably. 'I think he gets embarrassed on these occasions because he doesn't drink.'

'And,' practical, rather than charitable, me, 'he doesn't like the idea of a traffic man flourishing a breathalyser at one of us, and him becoming officially involved.'

'He hasn't got much in the way of small talk, either.' Cynicism was out today; she looked across at me, far from pleased. 'Meals out, bonding, professional back-slapping; it just isn't his thing. It took him all his time to ask me whether we wanted a boy or a girl this morning, and I bet he'd been psyching himself up to say something like that for hours. Hoped we both got what we wanted, anyway.'

'Twins?'

She smiled a trifle formally in return. A fairly well-publicised split in the Andy and Paula household: he wanted a boy and she a girl.

'No twins; that's something at any rate.'

'Anyway,' I back-tracked on my little faux pas. 'This is going to be a very upmarket Country Club luncheon party for the supervisory *crème de la crème*. Food, a few insincere smiles, one or two promises about interdepartmental and interdivisional cooperation between us and the senior uniforms, and about a glass and a half of white wine. Teddy knew that; it's not a boozy do.'

'I'm going to miss all this.' She glanced out of the window at the passing scene, but she wasn't referring to the ragged hedge, several hundred acres of flat countryside, the single clump of trees and the solitary, slightly depressive, cow.

'You'll be back before you know it.'

Her eyes remained firmly fixed on the uninspiring view. 'Bob, was Angie scared?'

I took a deep breath; unexpected. Totally out of the blue.

'Well, yes, I suppose. A bit apprehensive; giving birth, and wondering whether the baby was going to have all its fingers and toes. You know.'

'That's it, I don't know. I'm scared stiff.'

Gloom descended; I did know, or, putting it more accurately, at least I had some idea. But whatever I had to say was hardly going to help. Angie had worried, I knew. About her age, about the birth, about the baby. About ... I wasn't exactly fond of my mother-in-law, but the long-distance line had been pretty red hot. At least she'd talked to her mum.

'You've, er, spoken to your family about all this?'

'I've got one brother,' she said flatly. 'He lives and works in Wales.'

'Andy's mother?'

'She's pleasant enough; but she obviously thinks I'm too old for him. The designing woman who took away her son.'

I remembered: Andy had been twenty-five when they married; Paula thirty-three.

'Angie was fine,' I said, trying to lift the atmosphere and

injecting what I hoped was a note of optimism into my voice. Nobody had ever sent me on a course for things like this. 'She sailed through it in the end; everything was pretty straight-forward, and she's nearly five years older than you.'

Fractionally, she relaxed, 'That old, huh? She's really going to thank you for telling me that.'

'You could—' I said.

'I hardly know her.'

'You've spoken to your doctor?'

'He's always busy, and besides he called me a *prima gravida*. I looked it up.' I let that one slide, since I was going to have to do the same.

'What about the people at the clinic?'

She shrugged. 'The trouble is,' she said, 'that the job always seems enough. That, and Andy when we're at home. Otherwise, especially when you're trying to get on, you don't always make the effort to make outside friends.'

'Yeah.' I knew what she meant. The number of retired cops who anxiously buttonhole former colleagues in the street. I did a quick body count on my own behalf: acquaintances by the dozen. Close friends: not a lot.

Mentally, I blessed Angela and her former profession. At least there weren't two coppers in the same household; a pair of dedicated professionals sharing the same socially isolated boat.

'I'm sure,' I said weakly, 'that everything's going to be all right.'

She nodded dumbly; foolish remark number one. I felt thoroughly ashamed.

'You're right, Paula, I'm useless at this, but Angie really would be delighted to talk babies, eh?'

'You reckon?'

'Get her to ring you?'

Long pause.

'OK.'

I brooded in silence. Another well-known senior officer's

ceremony completed; captain abandons ship. And not, I had good cause to believe, my very finest hour.

'D'you think we can apply to you for the staunch but inarticulate Godfather stuff in due course?'

'Not if you're going to call him Alfonso,' I said, giving way to spur of the moment shock.

A proper smile this time, and she stopped paying such fixed attention to the countryside to her left, while I experienced this warm, thoroughly idiotic glow.

'Nice lunch? Charmed all the wooden-tops, and then you got your wicked way, I hope?'

Fairfield at his sarcastic best; he'd been waiting, according to my information, for nearly an hour, and I assumed he was killing two birds with one stone. Selfish buggers taking a two-hour lunch, leaving a major enquiry to run itself, and a quick hint of something dodgy going on between an over-promoted woman and his local DCI.

What's more he was in my chair again, with a scattering of papers all over my desk. I sat myself down opposite, and looked him straight in the eye.

'Very pleasant, sir, thanks.' Straight answer to a straight question: ignore the crack.

'Bit of a balls-up here.'

'While I've been out?'

'Not unless you've been out all week. I've been taking a look at your undetected murder, lad.'

'Sir?'

'Why is it that your enquiries never focus inwards, Bob? They always seem to go raving off in every direction at once.'

'I don't quite follow, boss.'

'Murder enquiries; how many do we get? Twelve to fifteen a year at the most, Force-wide? And most of 'em go the same way – body, background, suspect, evidence, interview. All done and dusted, right?'

The gears engaged with a dim and distant clunk. He'd made a recent visit to Aylfleet, and no prizes for guessing the name of the person who'd been bending his ear; Dorothea Spinks.

'Depends on the circumstances, sir. I assume we're talking domestic crime?'

'I assume we are.' He was looking something less than bucolic today, and he was putting that one down to downright cheek. 'You go in for sex crimes with invisible rapists instead, and offenders' wives who disappear. Can I also assume that there are no signs of her, either?'

'A possible sighting of her at the bus station on Tuesday, apparently talking to a man.'

'So, she could have decamped with our chief suspect once Davinia West was dead?'

'Look, sir; I've got a team on this, but there's no evidence so far that Pykett was ever in town. Nor, for that matter, do we know whether the woman at the bus station was his ex-wife.'

'But she *is* his ex-wife. Your team did get that far; nearly a week's work and all they've come up with are a marriage certificate, and this!'

He picked up a brand-new fax from my In tray and waved it under my nose: In The Salford County Court, Maureen Pykett, Petitioner, and Alan Albert Pykett, Respondent; the marriage solemnised at the Registrar's Office in the District of Salford, on ... be dissolved ... and made final and absolute ... dated 23rd July, 1984.

A long time ago, and Maureen had never got married again. Nice, too, the way I was having to decipher it while it was being wafted gently back and forth.

'You know,' I said unwillingly, 'I grant you that he's done the best part of a ten-year sentence in the meantime, but it's strange if he's still determined to come after her after all this time.'

'Well, she was damn well scared of *somebody*, however well she tried to conceal it with you; he's a brutal bastard, and people like that are frequently obsessed.

'Besides, why should they both come to live in our county if the connection was completely broken after the divorce? Funny coincidence, huh?'

'Speculative,' I murmured, but not wanting to have the head blown off my shoulders, I said it under my breath.

'Anyway,' he hadn't finished yet. 'We want Pykett himself, not a shower of paper confetti from your team.

'And that reminds me,' he continued, with another burst of heavy sarcasm. 'Have you got a similar gang of paper tigers working on lying theatrical toe-rags, and absent boyfriends with seagoing boats?'

'Lying?'

'That other sex maniac. He never said a word about the missing purse.'

Convoluted, but not too hard to work it out. Sex maniac: he'd not only been talking to Thea; that appointment at Headquarters, he'd been chatting up Teddy Baring as well.

'Paulie Parkes?'

'Paulie ruddy Parkes. I've been reading his statement; he stinks. All that crap about a prowler at the theatre on Saturday night. Some unknown toe-rag who just might have been a stalker or a pervert, oh yeah?

'Turns out to be a silly bloody purse thief, and your Mr Parkes was just winding you up; he never said a word to you about theft.'

'He might not have known at the time,' I said mildly. 'In any case, he's going to be seen again.'

'He might,' said Fairfield coldly, 'be trying to be making a clumsy attempt to divert suspicion from himself. Prowlers, Colin Critchley, and so on. Parkes tried to mount her, didn't he? And what about the jealous ex-boyfriend, come to that?'

One thing about Peter Fairfield, he has such a subtle attitude; deploys such a gentlemanly turn of phrase. Fortunately, however, if this was meant to be an attack on my failing to focus, he'd just joined the same club.

'And as you say, sir, there's Sheppard, the man with the seagoing boat.'

'And your unknown stalker who might be—'

'Pykett?'

Circuit complete, and I swear I played it straight: no grin, no smile, not even a twitch.

He glared at me with open suspicion; no irony traced. Satisfied, he bared his teeth, 'It's a bastard,' he said.

A concession at last. Nowhere near as blameworthy as a Graham personal balls-up: good. Taking into account his apparent visit to Aylfleet and his almost unprecedented conversation with Thea, however, I guessed that there was more to come.

'I was going to ask you to do a bit of a delicate job.'

'Sir?'

'Until I spoke to Mr Baring at lunchtime, that is, and discovered you had a similar problem, yourself.'

Slowly, reluctantly, he took two slim, plastic-wrapped packages from his briefcase, concealing the contents of the letter itself by placing it face down in front of him on the desk.

'Envelope postmarked Eddathorpe,' he said. 'Snap?'

Momentarily, he touched the letter. Then, having decided to keep it to himself, he compromised by handing me yet another cheap brown envelope with the familiar amateurish, hammered-home typescript, and a franked second-class stamp.

Posted Tuesday, addressed to him at Headquarters and marked 'Staff In Confidence,' the GPO could hardly be accused of having hurried itself if he'd only received it today . . .

'Snap,' I agreed. A determined troublemaker at any rate. Who next?

'Before taking action,' he said, 'I thought I ought to consult Miss Spinks, so I went over to see her first thing.'

He eyed me covertly for a moment; what did he expect? Signs of ill-concealed amusement, a knowing burst of ho! ho! ho! about the rumours of his long-dead affair with Thea Spinks? Albert had received a nastily worded version of the truth; Andy Spriggs had opened up a downright lie. True or false, whatever his letter had contained, it was not a subject for fun.

'You, er, said you wanted me ...'

'To put out a few feelers at first; I thought I could rely on you not to bandy things about.'

'And now you can't?'

'Don't be a bigger bloody fool than God made you, Bob.' Despite the insult, fellow feeling blossomed; he sounded as irritated as I felt. 'It's nothing to do with that. If you're another victim, I don't want to see you making any enquiries; I want you to keep well away.'

'But I've already done a spot of checking, here and there.'

'Typewriters: you did Eddathorpe, that's all. Paula Bail-Mrs Thingummyjig, arranged to do Retton police station, or so Mr Baring tells me, and I've done Aylfleet, today.

'They're all a dead end, so now it's got to stop. Somebody neutral ought to take it on, somebody discreet.'

I mulled that one over. Originally, I'd almost wanted to take Albert Flaxman's advice: burn it and forget. The only thing that had prevented me was a realisation that the letter-writer was only too likely to start again.

Then, for as long as it only affected me and mine, I'd kept matters to myself until the letter addressed to Andy had forced my hand. And now, in his turn, Teddy had felt obliged to pass it on.

Fairfield was talking sense. Any further personal involvement, and we could be properly accused at some later stage of persecuting somebody rather than making a legitimate enquiry; of running a feud.

'Who do you have in mind?'

'The obvious choice, the letters originate in Eddathorpe, so it's down to Detective Sergeant Caunt.'

George, my closest associate, not to mention the husband of Sarah, the biggest gossip in town. Absolutely great!

No consolation prize for me, either: our beloved leader was

operating on a strictly need-to-know basis. I was being excluded from whatever had or had not happened between Peter Fairfield and a younger, presumably livelier, Dorothea Spinks.

One bollocking for an undetected murder, every chance of starring in a round of canteen gossip, and I wasn't even in on the whole story. My cup definitely runneth over, as Teddy might have said.

# Chapter Thirteen

Bold, bad George; it's not often that detective sergeants have the chance to make their own executive decisions and embarrass detective chief superintendents by allowing third parties to read their private mail.

'You sure?'

'Maybe,' said George disingenuously, 'he was just embarrassed to show it to you himself. Probably expected me to do the honours, him being so shy.'

'He's not the only one.'

George paused in the act of withdrawing Fairfield's letter from the folder. 'Embarrassed about your past? Think I didn't know? Believe me, boss, that story had followed you before you'd been here a week.'

'Angie . . .'

'For Chrissake, it's all water under the bridge. She went, she came back, and now you've both had a kid.' He looked me straight in the eye. The immutable word according to Caunt; no additions, amendments or other interpretations allowed.

'The world goes on,' he said, 'OK, it's a story that did the rounds at the time. But it's not something they think about first thing in the morning when they come to work, and last thing at night before they go to bed: It's yesterday's news.'

'Until somebody—'

'Stirs it up. That's what Peter Fairfield's thinking. All the old hands know about him and Thea, so does his wife, but that's no reason for the younger generation to go around laughing at his expense. Especially,' he added cruelly, 'now Thea's so old and fat.'

'She'd kill you if she heard you say that.'

'Very likely. There you are, boss, now you've got something on me!'

I took the proffered note.

A single sheet of paper once again; another picture pasted at the top. Colour, roughly six by four, and clipped from a top shelf magazine. A female, probably one of those unfortunate readers' wives. Definitely a size twenty, with bulging, unsupported breasts, garter belt, black stockings, ridiculous spiky shoes and the feminine version of brewer's belly rolling over a minimal pair of flame-coloured briefs.

Big is not invariably beautiful, and without wishing to poke my head too far above the parapet as an unregenerate MCP, this was sad.

'THEODORA,' announced the caption,
'HOW WISE OF YOU TO MAKE HER REMOVE
HER CAP!'

The accompanying message was short, and equally to the point, 'YOU'RE A PIG SHE'S A SOW. YOU'RE BOTH MORALLY UNFIT TO DO YOUR OFFICIAL JOB. SMUG BASTARD YOU WILL SOON BE EXPOSED FOR WHAT YOU ARE.'

If only we could find the typewriter; two damaged letters, and a typist meticulous, or even obsessive enough, to double-strike.

One late thought, and I felt a bit of a fool. Paula, Peter Fairfield and me; the three of us had probably been wasting our time. Police stations might be shabby and frequently ill-equipped, but who would have the patience to play with a junk machine when there were others available, and put up with results like that?

'An unpleasant sort of nutter,' muttered George inadequately. 'Wouldn't you say?'

'But not all that likely, thank God, to be one of ours.' Theodora, not Dorothea, too, but the assured professionalism of the 'Staff in Confidence' envelope had initially come as a nasty shock.

'You had somebody in mind?'

'At first I thought it was likely to be a woman, but then when I heard about Fairfield's problem I changed my mind. I thought it had to be Malc.'

He looked at me as if I'd been shooting kittens for fun, 'Why's that?'

'Well,' I said, wishing I'd never said it, and feeling more than slightly ashamed. 'Peter Fairfield passed on some information about his debts, and I ended up having a few words with Malc.'

'I doubt it; he's grateful, didn't you know? The Welfare Officer's pulling a few strings on his behalf.' George, the first-line supervisor with his ear well and truly to the ground.

'He never said.'

'Perhaps *he's* a bit embarrassed,' said George. Then, having given me a few seconds to digest the criticism, 'Anyway, the Benevolent Fund's got it in hand, but their committee don't meet until sometime next week.'

'The envelope, though ...' I said, deliberately letting George pick up the thought.

'Yeah, somebody who knows a bit about us and the way we work. They're not proper insiders, though; ignorant enough to think that "Thea" is short for Theodora.'

'Or careless, or cunning, anyway.'

'Which might bring us back to a copper. I shouldn't try to

dig too deep if I were you.' He looked old and fatherly, and wise; he's good at that. 'If you go too far you start looking for conspiracy theories, and then you end up as confused and twisted as them.'

I stared at him; a platitude, but the jumping-off point for one of those leaps in the dark.

'Twisted?'

Uncomprehending, he didn't reply.

'I know it's not going to be nice,' I said slowly, 'and I'm sorry it's down to you. There's not a shred of evidence at this stage, of course ... A lot would depend on what he might have said, and her own mood at the ti—'

The lights came on.

'Twisted is right.' He regarded me without favour. 'And what's more, boss, you've just handed me one bloody awful job.'

According to the *Green Fairy Book*, a tome compiled by the Home Office in an unjustifiably optimistic mood, any form of oppressive police conduct is O.U.T. Do not belt 'em, do not bully; no threats of prejudice, no hopes of advantage and no promises of reward. All must be voluntary, fair, recorded, and conducted strictly in accordance with the Queensberry Rules. Not that I'd ever do anything to scandalise a *Guardian* reader: there's more than one way of skinning a cat.

And as for unlawful oppression and so on: well, there's nothing in the *Home Office Codes of Practice* about inviting a ham actor down to the police station, a few hours before his big Saturday night extravaganza is due to start ...

'I can't stay long.' Paulie Parkes in plaintive mode, as if we didn't know.

'You're not under any kind of pressure or constraint,' said George mendaciously, 'and you can always have a solicitor, if you want.'

'Why should I want a solicitor, sergeant?'

'I was only trying to be helpful,' explained George Caunt. 'Some people become unnecessarily nervous,' and he smiled.

'I'm not.' The smile hadn't gone unnoticed; Paulie looked none too sure.

'Good.'

'But you're still absolutely positive?' I asked.

'About what?'

'The solicitor.'

'You on commission, or what?'

'I was just trying to reassure you, Mr Parkes.'

Something of a hiatus occurred.

'Just one or two points; last Monday night, for example,' I said. 'What time did you say you left the theatre?'

'It's in my statement; just after half past ten.'

'Right,' I ruffled unnecessarily through my notes. 'And you went with, er, Miss Lindsey Preston to a restaurant called the Green Parakeet.'

'With others, yes.'

'Where you arrived at something after eleven o'clock.'

'Yes?'

'It's only ten minutes walk from the theatre, Mr Parkes.'

'All right, I was a few minutes later than I said.'

'That's partly what I'm getting at; a number of your times seem to be a bit out. For example, Miss Preston believes that after having a drink or two and a meal, you both arrived at your apartment around twenty past twelve, and that she left before a quarter past one.'

'Later, I would have thought.'

'Not according to her taxi-driver,' I said.

'Ye gods! You've gone that far, dear fellow? You don't think I did it, do you?'

Ignore that. It should produce its own effect.

'There's a big difference between a quarter past one and ten minutes to two.'

'Eh?'

'Ten minutes to two; that's the time of her leaving, so you said.'

'So what? Look, you caught me on the hop the other day; I wasn't thinking, that's all.'

'OK; what did you do when she went?'

'I went to bed.'

'You're absolutely sure?' asked George. 'We didn't confuse you about that the other day? We didn't, ah, catch you on the hop?'

'What is all this?'

'Have you got a car?'

'Of course I've got a bloody car; it's a Merc.'

'C Reg,' said George in tones which might have suggested that he, personally, would not have settled for anything less than the latest gold-plated Rolls-Royce.

'Where do you keep it?'

'In one of the garages downstairs.'

'So you could have gone out – been near Howlett Street, for example, at about half-one.'

'Why the hell would I want to go to Howlett Street, of all places?'

'You know it, then?'

'Of course I do, I've been living in this ruddy town for the past four and a half years!'

'Bit scruffy?' suggested George. 'Better in Cranbourne Avenue, eh?'

Parkes stiffened, 'I wouldn't know.'

'You don't know it?' George sounded genuinely surprised, 'but it's just around the corner from Howlett Street, and you say you've lived—'

'Of course I know it.'

'But you just said you didn't.'

'I mean I've never been to Davinia West's flat. That's what you were getting at, isn't it?'

'Not at all; I was just comparing the state of the houses on

Howlett Street with those on Cranbourne Avenue. What's all this about Davinia West?'

Parkes glared at him in baffled rage.

'Just as a matter of interest . . .' I started.

'No!'

'I'm sorry?'

'You were going to ask me if I'd ever been to see Davinia, as well. The answer is still no!'

'You tend to jump to conclusions rather too quickly, Mr Parkes. I made a passing reference to a minor incident which occurred on Howlett Street, but you do seem to be just a tiny bit obsessed by Davinia West.'

'Me, obsessed! But you're the ones who're supposed to be running the murder enquiry, and that's why I'm here.'

'Quite. Anyway, you'd like to voluntarily assure us that you've never been to her flat?'

Paulie Parkes began to breathe heavily, 'It was you who asked me whether—'

'You'd been to Howlett Street in the early hours of Tuesday morning where a policeman became entangled with a Peeping Tom. We never said a word about Davinia West.'

'But you were going to.'

'What?'

'Ask me if I'd ever been to see Davinia at home.'

'But you'd like to volunteer that you hadn't?'

'For Christ's sake, never. No!'

'So there couldn't possibly be any traces of your presence in her flat?'

'Who said there was?'

'You've never brought her a present, for example?'

He rolled his eyes upwards, and gave a deep, impatient sigh. Ham actor to the last.

'So that's what it's all about; yes, I gave her a so-called present. Price sixteen-and-a-half quid. She collected the bloody things for Chrissake! or so she said.'

'Collected what?'

'She told me that she collected cuddly toys; dolls.'

'You gave her a doll?' I began to brighten up.

'A big pink rabbit, as a matter of fact.' Not the answer I wanted; it figured all the same. A monstrous thing with buck teeth; I remembered seeing it on Davinia's shelf.

'When?'

'Look, it was just a gesture, I gave it to her when she won the quarter-final on the Saturday night.'

'Ah,' said George, 'you mean you bought it in advance?'

Paulie Parkes hesitated; we exchanged understanding glances; he blushed.

'I'm glad I'm not one of the unsuccessful contestants,' said George.

'OK,' he looked shifty. 'So I gave the girl a bit of a boost, so what? It's a relief to find a kid like Davinia. You want to see some of 'em strutting their stuff week after week; they're real dogs! But I've never been to her place. Whatever makes you think I've ever been to her flat?'

'Nothing; I mean, we haven't taken any samples from you, have we? Conducted any forensic tests?'

'You can do what you like.' The moment it was out, his mouth shut with a snap.

'Well, just a set of fingerprints,' I said swiftly, 'and samples for DNA. It's really very generous of you, Mr Parkes; just for elimination purposes, of course.' Not that we'd heard anything positive from Scenes of Crime, and we might as well be waiting on Santa Claus, as the results from a Home Office Lab.

Comprehension dawned, nevertheless; he'd just been conned into something he hadn't meant to say. A touch of spurious reassurance at this stage might help.

'And it's all perfectly OK from your point of view, if you've never been to her flat.'

'Absolutely not!' Once again he flushed.

George nodded, and carefully wrote it down, 'For elimination only. No possibility whatsoever of any forensic trace.'

'That's all right, then,' I reiterated.

If looks could have killed.

'And, equally, there's no chance you were anywhere near Howlett Street in the early hours of Tuesday morning?'

'What the hell is this? Do you seriously take me for some sort of Peeping Tom?'

'To be fair, he's not much like the description,' said George.

'What description?' It was just as if he was watching a tennis match. By this time his head was swinging backwards and forwards between us; left to right, right to left at every thwack of the conversational ball.

'The description of the man caught peeking through the windows in Howlett Street. The one who assaulted our PC,' added George helpfully. 'What about the purse?'

'What fucking purse? You know what I think? I think you're both mad!'

George looked suitably stricken, and I condescended to explain. 'Sergeant Caunt is talking about the purse stolen from the theatre last Saturday night. You recall your telephone call to Mr Baring, don't you?'

'Of course I bloody do.'

'And do you recall telling him about the fat, middle-aged man who'd managed to sneak backstage?'

'Yes.'

'Some sort of Peeping Tom, or sexual pervert, you said?'

'Not a pervert, I didn't say that. Bit of a dirty old man, perhaps.'

'But he wasn't, was he? A purse went missing; he sounds much more like a plain old-fashioned thief.'

'Not necessarily, I think he was taking a look at the girls. There's no proof he was anything to do with the purse. I'd forgotten about it; there's always little things going astray.'

'You chose to recall him as some sort of pervert, Mr Parkes.'

'What are you getting at? Are you hinting . . .'

'You've been doing the hinting; what did you say about young Critchley?'

'I just mentioned him as a possibility, that's all.'

'And when you saw him, you scared the life out of him, didn't you?'

'I wouldn't say that.'

'You seem to have been a trifle eager to push us in the direction of dirty old men, or Critchley, or anybody other than yourself.'

'Now just you look here, you—'

'You've been a bit of a lad, eh? In your time. Showgirls, and stuff?'

'With Davinia,' suggested George.

'But not with Lindsey Preston,' I said smilingly. 'Not on Monday, anyway. She left you in the lurch.'

'Perhaps you were feeling a bit frustrated, after that. Perfectly understandable; perhaps you went out?'

'No, I did not! I never saw her that night: after that little chippy left, I went to bed.'

'Didn't see whom?'

'Davinia, you know perfectly well who I mean. I didn't see Davinia West.'

'Pay for her supper, did you?' asked George.

'What?'

'Lindsey Preston. Took her home for a nightcap, and then she wouldn't come across?'

'That little chippy,' I explained. 'The one whose meal you paid for; unreliable, eh?'

His head stopped moving, the muscles in his face contracted, and his mouth twisted into a knowing sneer. 'You bastards, you double-dyed bastards. So that's what it's all about.'

'Sorry?'

'You treacherous scumbags have kept the records, right? Even after all these years. Not guilty is supposed to mean not guilty, you sods. No record: nothing. A clean slate.'

'Oh, you mean that old rape allegation,' said George dismissively. 'A clean slate; that's exactly what you've got, in law.'

'A clean slate,' I confirmed, 'and that goes for Davinia, too. Remember what you told us about your little bit of fun? Davinia, apparently, couldn't see the joke. She complained to a friend, but it doesn't matter, does it? She's dead.'

His face working, he opened and shut his mouth. The skin looked dead under his tan, and for a good ten seconds the words just wouldn't come. 'Critchley,' he choked finally. 'Colin Critchley knew she was lying; she just wanted to worm her way back into his good books.

'And as for you, you rake something up, drag in a victim, and screw him to the floor. That's the way you work, isn't it? Just like the Birmingham Six.'

'How did you know?' I asked, ignoring the sticks and stones.

'Know what?'

'That Davinia told Critchley about your, ah, sexual assault?'

'Once and for all, she was perfectly willing, it didn't go far and it *wasn't a sexual assault!*' His voice rose to a scream.

'But he told you what she'd said?'

'He accused me, damn you; just like you.'

'When?'

'When ... when I had a bit of a go at him, the other night.'

'I suppose you mean the evening after we first saw you; the time you tried to convince him that the police were after him for the murder of his ex-girlfriend, huh?'

Silence.

'Anyway, said George, 'she lied about you?'

'Yes.'

'Spoke to Critchley; practically accused you of attempted rape?'

'It was nothing of the sort! She was perfectly happy, and ask Critchley, it was only a bit of a snog.'

'So she lied — to get back in his good books, eh?'

'Yes.'

'Not the sort of girl for the friendly gesture, I would have thought. Not the big pink rabbit award.'

A longer silence this time, then a slow, reluctant grunt, 'She was useful,' he said. Then, a thought having occurred, 'Besides, I could have handed over the rabbit to the winning contestant, whoever won!'

We made our appraisal, and took a cold constabulary look at the Eddathorpe One. He stared dumbly back: fame at last. No more dear fellows, now.

'Not very satisfactory, is it?'

Slowly, infinitely slowly, Paulie Parkes's hands clenched, the fingers squeezed together, the knuckles whitened, and his eyes filled with angry, self-pitying tears.

'Maybe we ought to caution him, after all.' said George.

So we did, but Paulie Parkes, just like Miss Lindsey Preston, apparently, and despite our best efforts and his own self-contradictions, failed to come across.

# Chapter Fourteen

More of a demonstration than a riot, I decided, from the moment we pulled up outside the entrance to the pier. Well, a demonstration accompanied by an entirely separate Breach of the Peace, as things turned out.

The demonstration was moving backwards and forwards quite nicely when George parked the CID car on a convenient double yellow line. No obstruction of the wooden broadwalk outside the theatre, placards well to the fore. No written obscenities, either; nothing to offend the old ladies of either sex. Civil libel affecting the lesee of the Pavilion Theatre was none of our affair, and the potential theatregoers appeared to be enjoying reading the signs.

Not that Paulie Parkes didn't try to use the police to get it all stopped: served me right, I suppose, for turning soft twenty minutes before show-time, and giving him a lift.

By the time we arrived outside the Pavilion, the chanting was warming up, twenty or thirty women in two distinct groups. '*Who do we want, Paulie Parkes! Where do we want him, OUT!*' had established itself as a solid favourite with the first and larger group, while the second, only loosely associated with the livelier element, favoured the dignified, anti-apartheid, Black Sash approach. The rest of the public seemed to be clustering around a lone uniformed constable surveying the scene from the shallow theatre steps.

Adele Simpson and her crowd, conservatives to a woman with both a big and a little c, gave every indication of being embarrassed by the nature of their more vociferous support. Bernice, and to a lesser extent Beryl Matthews, her matchstick legs encased in tight grey leggings and with FREEDOM! emblazoned across the heavy sweater sagging from her less than ample chest, suffered from no such middle-class constraints.

'Coo-eee! Inspec-torr! Come and join the cause!' carolled Beryl, the second I left the car.

'There's Parkes. Get him!' yelled Bernice, a far more practical type. Paulie took one look at the reception committee and made a dive for the narrow walkway leading to the stage door like a startled rabbit.

'I'm late, I'm late! and now you've ruined me!' he screamed over one shoulder as he disappeared. The door slammed, the bolts drove home, and we were left to face the bolder spirits and their placards from the shallow porch. 'And thank you very much for the lift,' muttered George, turning sour. Personally, I hadn't expected a lot of gratitude from Paulie. Not even after we'd released him. Not after what we'd said and done.

'We only wanted to talk to him; we're strictly non-violent, us,' claimed Bernice, Beryl and half a dozen supporters crowding the dangerously narrow gap between stage door, guardrail and sea.

'Helping the police with their enquiries, was he?' asked Beryl in a certain tone of voice. The supporters, not all of whom appeared to be totally dedicated to the principles of the late Mahatma Gandhi, growled.

'No, just giving the man a lift,' I said hastily. 'He was late.'

'All right for some; taxi at public expense.'

'All chauvinist pigs stick together,' snapped another anony-mous voice. 'Hadn't ought to be allowed: Bloody men!'

'If you'd like to move back ladies ...' I had visions of somebody going over the side of the pier; Royal Humane Society material I am not.

There was the sound of breaking glass from the direction of the front entrance, followed by a few disjointed shouts.

We began to push forward quickly, making for the scene of the strife.

'It'll be nothing to do with us,' bawled Bernice approximately four inches from my left ear. 'It's that ganga Nazis from the other night.'

We popped out of the narrow confines of the walkway like a couple of corks from a bottle, still accompanied by an audience seeking sensation wherever it could. Adele Simpson and her associates had come to a confused halt, staring at the closed glass-panelled doors of the theatre front, while a gaggle of potential customers, looking apprehensive, kept well away from the steps. The rest of Bernice's party was keeping back for the time being, but the occasional placard was swinging negligently in more than one female demonstrator's fist.

On the steps of the main entrance the constable was struggling with a stocky, wildly-swearing figure, while four or five other men, cropped hair and denims mostly, were trying to haul him away. A couple of dinner-jacketed figures could be seen struggling to bolt the foyer doors from the inside, beyond the glass.

'Let 'im go! Let 'im go, copper: he's got a right!'

'Rat-faced perverts! What about me compensation, yer snot-gobbling bastards?' The prisoner was wrestling with his captor, and still lashing out with both feet, shards of glass on the steps providing ample evidence of an earlier success.

'Police!' shouted George, and grabbed the shoulder of one of the combatants to haul him back. The man abandoned his part in the rescue and rewarded George with a fist in the face.

Never a fan of the fancy holds and armlocks, I promptly kicked him behind the knee; his right leg collapsed beneath him, and he fell down the steps amidst a flurry of stonewashed denim and splinters of broken glass.

'Ooooh!' breathed the scandalised representatives of the libertarian middle-class.

'Now boot 'im in the crutch!' advised a more practical female voice. A group of placard swingers surged forward.

'Fascists!' And for once they didn't mean us.

The uniform man kept a determined hold on his prisoner, gabbling urgently into his personal radio at the same time, while George and I dragged our own assault merchant to his feet.

Battle was joined, and amidst a concentrated roar of rage, unchivalrous fists flew, while placards rose and fell. For reasons known best to themselves, the direct-action party had no intention of making common cause with the denims, earrings and cropped heads. They obviously hated the would-be vigilantes far more than they disliked the demeaning goings-on at the Saturday night performance of *Eddathorpe Rocks!*

Once on his feet, our prisoner screamed and struggled furiously, spattering drops of blood from his glass-damaged hands. It was as much as we could do to hang on; George, groggy, a nasty swelling developing over his upper-right cheek bone, was not at his best.

Amidst the mayhem, men and women fighting, and with would-be theatregoers in precipitate retreat, a new denim-clad, yellow shirted figure made a dash for the main doors.

'Oi, you!' Unwisely, the constable tried to intercept. With a wriggle and a curse, the originator of all the trouble wrenched himself free, and hurled himself into the crowd, taking a shrewd bat in the face from a placard en-route.

'I think,' said George with a degree of melancholy satisfaction, 'that the wooden-top has just lost Davinia's dad.'

In the midst of our own personal struggles, I took a quick glance towards the beleaguered uniform figure at the top of the steps. The constable, frustrated, had grabbed yellow-shirt instead.

'Leggo, leggo; I'm trying to get in!'

'Oh no you don't!'

'I'm late, I'm Nigel Laud, you pillock. I'm with the *Immortal Sins!*'

Resenting the slur, and having lost one prisoner already, the uniform merely tightened his grip. 'It's mortal, not immortal, and I can well believe you're one of 'em,' replied the angry cop.

It was only then that the distant woo-woo-woo of our new Federal sirens, the police equivalent of the much-clichéd cavalry trumpet, began to promise imminent relief.

'But it's Sunday morning!' protested Angie.

'No peace for the wicked,' I said.

'And when did you last have a proper day off? Last week, you were – Oh, never mind.'

'Just this morning,' I wheedled. 'No need to cook, I'll take you both out to lunch.'

'Promises, promises. I know you; once you get stuck in that place, you'll never come home.'

'Look,' I said. 'There's this man I've got to see. He's been away, and he only came back late last night. He rang Roger; he's an Aylfleet man.'

'Roger?'

'Detective Sergeant Prentice.'

'Oh.'

'One o'clock at the latest. Have a lazy morning, get Laura ready, and you could always call up Paula Spriggs for a chat.'

'Lady of the manor, eh? My voluntary social work?'

'Don't be mean; you love a spot of baby talk.'

'Oh all right.' Then she fired her Parthian shot. 'Believe me, laddo; it's going to be a very expensive lunch.'

Roger Prentice was hardly in the best of moods. He was dividing Action forms, tearing them off the printer, attaching questionnaires, adding descriptive forms, and pinning the results together ready for the Monday morning enquiry teams when I entered the incident room. Only two other people present; he was operating with a skeleton staff.

'Sunday, bloody Sunday,' he said.

'Morning, Roger: fancy a trip out?'

'I assume,' he muttered, only one degree short of sarcasm, 'that Detective Sergeant Caunt is enjoying his day off?'

Deliberately, I didn't pick it up. The disappointed candidate: George, aging George, was in line for the acting rank once Paula left. But George wasn't qualified, and ambitious Roger had passed his inspector's exams. In his own opinion, at least, Roger should have been fully operational, ready to take over the acting rank while somebody, anybody, ought to have been sitting around in the office slaving over a hot computer screen. But I hadn't come in to soothe his ruffled feelings. Tough.

'Anybody out on the street?'

No consolation prizes; no ego-stroking promises. He understood. He glanced at the duty board, instead. 'Three teams, boss, that's all. Stuff from the house-to-house. Appointments with people they couldn't see during the week. It's nothing especially exciting, just a process of taking statements and tidying-up.'

'Well,' I said, 'if things are so steady, what about a trip out?'

'To see Ralph Sheppard?'

'Yeah.'

'Funny bugger, that.'

'You know him, then?'

'Yep, puts himself about a bit does Ralph. The playboy millionaire.'

I raised my eyebrows.

'Well, not exactly, no.' For the first time that morning Roger began to relax. He even looked amused. 'He's got a bob or two, though. Buys a few rounds; back-slapper. Bit of a rugger-bugger, if you know what I mean.'

'You don't like him?'

'I wouldn't say that. He's alright, I suppose.' Suddenly, he grinned, 'After all, like I said, he does stand his round.'

'What does he do for a living?'

'Calls himself a business consultant, and that covers a multitude of sins.' He paused again, 'You're right, I'm being unfair. He owns a restaurant and a nine-hole golf course, somewhere up in Humberside; he leases 'em out. Finger in one or two other pies, as well. Bloaters, for one.'

'Bloaters?'

'Aylfleet's very own disco, boss. Wall to wall with sweaty schoolkids every Saturday night. One million decibels, and believe me, you wouldn't want to know.'

'It's only open at weekends?'

'Nah, but Friday and Saturday are the worst. Unless you count Thursdays – that's grab a granny night.' He leered suggestively. 'Gentlemen five pounds; *Ladies* free. Aging slags without hubby, usually hunting in pairs.'

'What exactly did he say when he rang you last night?'

'Said that somebody told him you wanted to see him, that's about all.'

'No outrage; no shock; no questions? Nothing at all about Davinia West?'

'No,' Roger Prentice hesitated momentarily. 'Somebody must have filled him in already, he never said a word.'

'It's raining again, Roger. Like to get your coat?'

Definitely, but definitely an upmarket gin palace here. *The Blue Marlin* was something of a misnomer; long-prowed and sharp all right, just like the fish, but it had a gleaming white hull, and only the thinnest of blue lines and the sky blue image of a fish on the stern to justify the rest of the name.

Ralph Sheppard looked as sharp as his boat; not exactly forty any more, but fortyish, crew-cut, gleaming teeth and a glowing, healthy face. Another one who obviously liked to keep himself trim.

'Coffee?' He asked. 'Decaff?'

I lowered my bulkier, softer body into the leather Chesterfield in the aft saloon. The sofa sighed luxuriously as it accepted my weight: money, money, it whispered. Roger Prentice took a long, lingering look at the glass, chrome and rosewood fittings: he too was impressed.

'Yes, please.'

Roger nodded; a healthy choice, and a distinct improvement on a taste for mid-morning Malt. Sheppard poured; he almost reminded me of a younger, better muscled version of Paulie Parkes; almost, but not quite. A second showman in his way, but this one was brisk, no flannel, very likely tough.

Gently, he replaced the cafetière on the thick glass table top and indicated sugar and cream. 'I only heard about Davinia's death on Thursday,' he said. 'Very sorry, and all that: my manager gave me a bell.'

'Bloaters?'

'Yes, that's right.'

'And you were, er, where?'

'Amsterdam; at the time. Mixing business with pleasure.' He winked. 'You'll want to know when I went. I left for Zeebrugge on Tuesday morning, and did a deal. Hired a car, and spent Thursday and Friday in Amsterdam and got back last night. Sorry of course, nice lass, but nothing to do with me.'

'Tuesday?' Asked Prentice.

'That's right.'

'You don't sound all that concerned.'

'I'm not a hypocrite, and it was all a bit casual.' He shrugged.

All right, if that's the way he wanted it: a spot of straight John Bull. 'We'd like to know about your movements on Monday night.'

Slowly, he replaced his coffee cup on the table, 'Come on now, gents; it happened on Tuesday afternoon, OK?'

'Tuesday was when we found her,' I explained.

'Oh.'

'Can we start at the beginning, Mr Sheppard; when did you first meet Davinia, or maybe Shirley West?'

He nodded soberly, 'Down at the club.'

'Bloaters?'

'No, no, here at the Marina; strictly weekends only stuff. She was here with Colin and his boss. Well, Colin really, but he had to sign 'em in.'

'So you know Paulie Parkes?'

'Not very well.' He looked suitably vague, 'I've seen him around of course; he owns *Seasprite*, and Colin Critchley rents it out.' He snorted with sudden amusement. 'He uses it as a houseboat. I don't think he even knows how to cast off the ruddy thing.'

'How long ago was this?'

He shrugged, 'Seven or eight weeks, who knows? About the time she won the first beauty heat; coupla weeks before Colin gave her the great big E.'

'You knew about that?'

'About Paulie? sure; little Davinia was sweet, but she always had one eye on the main chance.' He waved one expansive hand around the immaculately appointed saloon.

'And that's how you stepped in, Ralph?' Roger Prentice chipped-in for the first time. 'Because she was looking for a rich boyfriend?'

'Not exactly, no.' Sheppard kept his even, amiable tone. 'She wasn't as obvious as all that, and just for your information, Rog, I'm comfortable, but I'm not rich. Besides, I offered her a job.'

Prentice looked uncomfortable, 'A job?'

'Yeah; at Bloaters, part time. Bit of moving and shaking at weekends. Local talent to cheer up the lads on a Friday and Saturday night.'

'Sort of go-go stuff?'

'That's right; nothing wrong with that. Wiggle-wriggle in long boots and a little gold lamé dress for a performance or two, that's all.

'Anyway, she said she needed to do more hours than I offered, and that pub feller insisted on keeping her at weekends, bit of a dog in the manger type, so she turned it down.'

'But you, er . . .' said Prentice.

'Took her out and about.' Sheppard supplied him with another wink and a cheeky grin. 'Why not? A few drinks, a meal here and there, and all aboard for the skylark now and again!'

'Not serious?'

'You have to be joking; she wasn't exactly the sort to take home to mum.'

'You've got a mum?' Prentice introduced a note of total incredulity into his voice.

'Hey, watch it.' Sheppard kept his smile. 'You know exactly what I mean.'

'Anyway,' I said hastily, 'you took her abroad, as well?'

'Yeah; oh yeah, I see what you mean, but not on the boat.'

'No?'

'No, a half-day along the coast was her limit; a bit ikky whenever she went to sea, but I took her for a long weekend to Bruges by air.' He winked again.

'The Venice of the North,' I quoted. 'A *close* friendship, eh?'

'You could say that.' A knowing grin this time. Boys in the locker-room together: a rugger-bugger all right.

'When did you last see her?'

No thought, no hesitation, 'Sunday; her day off. Took her to lunch, brought her back here for a couple of hours,' another wink, 'and an hour or so at Bloaters on Sunday evening. Killed two birds with one stone so to speak. Whoops! sorry for that, not, I assure you, a Freudian slip.'

'*Two* birds?'

'Gavin, my manager; I looked in. First principle of business, Chief; keep an eye on the till. Left about eleven, and ran her home. I didn't go inside.'

'A spot of safe sex,' asked Roger, picking up on the earlier wink. 'On the Sunday afternoon?'

'There are,' said Sheppard smoothly, 'one or two of us old-fashioned buggers who call it making love.'

'But sensible people,' said Roger, equally smoothly, 'take care to protect their, er, assets, in these unromantic times. What brand? I assume you've got a packet or two in here?'

'Like that, is it?'

For a moment I thought he was going to refuse, then he shrugged. 'Bedside cabinet, through there.' He indicated with his thumb. 'Top right-hand drawer, look for yourself, though with tens of millions of rubbers on the market, Sunshine, I cannot for the life of me think why.'

Then, as Roger made to leave, he made a half-swallowed comment, designed to turn any sense of embarrassment on to the crude, insensitive rozzer. 'Liberty Hall, here, don't ya know, Sergeant; whenever you're caught short, I'm always willing to help when the barber shops are shut.'

Roger said nothing; he simply awarded him a modified version of the CID Glare as he exited to look. He was, I think, responding in kind to the general attitude of our host.

'She never made any kind of complaint to you?' I tried a different tack.

'About what?'

'Sexual harassment, for example?'

His eyes narrowed, 'By whom? Colin? Paulie Parkes?' Suddenly, the smile was gone. 'No, never. You reckon that's what this bloody awful mess is all about?'

I shrugged; he leaned forward. 'Nothing in the press, but she was interfered with, huh?' A strangely old-fashioned phrase; the *News of the World* had given that one up about the time I'd entered puberty. What were we dealing with here, a greying Jack-the-lad, or another Puritan-at-heart?

'She never mentioned that somebody peeked through her window, or that she'd been followed home?'

'Oh, that! She did mention it, as a matter of fact. Nothing

serious, she said. Some chancer, and she was going to fix him good, if he ever came back.'

'In what way?'

'We-ll,' he hesitated. 'A big squeezy bottle of bleach, for one thing. And I always had the impression that she could look after herself.'

'Anything else?'

He hesitated again, then, slowly, carefully, 'She, er, sort of gave me the impression she had a knife.'

But not at the time she'd been murdered, thanks to us.

'She never showed it to you?'

'No.'

'When did you last go to her flat?'

'Sorry, she always came here.'

'Then how did you know—'

'About the bleach? She reckoned she saw a blob at her window, and I'm just going on what she said.'

'And you never went to her flat; not on Monday night?'

'I was at home on Monday night.'

I glanced around the saloon.

'I don't live here permanently, you know. I've got an apartment above the caff.'

'Caff?'

The smile was back, 'That's what I call it, just to get the customers' goat. The Blue Marlin restaurant up in Grimsby; that's why I re-named this.'

Roger Prentice returned, oblivious to the finer feelings of others to the last. He looked at me, 'Not what we want. The *Featherlite* version of a very well-known brand,' he said.

Sheppard wrinkled his nose fastidiously; just for the moment he was ignoring the working class. 'The boat was called *Carole-Anne*, originally. I bought it from the receivers a couple of years ago, when a builder I knew went bust. Seventy-eight thousand quid's-worth, and I got it for less than half.'

I smiled noncommittally, but I think we were both expected

to congratulate him for that. The man was a bit of a mixture; not smarmy, not evasive exactly, but on the edge of villainy, all the same.

'You can substantiate your movements, last Monday night?'

'I didn't have Securicor guarding me, if that's what you mean. But the restaurant manager saw me passing in and out. So did the waiters and the chef.'

'What time do you close?'

'*They* close. They run it, I'm the boss. They shut at eleven on a Monday night; half to three-quarters of an hour to clear the place, and that's it. I spoke to the manager just before closing, and then I went to bed.'

'Alone?'

'Sadly, yes. I needed my beauty sleep,' he added ironically, 'I'd got a long day ahead.'

'Talking of long days …' said Roger Prentice; it was his version of being smooth.

'I knew that was coming; why did I go to Zeebrugge, etcetera? Business with pleasure, just as I said. What business, Roger? Now there you've got me, mate.'

'Why's that?'

''Cos I went to buy a load of naughty books. Not for me,' he said hastily, holding up his hands in mock-horror, 'and they're not hard porn. Just a bit of Scandinavian tit and beaver to enliven the punters in the sticks.'

'Didn't know you were into that sort of thing, Ralph.'

'I'm not; it just so happens that I know a man who is, if you see what I mean. He's got a chain of newsagents' shops.

'It's all going to be imported through Hull; fair and square to the last. Proper invoices, and the Customs boys can goggle as much as they like.'

'Glad to hear it.'

'Hey, now, don't be like that. You've got to turn an honest bob these days, wherever you can.'

'Don't worry about the Customs,' I threatened. 'Wait till the Eddathorpe and District feminists get on your track.'

'Yeah,' there was a distinct broadening of the slow, confident grin. 'I heard about last night; Paulie's show, and the girls-against-glamour riot. News travels fast around here.'

'Well,' asked Roger Prentice afterwards. 'What d'you think of what he says?'

'A bit confusing,' I admitted. 'He's shrewd. But too fond of playing the likable rogue for his own good.'

'I'll do the action forms; see they check everything out.'

'Tell 'em to dig deep; pin down everything he says in his statement, and a quick word with Customs and Excise wouldn't come amiss.'

'Funny bugger, isn't he?' The second time around.

'The type,' I agreed semi-seriously, 'to chuckle all the way to HMP Ford, or even, if he's lucky, the House of Lords.'

# Chapter Fifteen

Mini-skirted as usual, but as crisp and pert as somebody's Monday morning secretary-bird in a neat blue suit and a white high-necked blouse. Early, too. Not yet nine-fifteen, and she was already seated in my office, staring at me over the top of her handbag, knees tightly together, the toes of her shoes turned inwards. A new experience; Beryl making a State visit to the nick.

'It got,' she admitted sorrowfully, 'a bit out of hand the other night.'

I looked thoughtfully at her outfit, down to the matching two-inch heels and the discreet piece of costume jewellery on the lapel of her coat. It was so un-Beryl that it could have been deliberate; she could almost have been taking the mick. 'Are you an official delegation, by any chance?'

She glanced complacently downwards, 'Nope, but me mum bought it for Christmas. Nice, in' it?'

It figured. I began to like Beryl; the grateful type. Happy with a present which couldn't have been purchased for her by anybody under the age of forty-five.

'Fantastic,' I said. Then I waited.

'The other night.'

'The riot?' I asked unhelpfully. No point in letting an advantage slip away.

'Nah, not then.' she dismissed such a minor consideration out of hand. 'The night when your copper got hurt.'

'P.C. Appleby?'

'Right, but them fake Nazis reckon that your lot call him Domestos,' she nodded, 'because—'

'No.'

'No need to bite my head off, is there? I'll believe you, OK?' She stared at me in a way that made it perfectly clear that she didn't. One-up to Beryl: group solidarity to the point of idiocy, and I felt a complete fool.

'Sorry,' I said, 'but you wouldn't like to be called Domestos, especially if—'

'I was big and thick?'

'Thick and strong, actually.' Then, as her lips twitched wickedly, I realised what I'd done. Two – nil, and she hadn't even tried. 'Anyway, he's back at work this morning; light duties until his ankle's OK.'

'Good. And I'm not exactly sure about this.'

'Sure about what?'

'Your Peeping Tom. There was something familiar about him, that's all.'

'Take a deep breath, Beryl,' I advised, 'and tell me what you mean. Pretend that I'm big and thick.'

She opened her mouth to say something; then she changed her mind. 'Saturday night,' she said meekly, 'outside the Pavilion Theatre, when your constable lost Davinia's dad.'

'Stepdad. You know about him?'

'He's been drinking and yawping in the bar at the Standard,' she said contemptuously, 'last week. Four ounces of nothing: even Danny can throw him out.'

'OK.'

'Anyway, Saturday night. We followed you out of that walkway at the side of the stage door, right? And then there was the argy-bargy with all them Nazis on the steps.'

'Vigilantes,' I corrected. 'Just a few of Buchanan's heroes; big mouths, smelly denims, earrings and lots of tattoos.'

'Not according to Bernice; she reckons they're proper activists. Something to the right of Ghengis Khan.'

'Bernice,' I said irreverently, 'has an imagination all her own.'

'Please yourself. Anyway, you were all fighting on the steps, and then this feller made a dive for the doors. He was wearing a yellow shirt.'

'Yeah, I remember. Turned out he was one of the band.' Colin Critchley's sub-tenant, Nigel, as I remembered. A young man who'd made a fuss. All part of the great Saturday night disaster: he'd had to be un-arrested pretty damn quick.

'Well; I thought he looked familiar. Seen him in the Stand-ard, right?'

'Very likely,' I said noncommittally. 'Go on.'

'An' I've been thinking about it since. I reckon he could have been the one I saw that night going over the fence.'

'All you said,' I reminded her patiently, 'was something about getting to the window just in time to see somebody making an exit, and a swinging backside.'

'Maybe I saw more than I realised at the time.'

'Maybe.' I restrained myself: had it, I wondered rudely, been a particularly attractive, even sexy male bum? Is that what had stuck in her mind?

'He was young.'

'Yes.' He would have to be; I wouldn't have fancied tackling Police Constable Clifford Appleby, prior to leaping and wreck-ing an eight-foot fence, even at my relatively modest age.

'I don't know why, but I think it might have been him.'

'Well, stranger things have happened, and thanks, Beryl, for taking the time and coming in.'

'You are going to follow this up?' She didn't look happy: she stared at me through instantly beady eyes.

'Of course.'

'When?'

Oh God, women.

'I'll put somebody on to it, right away.'

The computer actions were filed on a priority basis of one to six; I might possibly be persuaded to slot it in on a number five, once I could find the name and number of a very, very junior DC.

'Why don't you do it yourself?'

What was his name, now – Nigel Laud? I remembered him, alright. Fresh from false arrest, and he'd been pretty cross.

*Hello, Nigel, I could say. Can you spare me a few minutes? I'm a real, live chief inspector, and I want to waste my time and talk to you about the size and shape of your bum.*

I stared at her levelly. Now why hadn't I seriously thought of doing that?

'What time is the inquest?' asked Teddy.

'Two-fifteen, sir. Just identification, and a brief résumé by Professor Lawrence as to the cause of death.'

'And who's doing the ID?'

I hesitated; a bit of a crippler, that. Ideally, it was supposed to be a relative, and in this case it should have been Davinia's stepdad; the wanted man.

'Er,' I said, 'It was supposed to be Gordon West. Originally, that is.'

'Her stepfather?'

'Yes.'

'And nobody's seen him since Saturday night.'

'I could always ask her former employer, Danny Smith.'

'The landlord.' Teddy crinkled his nose in distaste. 'And he knew her for what, three months, four at the most?'

'The beginning of April,' I agreed.

'Doesn't look too good, does it? The Coroner isn't going to like that.'

Nor, according to the lads who'd already been round to

see him, did Danny Smith. No, he did not wish to view the body, however great the emergency. Nor did he wish to make a statement afterwards. He had never seen a corpse, and he didn't wish to break the habit of a lifetime, just for us.

Danny Smith was a sullen grouch, but that didn't prevent me from sympathising with him, up to a point. Not, however, to the extent of letting him off the hook. I had intended to lean on him myself: view body, give statement, followed by a session in the witness box to do the ID. Sorry, Danny; needs must when Her Majesty's Coroner drives. There was no need to inform the superintendent of our initial lack of success.

'You'd think,' said Teddy almost wistfully, 'that you could find one minor toe-rag whenever you wanted him, in a small town like this.'

Oh, right, that's it, then. Gordon West is wanted; Gordon West is missing; blame the CID.

'The uniforms tried his lodgings on Saturday night.'

Implying that it was none of my business. A remark I should have put another way.

'And what about all those detectives you've got?'

'He's only wanted for a petty criminal damage, boss.'

Teddy fixed me with a very jaundiced eye, 'He's your witness for identification, Bob. Surely, that's far more important than a broken pane of glass?'

'Yessir.'

'Find him then, will you?'

'Yes, sir.'

'And preferably prior to two-fifteen.'

'Cutting it a bit fine, aren't you?' asked George.

'Never mind that,' I wasn't in the receiving-criticism mood. 'Just find somebody nasty to go round to the Standard again, and lean on Danny Smith. Get them to drag him along to the hospital mortuary to do a formal ID. Then get 'em to take a statement, just in case we can't find Davinia's dad.'

'Somebody nasty,' muttered my detective inspector designate reflectively. 'Would Roger Prentice do?'

'If you like.' I hadn't the time to make enquiries into the state of the Caunt versus Prentice feud. 'In the meantime we're going to have a go at Buchanan and one or two of his little-Hitler pals.'

'Vigilantes,' corrected George.

'That was before they managed to upset me,' I explained.

It wasn't all that far to the High Street and Buchanan's double-fronted shop, but we took a CID car all the same. We weren't, all circumstances considered, entirely sure that we wouldn't have Ian Buchanan as an unwilling passenger on the way back. Besides, there's a certain *frisson* to be obtained from indulging in unauthorised parking on single yellow lines. NO PARKING BETWEEN THE 1st OF MAY AND THE 30th OF SEPTEMBER, according to the notice on the post.

'All right, me love!' shouted my detective sergeant the moment he hit the pavement, eliciting a startled, probably gratified, response from a dozen turning female heads.

Twenty yards away, a Traffic Warden put away her notebook, waved to him and grinned. He'd probably had a harem in a previous life, I decided. Much-married me, and duty or not, she'd have delighted in sticking a fixed penalty notice on the car.

Once inside Buchanan's Emporium, *Go No Further For All Your Gifts!* the atmosphere stiffened the moment we stepped through the door.

'What d'ye want?' and 'Ye'd better come through,' indicated to a short queue of shoppers and a couple of young assistants that we were about as welcome on his premises as the return of bubonic plague. Previous experience had shown me that Ian Buchanan, forty years awa' frae hame, laid on the aggressive Scottish accent whenever he was feeling cross.

Carefully, we squeezed our way through the piled-high shelves of glass, tat and pot, and there was, I noted, a fair selection of dolls and cuddly toys. Distinctly unhelpful, however; *Please, Mr Buchanan, can you give me the run down on how many hundreds of these you've sold over the past four months?*

George, however, had other ideas, 'You don't by any chance sell milkmaids?' he asked.

'Milkmaids?' Buchanan sounded just the least bit tense; almost as if he was being accused of making his living out of procuring innocent country girls.

'You know, dolls. Aprons, buckets, little yokes. Ribbons in their hair?'

'Don't sell 'em,' said Buchanan briefly. 'And I never had you figured for the grandfatherly type.'

I didn't dare look at George; instead I concentrated on making my way through the narrow aisles unscathed. One careless brush against a precariously balanced musical decanter or a tastefully decorated piece of Eddathorpe's ceramic art could easily cost us anything between fifty pence and an outrageous twenty-five quid.

Breakages, threatened the prominently displayed notices, had to be paid for. Probably the only way that he was ever going to realise a profit on most of the crude, highly-coloured trash which tottered on either side of us as we cautiously made our way to his office at the back of the shop.

The Buchanan sanctuary was an eight-foot square rabbit hutch carved out of the store room and surrounded by hardboard, containing one miserable glazed slit of glass through which he could spy on his staff. Probably untrue that last one; it's just that I can be as big a bigot as he is when I try.

Three overweight men, one desk, one chair, a telephone and a filing cabinet; it's a wonder the walls didn't bulge. Our host appropriated the chair.

'Have ye come to apologise?' He tried an aggressive blue-eyed stare through a forest of grey, unbarbered eyebrows.

'About what?'

'Your gross dereliction of duty the other night,' the Lowland rrrs rolled, and he hunched forward to rest his belly comfortably on the edge of the desk. Surely, even Ian couldn't believe anything as unlikely as that?

'The meeting, Mr Buchanan? Superintendent Baring told you, it's the chairman's task to control it. I thought you did very well,' bland, just this side of patronising, 'on the whole.'

'Graham,' he rolled my surname around in his mouth like a poisoned pill. 'Baring as well. I'll no' forget the favour in a hurry, Ah'll tell you that.'

'You realise, I suppose, that your meeting resulted in something like a riot outside the Pavilion Theatre on Saturday night?'

'I was nowhere near the Theatre on Saturday night.' Suddenly, scenting danger, the accent readjusted itself to a close approximation of BBC English, overlaid with a touch of East coast.

'No, but a number of your associates were.'

'What d'you mean by that?'

'I'm sure you've heard; on Saturday night Adele Simpson's crowd held a peaceful demonstration before the start of *Eddathorpe Rocks!* Some of the young men I saw supporting you at that meeting were present, they were anything but peaceful. Police were assaulted; a window got smashed.'

'One's in court this morning. Hooligan.' Tenderly, George touched one still-swollen cheek.

'Just because he's alleged to have hit you. He's not a hooligan until he's found guilty, and that's a very defamatory remark.'

'So you *have* heard all about it, and you're the one who stirred up this vigilante nonsense in the first place,' said George.

'Now, just a minute—'

'We didn't really come here to talk about that,' I said quickly, in a vain attempt to stifle George's civil liberties, especially his freedom of speech.

'Well, not entirely, anyway,' amended Detective Sergeant Caunt in a voice which did nothing for the state of Ian

Buchanan's nerves. 'We want to talk to Gordon, actually. Gordon West, you know?'

'Now there's another thing.' It was out before he'd taken thought. 'You're out to persecute a man whose just suffered a tremendous personal loss.'

'Ah, yes,' I said. 'I'd almost forgotten, you know him, of course. He apparently went to get some money out of the management at the Pavilion on Saturday night. Reckons he was due financial compensation; I can't think why.'

'He was accompanied by a group of your ruddy skinheads,' added George unnecessarily. 'Lovely feller, Gordon; fighting with coppers, vandalising glass.'

'They're not,' said Buchanan, dragging the threads of his dignity around him, 'my skinheads. And one or two of them might be politically active, yes. But I'll tell ye this, I don't necessarily agree with everything they say, but they've got a right to express their opinions, and they've got a greater sense of civic responsibility than some people I could mention.'

'It's a wonder you aren't there in court this morning; a character witness for the one we locked up.'

'It's a remand hearing this morning; I might just do that, once this comes to trial. The lad was provoked!'

There was an uncomfortable silence; scowls all round, while I stared thoughtfully at our pillar of Eddathorpe life. I'd had him down as nothing more than a pompous, self-important ass; now, I wondered. Glib, almost practised, that convenient little dig about freedom of speech. Provocation, too; echoes of excuses I'd heard before.

'You've got the names and addresses of the people you've recruited, I suppose?'

He looked startled, almost guilty, 'What makes you think that?'

'You held a public meeting,' I reminded him blandly. 'That was the object of the exercise, wasn't it? To recruit a sort of, er, mobile neighbourhood watch?'

'Weel,' the ageing, honest Scot was back, reluctant though. 'Ah suppose . . .'

'The inquest is this afternoon,' I said. 'Gordon isn't at his lodgings. He should be there to identify her, as the victim's closest kin.'

No need for a further mention of Criminal Damage, or the probability of an unpleasant interview between the bereaved and the uniformed branch down at Eddathorpe nick.

'And you think that these lads might be—'

'Looking after him,' suggested George.

'Weel . . .' He'd said that before. We waited: given time, I was confident that his own sense of civic responsibility would somehow struggle to the forefront of his mind. He knew it, we knew it; he knew we knew it. Nothing too direct, but we'd obviously flushed him out. Not that he was doing anything illegal; merely following his own convictions. We were, as he would no doubt have told us, living in a democracy, after all . . .

Slowly, reluctantly, his hand moved in the direction of his top right-hand drawer. He opened it, fumbled ineffectually with its contents for a while, and eventually brought out a black plastic folder which he then held shyly on his knee behind his desk.

Oddly, almost as if he wanted to draw out the process even by a second or two, he slowly reached across the desk and handed the sheet of paper he extracted to George.

'They're all good citizens,' he said emphatically. 'I don't know whether they know where Mr West is, but I'm sure they'd want to help.'

We tried to look suitably impressed. And by the time we'd finished, both George and I knew we'd be equally sure ourselves.

# Chapter Sixteen

We now had, as The Lord High Executioner sometime sang, our very own little list; and for very similar purposes, too. Not that we needed it straight away, after all.

'Control to any units in the area of Eddathorpe High street,' blared the control room despatcher as we settled into the car.

I picked up the handset, 'DCI Graham; go ahead.'

There was a shocked silence at the other end. Never in the history of ... A CID man voluntarily answering his radio; a supervisory officer inclined to *work?*

'Is that a Charlie Sierra vehicle calling?' squeaked the voice doubtfully, Charlie being the call-sign for the divisional CID, and S for Sierra indicating a supervisor on board.

'Charlie Sierra one – zero,' I said ritualistically. 'Affirmative, Control.'

'Was that Charlie Sierra one – zero?' persisted the voice. 'Repeat please. Your signals are at about R three level and breaking-up.'

'Aw, Gawd,' moaned George, 'don't let 'em get away with that. It makes us sound like *Top Gun*.'

'They should be so lucky!' I made another grab for the handset. 'This is DCI Graham in a CID car, now pass your message and stop buggering me about!'

'Charlie Sierra one – zero; please observe message protocols,' snapped the very offended voice.

'Ignore him, boss; it's that fat fart Forster in the Control Room,' George advised.

Bloody cheek: this time I left the handset severely alone, while plotting revenge on Eric Forster as soon as I got back to the nick.

'Any unit, High Street,' bleated the voice. 'Please visit premises of DSS: disturbance. Acknowledge, please.'

'Attending,' I said into the mike.

'Less than a hundred yards,' murmured George with satisfaction, as he checked his mirror, flicked his indicator switch and put the car into gear.

'Mobile calling, please repeat your call sign and—'

Enough is definitely as good as a feast. I made the standard derogatory gesture in the direction of the radio, and switched it off.

Apart from the metal-framed windows and the doorways surrounded by a minimal riveting of Portland stone, the building occupied by the Department of Social Security looked like a large public lavatory constructed in bilious yellow brick. Forty years before, its planners appeared to have gone to a great deal of trouble to find a building material unique in the architectural history of what was otherwise a warm, red-brick town.

''Ere,' said our friendly female Traffic Warden as we drew up outside, 'there's some sorta row going on, inside.'

'Isn't there always, love?' asked George.

Two shabbily dressed, pushchair-toting women and a brace of elderly men hovered in the doorway, 'Told ya they'd call the cops,' said one woman to the other as we made our way between them and through the door.

Once inside the building, disturbance or not, doom and gloom descended, reinforced by the sight of the chipped, cream painted walls of the waiting room. Above all, faint but distinct, we caught a whiff of that unique odour of disinfectant, subtly blended with a touch of dead floor mop, thoughtfully provided by government departments for the benefit of the no-account and poor.

A scattered group of potential customers sat or sprawled across the rows of pew-like benches, inadequately upholstered in brown leatherette. They were all staring in the same direction, each clutching a numbered plastic docket, while they watched and listened to the fun.

In front of the sectioned-off, glass-protected counter, a semi-shoeless male figure was limping backwards and forwards clutching the other half of his footwear, and hammering ineffectually on the reinforced glass.

'You whey-faced bastards!' he was bawling. 'Come on then, all of you! Come on out and fight!'

On the other side of the screen three male and two female members of staff seemed disinclined to take him up, while on the wall above, the red lights on an electronic counter flickered madly, 998 ... 999 ... 000 ... 001 ... 002 ... 003 ... *Next Customer, Please!*

The docket holders, having decided that there was entertainment as well as safety in numbers, made absolutely no effort to move.

'Oh, dear,' said George, as we marched briskly across the scuffed parquet floor towards the scene of the action. 'He appears to have broken their machine.'

The situation was familiar, and so was the man; short, stocky, fifties, with an enpurpled face, wide shoulders and a swollen pigeon chest.

'Police! Put your shoe on, Mr West, and calm down.'

It sounds all right, but it is not, perhaps, the wisest thing to say. All too often it only seems to stir 'em up. Exhorted to calm, Gordon West swung round and prepared to use his shoe. As he lifted it high, I stepped in, and using my left forearm as a bar, I blocked it as it came down, brought my right hand under and through his upper arm, clasped my own wrist, took another step forward, pushed firmly and Gordon was on the floor.

'I've got witnesses, I've got witnesses! That was police assault!'

George grabbed a spare arm, confiscated the shoe and we dragged him smartly to his feet. 'Boss,' he said, 'I don't suppose you're carrying a set of handcuffs, by any chance?'

'No, are you?'

He shook his head, then, ironically, 'Join Britain's modern police!'

'Hey,' said the prisoner indignantly, 'what am I supposed to have done?'

'It's not just 'cos we like you,' grunted George. 'What about Breach of the Peace?'

'And criminal damage on Saturday,' I murmured, 'and what about the DSS and their electronic—'

The Departmental manager, thirties, glasses, grey suit, unlocked the side door and emerged from his retreat. Following the direction of my gaze, he watched the whirling numbers for a few seconds, 'It's doing it again!'

He pointed to the lights, drew the attention of a colleague, and made a winding motion with one hand. One of his staff caught-on. He banged the counter vigorously with his fist: 431 . . . 432 . . . *Next* . . . Bang! again . . . *Customer, Please!* and it stopped.

The manager smiled nervously, 'Thank you very much,' he said to us, but he kept a good three or four paces back.

'What's it all about?'

'We told him he wouldn't get a Giro 'till Thursday,' he said almost plaintively, while the scattered group behind us, sensing the old official run-around, shifted uneasily and growled.

I nodded understandingly, I knew the score: a stranger off the street, and they'd wanted some sort of confirmation of identity and a postal address.

'I'm an emergency!' bawled Gordon, seeking the sympathy vote. 'What about immediate payments? I know my ri—'

George altered his grip, 'I haven't cautioned you, yet,' he said menacingly. 'Now shut up!'

'Er, look, I'm grateful,' said the manager, taking a backward pace, 'but do you have to make a charge? Time . . . going to court . . . staff shortages; you know how it is?' He glanced anxiously at his bunch of keys; obviously a man who would be far, far happier on the other side of his securely locked and bolted door.

'Oh, don't worry about that,' leered George, staring fixedly at the prisoner. 'After all, HM Coroner will soon be wanting him!'

Behind us, the audience, misinterpreting his sentiments, gave a collective gasp, and flinched.

It's a cliché that I've come to hate; the *all coppers are bastards!* bit. The trouble is, it trips so lightly off the tongue, and short of confirming them in their prejudices by delivering a short, sharp shock in the area of the left ear from time to time, it's difficult to break our customers of the habit. Besides, it's unwise to belt people in public, especially ten minutes before an inquest, in the waiting room of the Coroner's court.

'You bastards. You unutterable bastards!' screamed Danny Smith, 'Dragging me down to the mortuary, putting me through all that, and now you don't want me any more!'

'It's never very pleasant,' I said soothingly, 'viewing a body. Thank you very much for being a volunteer.'

'*Never very pleasant!*' He minced in a high falsetto voice. 'You bloody pouf! And what about that tame gorilla you sent along? A volunteer, was I? I said no, and he practically dragged me out of me own pub! So that's your idea of a fucking volunteer!'

'Shhhh!' said Roger Prentice. 'Remember where you are.'

'I know where I am, all right,' hissed Danny venomously through his teeth. 'I'm gonna tell the Coroner about you and your nasty sodding ways.'

'But you're no longer a witness; you're not needed now. Come quietly like a good lad, and I'll give you a lift home.' Roger Prentice put a companionable arm around Danny Smith's shoulders, and began to lead him away. I've no experience of gorillas, but I could see what the landlord meant.

'He's a wanker,' said Gordon West judicially, handcuffed to George at the other side of the waiting room, and almost certainly referring to our former witness for the ID.

Prentice paused at the door, 'Takes one to know one,' he snapped. Not the most tactful rejoinder he could have made in the presence of our erstwhile volunteer.

Professor Andrew Lawrence, awaiting the kick-off, and seated as far away as possible from George and his charge, pursed his lips. It confirmed everything he'd ever heard or thought of about the police.

I sat, I brooded; metaphorically, I twiddled my thumbs. The press were already in court; it was just about worth a paragraph, I supposed. But the scattering of the morbid, the downright ghoulish and the unemployed who were undoubtedly in the process of occupying the public gallery presented a puzzle all their own. It was the holiday season, the sun was shining – well, a bit. Why on earth would they want to stay and listen to a string of semi-comprehensible medical evidence? The possibility of gloating over a rape? Was that the attraction on a fine afternoon like this?

The Inquest, I knew, would take about twenty minutes: nothing exciting, a short but necessary bore. Finding the body, me; witness for identification, Shirley's, alias Davinia's, courtesy dad. The postmortem evidence would feature our professorial friend, and that would be it. A few encouraging words from the Coroner, and an adjournment *sine die* for police enquiries to take place.

Eddathorpe's magistrates court, once inconveniently, even riotously, held in the Town Hall, and mixing villain and coun- cillor in what some might regard as an entirely appropriate way, had now moved out leaving the premises for use as an occasional Coroner's court. This suited everybody, particularly the borough councillors, embarrassed for decades by defendants who hung about in the foyer claiming their elected representatives as close and influential friends.

Suddenly, the waiting room began to fill; a woman in her fifties, weeping, and accompanied by a subdued group of her female friends, together with a smartly-dressed managerial type, with a couple of men with jackets over their overalls in tow. Subdued greetings were exchanged, and I glanced across. Nothing to do with me: early arrivals for the next inquest, an industrial accident case.

Once they had settled, the emotional tension seemed to deflate. After a few moments of muttered conversation, they started looking around for something more exciting to see or do.

Men in handcuffs! Simultaneously, six or seven pairs of eyes fixed themselves excitedly on George who stared right back, silently daring each and every one of them to confuse the prisoner with the cop.

A quarter past two ... twenty-past ... twenty-five ... Time dragged; hurry up and wait. Lawrence, his eyes ostentatiously buried in his file for the last fifteen minutes, eventually closed it, replaced it in the expensive briefcase held across his knee, and signalled me with his eyes. Confidences, I gathered, ought to be exchanged.

Boredom, rather than expectation, drove me into the corridor where Lawrence, after looking around, drew me into an alcove formed by a sealed-off door next to the stairs.

'There's a full report on its way to you,' he said.

'Thanks.'

A young man mounted the stairs and brushed past us; scuffed bomber jacket and a yellow shirt. I turned, but not too quickly, just in time to see him enter the public gallery. My nod of acknowledgement was lost on his retreating back.

Surprised, but only mildly surprised to see him at the inquest. A man with a minimal acquaintance with Davinia, so far as I knew. The sighting, therefore, was only marginally more interesting to me than the pathologist's summons. Beryl, I recalled, had fancied Nigel Laud as a Peeping Tom, and having been reminded of his existence, I mentally advanced his interview priority by a single notch. Bored or not, petty-minded or not, we tend to clutch at these scraps and straws whenever and wherever we can.

'You got the preliminary all right?' Lawrence drew me back to the business in hand.

'Yes.'

'Sorry it's taken so long.'

'That's OK.'

'Mere formality today, of course.'

Inwardly, I sighed. He was bored; I was bored, and it was probably simple ennui that had driven him out of the waiting room to talk. No need for the secret-squirrel stuff, we could have exchanged platitudes while we were comfortably sitting down.

'Was there, er . . .' I said.

'As a matter of fact, there is. The Coroner has a copy, of the report, naturally, but I will not be mentioning it today in open court.'

'Oh, yes?'

'You did, ah, thoroughly search the victim's flat?'

'Yes, of course. And there was a full examination by SOCO, Scenes of Crime.'

'Good, good. And there are items outstanding – awaiting forensic examination, no doubt?'

'Yes, for one thing we submitted all the jewellery from her box,' I reassured him. 'They'll let me know if any of the remaining earrings contain traces of blood, and if she is likely to have damaged her ear lobe herself.'

'That's not what I had in mind. you'll need a forensic examination of her personal property; her handbag and purse, for example. There are traces of THC both in her urine and in the blood samples I took.'

'THC?'

'The active constituent in cannabis.' He looked at me severely. Ignorant copper: I'd failed my examination in elementary chemistry once again.

# Chapter Seventeen

Wild excitement at home, and silly games. Engaged in a crazy chase of round and round the furniture without touching the floor, Joe was behaving like the daftest, drunkest subaltern in the whole of the officers' mess.

On the forth or fifth circuit, I managed to grab the offender and hold him, shuddering, panting and wriggling, under one arm and squeeze him close to my chest. He struggled vigorously, whining to be let down.

Laura, who had been watching the proceedings and clinging wisely to one arm of the sofa in case of accidents, planted her feet firmly apart and grinned, 'Nice Joe; doggy play,' she said.

'That dog has been a ruddy pain all day.' Angie was of a different opinion, 'For goodness' sake give him some exercise, before he drives me mad. He's hardly been out of the house for the best part of a week.'

'He's been out first thing every morning,' I replied indignantly. 'Without fail.'

'And you've been coming home at all hours; he's had exactly one proper walk at night. He's getting on my nerves.'

I recognised the ploy; a Union meeting had been convened, and the official grievance procedure was being invoked.

Gingerly, with a quick ruffle to the ears I restored Joe to the carpet. For once he plumped himself down instead of doing his far-famed imitation of Concorde taking off. Clocking the general tone of the conversation, he cuddled close to his master, signalling the frequency with which he was subjected to unjustified verbal abuse.

Laura, seeing him settled, released her protective hold on the sofa and wandered across, the straps of her dungarees dangling around her elbows, to give him a pat.

'It's always the same in this house,' grumbled Angie unreasonably. 'You're hardly ever here, you never take any notice, and when you do arrive it's always the three of you ganging up.'

'I could always set the table,' I offered.

'Bob a job week, is it?'

'What on earth is the matter with you?'

'Look, why don't you do something useful, and take them both out for half an hour. Dinner will be ready when you get back, and she can go to bed.'

'Just tell me—'

'You ought to know already, Rob,' said Angie coldly. 'Except when it comes to that job of yours, you've got a memory like a sieve.'

'OK, so I've forgotten something, but we could always—'

'Tuesday; tomorrow is Tuesday. Doesn't that remind you of something?'

'No.'

'Like an interview? *My* interview?'

'Oh, God, I'm sorry; Sandiland's school. You must be feeling fraught.'

'A bit, and I wouldn't mind knowing what's going on.'

'The letters, you mean?'

She sighed heavily and glanced warningly at Laura, 'Yes, of course it's the letters. But little piggies have got big ears, so ...'

'It's a bit tricky, but George is going to sort it,' I said.

'George?' She advanced and swept up Laura under one arm, 'Playpen, darling. Five minutes with your toys, sweetie, eh?' She was out and back within thirty seconds, leaving a surprised, fortunately unprotesting, toddler contemplating an assortment of soft toys and a pile of bricks in the next room. 'I just don't believe this. *George?*'

'I had no alternative; I'm too personally involved.'

'First it was a local councillor and chairman of the school governors; that was bad enough. Then Fairfield, then Baring and Paula, or maybe it was the other way round. Now you're telling me it's been passed to George Caunt. Why don't you buy a megaphone, and broadcast it, Rob?'

'Once it started to snowball, Teddy Baring had to know. Fairfield and Paula are victims themselves, and George is very experienced, very discreet.'

'*Discreet!* George might be, but we don't need a newspaper in Eddathorpe, not as long as he's got that wife. Paula Spriggs,' she said, bringing up the heavy artillery, 'will probably skin you alive.'

'She's been round for coffee and sympathy, eh?'

'I talked to her about babies, and she filled me in on one or two bits and bobs she thought I ought to know.'

'Like?'

'Like the Eddathorpe International News Service,' said Angie tartly, 'otherwise known as Mrs Sarah Caunt.'

'George isn't an idiot; he doesn't tell her everything. In the same way,' I added with thoughtless accuracy, 'as I don't tell you.'

'Oh, so I'm a bigmouth too, am I?' Something to seize on at last.

'I don't mean that.'

'Then what do you mean?'

Patience, Robert, patience. She's got every right to be wound-up. A poison-pen: the possibility of tales spreading within a very tight and self-regarding club, and a job interview coming up the next day.

'It's extremely difficult, that's all. And what with the murder and everything, we just haven't got around to it, yet.'

'You've got a suspect, haven't you?'

I nodded.

'Somebody in your precious Force?'

'Poor old Malc Cartwright—'

'*HIM!*'

'No love, and we haven't any proof.'

'So it's somebody associated with him. If it's not him, it's Ginny, isn't it? It's his barmy wife.'

Chief Inspector Derek Paget stormed into my office at three minutes to eight, 'Thank God you've arrived!'

'Good morning, Derek.' Bring 'em up short, preserve the civilities, and impose that necessary touch of healing calm.

Distractedly, he ran one hand over his almost nonexistent hair. 'Oh,' slight traces of confusion as he signalled a rapid change of gear. 'G'morning,' he said.

'And what can I do for you?'

Obviously feeling that in some obscure way he'd lost the first round, he flopped into the visitors' chair, and did his panic-stricken best to look smug.

'More of a case of what I can do for you, Bob. Does the name Alan Alfred Pykett ring a bell?'

'Got him downstairs, huh?'

For an instant, amidst the air of hurry and scurry, a gleam of pure Thatcherite triumphalism lit his eye. I was obviously about to discover that in somewhere remote, in the constabulary equivalent of South Georgia, probably, Pykett was no longer free.

'Next best thing; he's in Casualty, having stitches put in a head wound right now. Cliff Appleby's there.'

'Domestos?'

His expression hardened, 'I'd heard you didn't approve of people using that particular name?'

'Sorry, Derek, you caught me on the hop, that's all. I didn't think he'd fully recovered yet. Never thought you'd got him out on the street.'

'Light duties only. He's on early mornings, so I sent him down to keep an eye on Pykett as soon as I heard. I suppose you'll want to get along yourself and see him *tout-bloody-suite?*'

'Tell me about it: how do we know it's Pykett, for a start?'

'Well,' Derek shuffled, and a trace of embarrassment crossed his face, 'That's what we were told.'

'Oh yeah?'

'Anonymous three nines call just before seven a.m. The caller said we were all useless, and a group of concerned citizens had been left to do our job.'

Nasty; an unexpected jolt. It sounded very much like Buchanan's Brownshirts, and I thought I'd settled that. Still, it was silver lining time, nevertheless: a three niner meant that the caller was recorded on tape.

'Go on.'

'He also said that they'd found Pykett, dealt with him last night, and dumped what was left to cool his heels in the Queen Victoria Memorial Park. That's what they said; all very formal, not just the Vikky Park. Two lads from the area car found him unconscious at the side of the bandstand, and sent for an ambulance straight away.'

'Bad?'

'Bad enough. He's had a good hammering. He's been sleeping rough, from what they tell me. Physically, he wasn't all that good in the first place, he's getting on and they've left him out all night.'

I reached for the file, 'According to this, he's fifty-one.'

Derek shrugged, 'Takes its toll; the best part of a ten-year sentence inside.'

'Six and a half; he had to do more than fifty percent of his time under the new rules, and now he's on parole. Or at least he was until he did a bunk. You've traced the origin of the call?'

'Phone box; not far from the Royal Standard pub.'

'Deliberate? Somebody making a point?'

Once again he shrugged.

'OK, thanks.' I extracted a copy of the photograph and descriptive form, and pocketed them both. 'I've got a bad feeling about this one, Derek; for starters, how did these bastards come to know?'

'About what?'

'About Pykett; we've never released his name. We never said a word about him, come to that, but Buchanan has been moaning-on about rapists being left on the loose by an incompetent police force, over the past few days.'

'We've got a leak?'

'Not exactly unique, is it? But what sort of copper goes around giving information to a gang of toe-rags like that?'

Slowly, cynically, as I made for the door, Derek Paget raised a rigid right arm, and placed the forefinger of his left hand across a thrust-out upper lip.

'That's very funny, Derek. Thanks a bunch!'

Casualty was crowded; nobody dying, but nearly every cubicle full of injured minibus passengers. Trippers versus an overnight delivery van, apparently. Amidst the organised chaos of doctors, nurses and orderlies, a pair of policemen, white-topped caps beside them, were slumped patiently on a couple of appropriated staffroom chairs, sipping tea, chewing gum and waiting: doing what the Traffic division does best.

One of them lumbered reluctantly to his feet when I entered; the other remained firmly glued to his seat. 'Yours is in there, sir.' He made a careless sideways gesture towards the extreme right-hand cubicle with his thumb.

'Thanks; can I—'

'Doctor's with him.'

'And have you seen—'

'Gone to fill the kettle for another cuppatea.'

Wonderful news: a wanted man receiving treatment in one part of the hospital, while his guardian searches out a kettle, and abandons him in favour of a hot drink.

Misinterpreting my scowl as a comment on the paucity of accommodation for senior officers, my informant promptly resumed his seat. ''Nother chair if you want it, in there.' He indicated the partially curtained-off staff room with the same ubiquitous thumb.

'No, thanks. What about the admissions—'

'Clerk? Buzzing around like a blue-arsed fly at the moment,' said my helpful volunteer. 'I should wait, if I was you. They'll all settle down in a bit.'

'Everybody's very busy,' rumbled his mate reproachfully, slumping forward, resting his elbows comfortably across his thighs and clutching a half-empty mug between his knees. I wouldn't have minded being the chief inspector of an outfit like theirs. It's not a bad old retirement job on the whole; a big, distinctive car, a free uniform and they still let you draw real police pay.

'Stay here and keep an eye on the prisoner,' I said, employing my own thumb.

'But we're both bus—' the rebel lifted his head from his steaming mug, and rapidly changed his mind. 'Yessir!'

'And you might tell the doctor I'd like a word, as soon as he comes out.' I tried my shark-like smile, and managed to make them both look glum.

'It's a Paki; Doctor Ben-something,' muttered my first volunteer, a note of resentment tinging his voice.

A bell rang somewhere at the back of my mind. Doctor Ben-something; unpronounceable name, pleasant manner, we'd met before. 'He's from Sri Lanka,' I said severely, 'And you're supposed to be a professional, constable, so watch your mouth.'

I only just caught the murmur of, 'Big-headed bastard,' as I passed vengefully down the corridor in search of my errant PC, but if you can't make grouchy bastards unhappy occasionally, what's the point?

Clifford Appleby, built, as some are liable to say, like a brick outhouse, with more than a hint of a double-chin at the age of twenty-one, was just on his way out of the kitchen as I approached, a kettle dangling carelessly from one massive paw.

Not exactly the Brain of Britain, he'd have conceded that himself, but he was not the size and kind of copper I'd have liked to have tangled with while playing Peeping Tom on a dark and dreary night.

'Want a cuppa, Boss?' At the sight of me his beefy face split into a guileless grin, and if he'd had one he'd have wagged his tail. His whole attitude was reminiscent of nothing so much as an overgrown Labrador pup.

'Did those two send you off to make the tea?' I flicked an over-the-shoulder nod down the corridor, in the direction of the flat-cap twins.

'Well, y'know,' he hesitated, wondering what on earth he might have done wrong. 'They thought that another one might be nice.'

'And they couldn't do it themselves because they're having such a busy day?'

'We-ll . . .' There was a whole world of amiable self-effacement in a single word.

I looked at his open, smiling features, and not for the first time I wondered how he'd ever passed through the training processes intact. Basic cunning, a nascent talent for self-preservation even, he simply hadn't got.

I took a deep breath, preparing to deliver a high-class bollocking, and all, I told myself, entirely for his own good.

*Clifford Appleby, you're an idiot; however you managed to get through your probationary training I'll never know* ... And the words just died. Somehow, not for the first time, and certainly not for the last, Cliff unconsciously deployed his single useful resource; the ability to avoid the standard supervisory bawling-out.

'Clifford,' I said, more-or-less gently, 'that's your prisoner back there, and he's your responsibility. What if you'd lost him? Didn't you ever think?'

'Oh, no, boss.' He was entirely unruffled; the grin remained firmly in place.

'What do you mean, *oh, no?*'

'He's not my prisoner, sir. They only told me to come down here to look after him, like.'

'But it's Alan Alfred Pykett, OK?'

'That's what they told me, boss.'

'He's a murder suspect, Cliff.'

'Yeah, but he's unconscious, so how could I tell him he was under arrest?'

He stared at me guilelessly. There was a twisted logic down there somewhere; buried far, far below the reach of a simplistic DCI.

'Tell me,' I said, 'what exactly have you done since you've been here; apart from filling the kettle to make the tea?'

'I had a word with Doctor Ben.'

'Good, and what did he say?'

'That he's not in very good shape, whoever he is. The man's had a good kicking, and he's been out all night.'

'You mean *Pykett*, yes?'

'I dunno, I'm not exactly sure.'

He fumbled in a side pocket of his tunic and produced a sheet of crumpled paper roughly wrapped in the inevitable polythene bag. Preserve for fingerprints: at least I was grateful to the instructor who'd managed to ram something into his less than sensitive skull.

'It doesn't look a lot like him, does it?'

'I don't know. I haven't seen him, yet.' Mechanically, I took the proffered sheet, and stared uncomprehendingly at a photocopied description of Pykett, complete with a poorly reproduced photograph at the top.

'Cliff,' I said. 'It's a copy of one of our own descriptive forms, probably yours. Why have you bothered bagging this?'

'It's certainly not mine!' For the first time a touch of asperity entered his voice. 'I found it stuffed in the breast pocket of the victim's jacket, boss.'

Proudly, he produced his pocket book, 'Look!' he said, 'you can't catch me out on his property. I found it, and listed it when I went through all his other junk!'

# Chapter Eighteen

'I've got another one!' Peter Fairfield breathing fire and slaughter down the phone at a quarter past ten.

'Another one what?'

My mind was still on the semi-comatose tramp, by now transferred from the Casualty department and on to a ward: Alan Alfred Pykett, or not? This man had had a good kicking all right, and the out-of-date police photograph of our suspect was not a lot of help. Fingerprints — but they would come later — were the ticket. In the meantime Police Constable Clifford Appleby was staying firmly in place.

'Another letter, of course. Bob, are you with us this morning? Not living in the same mundane world as the rest?'

'Sorry, sir. I was thinking about a GBH.'

'It all happens to you, doesn't it? Anybody we know?'

'It could be Pykett, boss, but we can't be sure, yet; the victim looks older, and he's pretty duffed-up.'

'Couldn't happen to a nicer chap!'

'Pykett's only fifty-one; this feller looks damn near sixty, if he's a day.'

'Maybe he's led a hard life; took a lot out of him, raping little girls.'

There was no reasoning with him in this mood, 'Yes,' I sighed, 'perhaps.'

'Anyway,' he said recklessly, 'keep me posted, eh? I'm glad you've cleared it up.'

'The murder?' Involuntarily, my voice rose. 'But I haven't—'

'Yes, well, I'm sure you'll sort it out. I want to talk to you about this letter, Bob.' Nothing unusual in that; a chief superintendent getting his priorities right once again.

'Yes, sir?'

'I'm not standing for it; the bugger's making personal threats. I want this animal squashing, right now.'

'Sir, we—'

'I appointed Caunt to sort this out. I appreciate your problem, Bob, and I want you to keep well out of it from a personal point of view. But he's your man; put a rocket up his bum!'

'These threats . . .'

'"*You are a fat, idle, immoral pig,*" and I quote.' The breathing became distinctly heavier at the other end of the line. '*Unless you are prepared to take action to clear the filth from your Augean stables immediately, every one of your own disgusting sexual habits will be fully exposed in the Press.*" What the fuck are the Augean stables, Bob?'

Sod him; I was feeling bolshie by this time. Let him look it up for himself. 'Something Greek, I think.'

'We got anybody of Greek extraction on the job?'

Another no-win situation.

'No, sir; not so far as I know.'

'Well tell Caunt to bear it in mind.'

'Sir.' Any last misty threads of thoughts of taking him into our confidence faded. Yes, George and I had a suspect, and yes, for the time being at least, we were going to keep her identity strictly to ourselves.

'I suppose you'll want the envelope and letter?'

'Please.' Well, well; something of a turn-up, here. He must have mellowed, having unsuccessfully tried to keep the first one on a strictly need-to-know.

'I'll have it sent over in a property envelope – make sure the plastic is intact when you receive it, eh?'

Property envelopes were fitted with a brittle plastic tag; once in place the package could not be opened without making it obvious that the confidentiality seal had been snapped. Detective Chief Superintendent Fairfield; a trusting sort of chap.

'The, er, letter,' I asked. 'I suppose the typeface is the same?'

'Yes,' said Fairfield shortly, 'think I'm daft?' 'Just checking, sir.' Then, realising the ambiguity of what I'd just said, I added hastily, 'Damage to the letter O?'

'I've already told you, Bob.' A note of exasperation entered his voice. Excellent: an entirely unintended insult, but he'd been too impatient to have picked it up. 'Oh, and by the way, I've had a word with the head of Scenes of Crime. He'll process all the letters for fingerprints personally, and in the strictest confidence, any time you like.'

'Thank you, sir. Oh, and if you're sending me a despatch, would you ask SOCO to send a copy of Pykett's fingerprints to me at the same time?'

'Surely, it's better if you take dabs from your passing tramp and send them over to HQ?'

'He's been well and truly thumped. If I go trying to take fingerprints at this stage, the hospital authorities won't be very chuffed. But if I've seen Pykett's marks I can visit the guy, and even I can take a preliminary look at his hands and . . .'

'Point taken. OK.'

George sidled into the room, and, seeing how I was employed, he did his elaborate pantomime of *Please, boss, I'm not here!* Entering into the conspiracy, I raised my eyes heavenwards and pointed to the visitors' chair. He sank down and eyed me with a suitably serious expression on his face.

Fairfield trundled on; the threat of unwelcome publicity, unlikely though it sounded, had caught him on the raw. Working, I gathered on the sound old principle that his gang was bigger than theirs, he wanted action *now!* Never mind the peripheries; restless natives, tramps in hospital, murdered girls. Just get this bugger put a stop to, *now!*

'Rank has its privileges,' said George sententiously, when I put the receiver down.

'Personally, I haven't noticed it much.'

'Oh, I dunno; want to try interviewing Ginny Cartwright yourself?'

'You got elected, mate. And,' I allowed a note of irritation to enter my voice, 'I can think of a lot of chief inspectors who'd take more than a touch of offence at that.'

'OK, sorry, boss. You'd do your bit if you weren't personally involved. But one thing you can tell me; how the hell am I supposed to tackle this?'

'Wait for Fairfield to send his latest epistle across. Then you've got a choice.' I was sounding brisk enough, but to be strictly honest, I couldn't quite meet his eye. Chief Superintendent or no Chief Superintendent, deep down, I still regarded this mess as mostly mine. It went against the grain to walk away.

'This choice?' said George.

'Yep; choice one, you can play it blunt. Collect your stuff together, find yourself a policewoman, brief her, and go and bang on Mrs Cartwright's door. Choice two; colleague to colleague first. Go and talk to Malc.'

'And if he turns nasty on Ginny's behalf? What happens if he kicks up a fuss?'

'Fairfield will do his nut, and I'll give him the short version of my lecture on decency and humanity, and tell him that it's what I told you to do.'

'That should make Fairfield *very* happy.' He stared at me levelly for a moment. 'Rank has its privileges, huh? Now d'you see what I mean!'

'Boss,' Detective Constable Patrick Goodall, no bombast, and with his face remarkably straight. 'I can't find George.'

'He's busy right now,' I said absently, still concentrating on the pile of statements littering my desk.

'I wonder ...' he was being diffident. Not something he normally does well.

'What is it, Pat?'

'Well, y'know that character, Nigel Laud?'

'Not intimately, why?' I regretted saying it almost straight away; he's young, he's loud, he can be trouble, but there's no need for the automatic touch of sarcasm whenever I speak to Pat.

'We've got him downstairs.' I looked up; alarm bells rang. He sounded embarrassed as well as pleased.

'Why?'

'He wouldn't talk to us, boss. Not a word, so we arrested him for assault on police.'

I stared at him incredulously; big, blond, blocking the light from my doorway, and now he was calmly telling me that he'd employed the oldest police chestnut in the book. Find a stroppy witness, lose your temper, start a row and promptly arrest him on a trumped-up charge of police assault.

Why me? Did I really have to put up with people who routinely deployed the social skills of Saddam Hussain? Of the tens of thousands of coppers who, faced with an awkward situation, employ a touch of civility, even charm, I get lumbered with Pat. I wondered, not for the first time, how he'd manage to wriggle out of the consequences of the all-too-likely police complaint.

'I don't exactly follow you,' I said.

'Last week, huh?'

I shook my head.

'Howlett Street; when poor old Domestos got thumped.'

Almost imperceptibly, I relaxed. Not, after all, an opportunistic misuse of police powers. Domestos, sorry, Clifford Appleby, had been the victim of a genuine police assault, and Patrick, for once, had only been doing his job.

'So, if Laud assaulted Appleby, he's also a stalker and the Peeping Tom?'

'Dunno; that's why I wanted George Caunt. Nigie-baby won't talk to us, boss.'

I was getting psychic. I stood up, no longer relaxed, and subject to an almost palpable sense of doom. 'And where's the evidence?'

'Well, that girl, Beryl, said it might be him, an' it should be OK when Cliff Appleby picks him out.' A new definition of evidence, apparently: that which you scrape together somehow whenever you don't get things all your own way.

'OK,' I said, 'I think I'd better come down. Just tell me, who went with you when you went to interview Laud?'

'That new lad from Aylfleet; the CID Aide.'

It all clicked together: another glorious cock-up in the Eddathorpe annals, with the blind leading the blind. I remembered the Aide all right; the lad on a free transfer from Dorothea Spinks.

Slim almost to emaciation, pale, with a shock of dark brown hair falling across his forehead, Nigel Laud sat well back in the interview-room chair, determined to give nothing away. He looked defiant, scared and very young. He was, I had to admit it, a trifle effete. Crude, cocksure Pat and his nickname, Nigie-baby, he wasn't far wrong.

Comparing him mentally with Clifford Appleby, I could only wonder; our uniformed victim could give him at least three inches in height and a good four stone. Suddenly, the interview room looked very overcrowded; me, Pat Goodall and the Aide; three on to one.

'Nigel,' I said quietly, 'these officers have cautioned you, and the custody sergeant has told you your rights?'

He nodded.

'For the tape please.'

'Yes.'

'And you don't want legal representation?'

'No.'

'You can change your mind, you know; any time you like.'

'I've already said.'

Five words on tape so far. And five more than he'd vouch-safed to Pat.

'Were you hanging about in Howlett Street in the early hours of last Tuesday, old son?'

No reply.

'Remember seeing a policeman going past?'

Nothing.

'Been hanging around there before, had you?'

Silence, and a marginal tightening of the arms folded across his chest.

'Maybe you've been doing it a lot over the past few weeks?'

'No.'

'The first time, was it?'

No reply.

'And once you thought the policeman had gone, you went round the back of a house.'

No reply.

'A bit naive, wasn't it? If you'd been a potential burglar you'd have run a mile once you saw a cop.'

He shrugged.

'I mean, that time of morning, and a policeman sees you, and he didn't even stop and pass the time of night?'

Another shrug.

'Didn't you stop to wonder why?'

'Giving me enough rope.'

'That's right; waiting to see whether you'd go round the back of a house, and you did.'

'I'm not a thief.'

'I've not suggested that, have I? But we've had some other complaints.'

I watched his chin droop down towards his chest.

'People following people; looking in their windows at night.'

'I only wanted to talk to her, that's all.'

'Girls don't like being followed like that, Nigel. Especially at night.'

'She's not a girl.'

'Beryl, the girl from the pub. She's hardly older than you.'

'No.'

'You didn't even go to the right house.'

'I don't know what you're talking about.'

'The policeman, PC Appleby, followed you into a back yard; it wasn't Beryl Matthews' house.'

He didn't answer, but he had every right to look glum.

'And then there's Davinia. You'd met her a few weeks ago, hadn't you, when you were there in the pub with Colin, your mate? She was his girlfriend for a while at the beginning of the season; did you fancy her, too?'

'No. I know what you're trying to do; she's dead, and it was nothing to do with her.'

'What wasn't?'

'What I was doing: nothing at all, and if I say anything you'll stitch me up.'

'So you didn't fancy Davinia?'

'No.'

'But you followed her, didn't you? And you went looking through the windows of her flat.'

A long hesitation, 'No. Just like I said; whatever I say you'll try to stitch me up.'

'Beryl, then?'

'That's the skinny one, isn't it? No.'

'But you did made a mistake, didn't you? On Tuesday morning, you went to the wrong house.'

'If you say so. Yes, alright, I did.'

'But you say you only wanted to talk to her; at half past one am, OK?'

A nod.

'Speak for the tape please, Nigel.'

'Yes, but it was nothing to do with that skinny kid.'

'Who then?' I paused. Kid of twenty fancies a buxom rising-forty with salt-and-pepper hair?

'So you knew that the, er, blond lady was staying with Beryl that night?'

'Maureen.'

'Yes, that's right, Maureen, but you went to the wrong house, and that's when PC Appleby caught you, eh?'

'I didn't mean to hurt him. I was just running away.'

'OK, we'll come back to that in a minute. Why did you want to talk to Maureen, Nigel?'

'I'm not a sex maniac, if that's what you mean.'

'But you'd been following her, hadn't you? She doesn't even live on Howlett Street. She'd moved in with Beryl Matthews that night because she was being stalked.'

'I wasn't stalking her.'

'What do you call it then?'

'I was going to knock.'

'Firstly, you were following her friends, then you drive her out of her own home, then you go round to the house where she's staying just to get out of your way. And finally, you were going to knock her up at half-one in the morning. But you weren't stalking her? OK, have it your way, but wouldn't you say that you were being a trifle obsessive, old son?'

'I wasn't what-you-call-it, stalking the others, either. They were her mates; I did hang around a bit, but I just wanted them to help.'

'Help you do what? get a date with Maureen, eh?' Twenty fancies nearly forty, and he was seeking assistance by sneaking around in the small hours, and plucking up courage to talk to her mates?

Not a tidy interview so far; confusing, even, but at least we had the makings of a long, productive chat. I glanced at Pat and his sidekick, their worries were apparently over: they were beginning to look as if they'd won the pools. My own professional expectations were rising by the second; we had a right little nutter here.

For the first time he looked at me directly, miserably, straight in the eye. Our joint expectations crashed.

'It's not what you think,' he muttered shamefacedly. 'I told her who I was. She was shocked, she cried, but she said she'd think about meeting me regularly. Now she says it's no good, an' she's refusing to have anything to do with me at all. She can't do that, can she? Not me Mum.'

# Chapter Nineteen

'Well?'

George avoided my eye, 'It was Ginny, all right. We grabbed the typewriter, boss; an old Underwood, practically an antique.' He stirred uneasily, and the young policewoman beside him, her lips pressed firmly together, didn't seem all that eager to support him in the role of conversational volunteer. I was feeling a bit monosyllabic myself.

'Unpleasant?'

'You could say that.'

'I'm sorry, George.'

'Good job you weren't involved,' he said generously. 'She really hates your guts.' Then, anxiety etching lines around his mouth he added, 'You'll never take it to court?'

'Not if I can help it.'

'Well, Andy and Paula won't want to: you reckon that Fairfield might push it, then?'

I glanced at the youngster beside him; no point in discretion at this late stage. Just out of her Probation, pretty in a dumpy sort of way. Sylvia Something-or-other; Sylvia Doyle: she didn't look the twittery, talkative type. Not happy, either; a trifle pale and shocked.

'I don't know. Perhaps.'

'He wouldn't be such a shit.'

Sylvia tugged nervously at the edge of her tunic. In too deep already for her own peace of mind, and she could do without the full and frank discussion between her seniors, thank you very much.

I didn't reply; I wouldn't have bet on it having listened to Fairfield on the subject of poison pen, but George had known him a lot longer than me.

I turned to our unwilling co-conspirator, 'Miss Doyle, have you completed your book?'

'My pocket book? Yessir, with Sergeant Caunt.'

'Thank you.' I took it out of her hand, signed it below the last entry, sealed it in an envelope, scribbled rapidly and dropped it into the top drawer of my desk.

'Go and see the duty inspector, will you? Ask him to issue you with a new book, and tell him the old one contains details of a confidential enquiry. Ask him to speak to me.'

She stared at me round-eyed, 'But I can't have a new one; that one isn't full.'

'Don't worry; it's just that I don't want the uniform supervisors reading it, otherwise the news will be all round the station in half an hour. Mr Fairfield wouldn't like that.'

'Oh.'

And nor, it went almost without saying, would I.

'And Miss Doyle,' her faced stiffened. She'd expected it; the bleat about secrecy, followed by a lecture on the strictness of the confidentiality, rounded off by an oblique senior officer threat. 'It couldn't have been a very nice experience for you; thank you very much.'

'Thank *you*, sir.' She gave me the ghost of a grin, and when she left there was almost a spring in her step.

The door closed behind her.

'You devious bugger,' admired George.

'Learned a lot of it from you.'

'Not the management strategies.'

'Otherwise known as passing the buck?'

'Sorry: anyway, I've already said it; far better it was nothing to do with you.'

There were still two opinions about that. I'd been more than reluctant to indulge in a spot of Do-It-Yourself in this particular case, and Peter Fairfield's attitude had certainly let me off the hook. Rank cowardice, however, isn't a pretty charge, especially when nobody is making it against you except yourself. What about the old leadership adage, never ask anybody else to go and do anything you wouldn't do yourself?

But I would have done it; of course I would, and once it was all over, from the point of view of my own peace of mind, a half-hour interview with the unbalanced wife of a colleague seemed a perfectly reasonable price to pay.

'I suppose—' I said.

'It was totally bloody awful,' interrupted George. 'Ginny clocked-on the second we entered the house. She went up to about thirty thousand feet and she came down screaming abuse – at Malcolm, mostly. Selfish of me, but I was glad he was there; he's used to it, and it took some of the pressure off us.'

'You, er, didn't arrest her, then?'

'What for? The letters come under the Post Office Act; not an arrestable offence. Mental Health Act or Breach of the Peace? Not likely, the last thing I wanted was Virginia Cartwright around our necks. Quick in, quick caution, interview, tell her the facts would be reported, and run away.'

'George,' I said, 'that's just not your style.'

'No? Well ... You're right to some extent, I didn't exactly leave Malc in the lurch. I tried to keep things reasonable, but there was no chance. It wasn't even an interview; she was more than willing to spill it all out.

'How much she despised Malc; how much she hated the police; how much she regretted marrying into the fucking pig force, full of arrogant fucking gits who couldn't keep their prick-like noses out of her affairs.'

'I thought it might be some sort of nutter with sexual hang-ups when I first saw the letters; the language helps confirm it. But why in particular does she have it in for me?'

I paused, I examined my conscience; what had I ever done to Ginny? She'd been down to the police station moaning on a couple of occasions; complaining about long hours, money, and an allegedly errant Malc. I'd been soothing, civil, and I'd calmed her down. I'd once seen her with a few doses of brandy and Babycham inside her, insulting Teddy at a Christmas bash, before she'd been hustled home.

That was the extent of my experience of Ginny, pretty well. Apart from the rumours, the tales, and that one, never-to-be forgotten occasion when George had shown me the luncheon of newspaper sandwiches lovingly prepared by his spouse, and discarded by Malcolm in the police station kitchen bin.

'She reckons that you made Malc cut up her credit cards, and you threatened him with the sack if she kept on getting him into debt.'

'She's got that back to front,' I said indignantly. 'The card companies had been on to Malc, long before I came on the scene. I never—'

'She also says,' continued George remorselessly, 'that Fairfield was behind you, and you'd snivel and crawl and do whatever he tells you for the sake of your own career. You're both hiding dirty secrets, but you'll go around destroying other people's lives because you enjoy sadistic power-games and playing God.'

'No wonder that uniform lass looked a bit shell-shocked. The truth at last about the upper echelons of the CID.' I attempted something that felt like a very sickly grin.

'And that.' said George bitterly, 'was before she really started to rant.'

'I suppose she got the basis of her stories from Malc?'

''Fraid so; like everybody else, he's gossiped with his wife over the years, and in her case she's twisted it all up and spewed it back in revenge.

'When he went home last week and told her about your

interview with him, and how they could make a new start once the Welfare Fund had helped him sort out their debts, she flipped. Took it as a personal attack, reckoned the withdrawal of her credit cards was down to you and mixed everything up in her own mind. The letters are the result.'

A sudden disastrous thought, 'His kid . . . ?'

George shook his head, 'OK; still away at school till the end of next week.'

'And Malcolm?'

'I told him to stay at home for as long as necessary; we've called out her GP. It looks as if she's in for another session of psychiatric help.'

'Poor woman; poor Malc.'

George stared at me levelly, tightening his lips, 'Glad you feel that way; thousands wouldn't, boss. It's a tough one, all right. Talk to Mr Fairfield, and try to make sure that him and his ex-lady-love come round to feel the same.'

The same damn Staff Nurse on the receiving ward; just as brisk, just as efficient, with a manner suggesting exactly the same degree of uncompromising starch.

'Back again, are we?' she said. It might have been my imagination, but she sounded as if I ought to be down on my knees in front of her, full of remorse and suffering from some painful, preferably terminal, disease. 'How are the eyes?'

'Great,' I replied enthusiastically. 'No problems whatsoever. Absolutely great!'

Professional flattery got me nowhere; she'd obviously no time for people who discharged themselves against medical advice. She allowed herself a chuck of the chin and a short expressive sniff. Tactfully, I refrained from asking after the health and wellbeing of her favourite consultant, the one I'd neglected to meet.

'Er, you've got a man in one of your amenity beds . . .' I said.

'Mr Wilson; your constable's with him. And about time too!'

'Sorry?'

'Police Constable Appleby; he's was supposed to be off duty hours ago, and he's had no relief. The poor man's been hanging about all day.'

'Paid overtime,' muttered George *sotto voce*, unwilling to make an enemy. He knows instinctively when he's well off.

'Are you sure his name's Wilson?'

'So he says. In my opinion he doesn't look much like the man you want.'

I sighed. Thank you very much Clifford Appleby: a few gossipy words, a quick flash of a photo, and the medical staff turn into a latterday version of Sherlock Holmes.

'Could we, er . . . ?'

'Next to my office; second door on the right.'

'Staff.' A brief acknowledgement and George sidled past; a good looking female all right, but for once a well-filled nurse's uniform didn't appear to turn him on.

Our tramp was sitting up in bed supported by pillows, practically the whole of one side of his face was a solid, swollen, purple bruise. He was breathing noisily, and he'd been well and truly kicked. Fortunately, whoever had done it had probably been wearing trainers or some other sort of soft-soled shoes. Even so, it hadn't been exactly half-hearted; the results spoke for themselves.

There was, in the midst of all the damage, some resemblance to our second-rate photograph of Pykett, I had to admit. Square-set turning to flab, thinning brown hair, and a rat-trap mouth. Even so, this man looked older; late, rather than early fifties, with deep lines etching one side of his mouth, and the other grotesquely swollen up. Not instantly recognisable, but swellings apart, it wasn't a bad match.

Clifford Appleby occupied an upright chair at the foot of the bed, not exactly lone and lorn, he was dunking biscuits in a large white hospital cup.

'Hello, sir. Hello, Sergeant Caunt.' He finished a soggy piece of biscuit before struggling reluctantly to his feet.

'I see she's looking after you all right.' There was, perhaps, a tinge of envy directed towards the more socially successful among us. He beamed back amiably; I could have told George, irony was still a waste of time with Constable Cliff.

'Gillian, sarge? Lovely lass.' Obviously on tea and sympathy terms with the attractive dragon; I didn't approve. In any case, she was far too old for him.

Our potential victim glared at us balefully through his one good eye; his head moving once, painfully, from side to side.

His speech was difficult and more than a little slurred, 'Thanks for asking how I feel, whoever you are,' he directed his complaint at me. 'I do-doan't feel very well.'

'Sorry about that, Mr, er, Pykett, is it? I'm DCI Graham, and this is Detective Sergeant Caunt.'

'Oh, Christ, not anoth-er one; me name's Wilson, Edward Wilson,' he said.

'Another one?' I moved round to the relatively unbruised side of his features to the right of the bed, and appropriated Police Constable Appleby's chair en route. Placing his empty cup on the bed tray with something of a clatter, he shuffled off in search of two more places to park.

'They reckoned me name was Pykett.'

'Who?'

'Just 'cos I used to go in there for a pint.'

'In the Standard?'

'Yeah.'

'Who?' I repeated.

'Them two as saw me in there; they reckoned as I was Maureen's chap.'

'And you're not?'

'Wouldn't mind.' Ten out of ten for trying. The wreck of his face transformed itself into something that might have been, under other circumstances, a parody of lust.

'So you admit knowing her, then?' George jumped in with both feet, the master interrogator was at work.

'C-course I bloody know her; she'll let me stand at the bar, an' it's more than you can say for some.'

I stared at him; stubbly but scrubbed, in a pair of striped hospital pyjamas that might once have been occupied by me. Still slightly dingy, perhaps; shaggy hair, and as for his yellow, tombstone teeth . . . All in all, however, he didn't look too bad. Dressed in whatever he normally dressed in, and sleeping rough, he probably presented a far more fearsome figure to the clientele of even the lowest bar.

'Kindly?' I offered.

'Eh?'

'Maureen, encouraging you at the Royal Standard pub. The motherly sort.'

'Toffee-nosed b-bastard; my money's as good as the rest!'

'Oy!' said George. 'No need for that. You keep a civil tongue in your head.'

'Danny Boy, the landlord; not 'im.' Despite his injuries, the figure in the bed managed to address me with a look of complete contempt. 'Since when was a copper bright enough to keep a pub?'

'Maybe you've got a point,' I agreed equiably, forestalling George. 'Now show me your hands.'

'Whaffor?'

'I tell fortunes in my spare time.'

'Funny bugger!' Nevertheless, he held out a pair of stubby-fingered, broken-nailed paws, the joints already knotting with arthritis. I didn't even bother to open my briefcase to examine the prints that Fairfield had despatched: nothing like Alan Pykett's marks: loops on his fingertips, not whorls.

Win a few, lose a few. 'You've had a rough time, Mr Wilson,' I said. 'Tell me about the feller who filled you in.'

'Two of 'em, like I said. Youngish, bomber jackets, squaddie haircuts. Thassall I know.'

'And they attacked you last night, in the park?'

'Just as I were settlin' down. Musta followed me from the pub.'

'Did you see them in there?'

'Told you; they're the pair what thought I was Maureen's chap.'

'So they spoke to you in the bar?'

'Yeah. Thought they was being sociable, but then they turned funny; wouldn't buy me a pint.'

'What sort of funny?'

'They were all right at first; chatty, like I said. Then they asked me about Maureen. I said I knew her, like. Then they asked me if I enjoyed shagging little girls.'

'And what did you say to that?'

'Nothing; thought they were looking for trouble. Drunks or nutters, or something. Time I baled out.'

'What time did you leave?'

'Just before ten: 'e only ever lets me have two pints, anyway. That's max, an' he always makes me stand on the mat by the door. Said 'e was doing everybody a favour by propping it open to get some fresh air.'

I followed the sudden switch. 'Danny Smith?'

'Who else?'

'A right bastard,' encouraged George. 'Why on earth do you put up with that?'

'Jokin' ain't cha?' He peered at us through his one good eye in weary defeat. 'Who else is gonna let me in, anyway? The manager of the Ritz?'

'Some people,' said George cautiously, 'drink in the park with their pals.'

'An' some people might be homeless, but they ain't scum. They still like to keep themselves to themselves; they doan't all fancy mixes of cider and meths.'

'You haven't been in custody, here in Eddathorpe?'

'No.'

'How long have you been around?'

'Six, seven weeks. I fancied a bit of seaside; I even 'ad a room for a bit.'

'You paid rent?' George's voice rose; not exactly the tactful type.

'Like I said; then I got the push. Still collect me Giro,
though.'

'How do you manage that?'

'Social don't know; they still s-send it to me old address. Mate
livin' there picks it up, an' I give 'im a quid or two from the dosh
to make sure it isn't pinched.'

'What happens when they check?'

'I'm entitled, aren't I? They're the bastards who insist you gotta
have an address.'

'And what about Housing Benefit?' I looked at George sharply;
totally irrelevant, anyway. I couldn't make up my mind whether
he was playing social worker or running a practice interview,
keeping his hand in on minor fraud.

'Never got it; no time to come through, after I filled in
the form.'

'These two men,' I said firmly, 'in the park.'

'Said they'd teach me to batten on women. Said I was a fughin'
waste of space.'

'Batten on?'

'And what about poor Maureen? Thass what they said.'

'Maureen?'

'They said they knew who I was, that I was a rapist, an' if
I weren't a killer, I was the next best thing. So first they were
sorting me themselves, an' afterwards they were maybe goin' to
leave a few little bits for the police.'

'Anything else?'

'They stuffed a bitta paper in my pocket, according to
your mate.'

I wasn't grateful: I scowled at Clifford Appleby, our amateur
newscaster, slumped in his newly-acquired chair by the door.

'And that was it?'

'Three broken ribs, concussion an' a fractured cheekbone. If
that's what you call "it," that's it.'

'Sorry.'

'Not as sorry as me.'

'Look, Ted ... you haven't been—'

'No.'

'Not even hanging around?'

'No.' A long pause, 'Well, up to a coupla weeks ago, I was sorta kipping in sheds.'

'What sheds?'

'Up in the backs not far from where that gal got killed.'

'Up to last week, you mean?'

'Yeah, I suppose so. Then when all them coppers started playing around, I kept away.'

'And you were shiking as well?'

'Never, never! No!'

'Come on, you might as well tell us, Ted.'

'I wasn't! I was only kipping. That's what the men who 'it me said, and they said I'd come back, an' that I was Maureen's chap.'

'You followed one or two women home, eh? Pressed your face up against a window now and again?'

'Not on your life, mister. You ain't gonna f-frame me!'

'You knew Maureen, and you knew Davinia, didn't you?'

'Who?'

'Used to call herself Shirley, as well. The barmaid who was killed.'

'Well, yeah; I told you, I'm p-pretty well a regular; she used to pull me a pint.'

'Talk to you, did she?'

'She wasn't s-snotty, if that's what you mean. Passed the time o'day.'

'She didn't make you stand on the doormat, like Danny?'

'I've said.'

It was difficult, more than difficult; the man was injured, it was hard to read his features, hard to interpret the uneasy movements of his head. We were vertical, looking down, he was almost horizontal, lying in bed. Even the hesitancy, the extra slur to his speech could be explained in terms of the hammering he'd received. Nevertheless ...

'So, you used to kip in some sheds.'

'Yeah.'

'At the back of Cranbourne Avenue?'

A nod.

'Near where the other barmaid used to live?'

Definitely a yes: a fixed, pseudo-sincere stare into my face, body tense.

'How did you know that? Followed her home?'

'No.'

Make it easy for him, 'Casual conversation, then?'

'Yeah, that's right,' he said eagerly. 'She must have said.'

'That's right, is it, Ted? *"Hello, darling; pull me a pint! Hello Ted! I hear we're neighbours — I live in a flat on Cranbourne Avenue, and now you've got a very desirable garden shed just down the road?"'*

'Sarky sod! She was ... she was sorta talking to somebody else.'

'About what?'

'About — about the empty flat.' A spur of the moment lie, if ever I'd heard one. Inspiration had struck.

'The one at the front of the house? Come off it, Ted.'

'Yeah ...' the word was little more than a sigh.

'Sorry, I didn't quite get that.'

'Yeah, all right. But I was looking for s-somewhere better than leaky old sheds.'

'But that's not why you followed her is it?'

'Partly.' It was pathetic.

'Ted,' I murmured. 'It doesn't even sound vaguely like the truth. I bet you never knew anything about the empty flat at the front of the house before you followed her home.'

'I suppose.'

'And after closing time, I suppose you followed her once or twice, and when you found she lived in a ground floor flat, you sneaked round the back to see whether you could see her strip?'

'Wha-what d'yer think I am?'

'Somebody,' said George coldly, 'who hadn't ought to be let loose on lemonade, let alone a couple of pints!'

# Chapter Twenty

———————◆———————

'Only two on the short-list,' announced Angie. 'Not all that much competition for a post in this one-horse hole.'

'I thought you liked Eddathorpe,' I said teasingly. 'A charming Edwardian seaside town.'

'I did; well, I do, come to that. Apart from the winters, the scandals, the nasty gossip, the grasping natives and whoever's sending out the poison-pen.'

'I take it,' I said sardonically, 'that you got the job?'

She did a twirl around the dining table, scattering dishes carelessly across the newly-set cloth en route, 'In a word, yes!'

'Good; congratulations, love. There won't be any more letters, either, you'll be pleased to know.'

'Ginny Cartwright?'

'George sorted it this morning; he interviewed her with a policewoman in the presence of Malc.'

'And?'

'She was more than pleased to admit it, I'm afraid. Revenge on Fairfield, revenge on me, for having a go at Malc about their debts.'

'I thought you were trying to help?'

'That's not how she saw it; anyway, she's out of circulation for a week or two, now.'

'Hospital?'

'Yes.'

'You're not,' she asked hesitantly, 'going to have to take her to court?' Dinner plates in hand, she came to an abrupt halt.

'Not if Peter Fairfield sees sense, and he will.'

She perked up immediately, 'You never did tell me what she might have had on him.'

'No,' I replied, bathing in an unaccustomed sense of moral virtue, 'I don't believe I did.'

'Prig,' said Angie.

And that's all the thanks you get. Right.

'Well,' said Pat Goodall the next morning, with what amounted to insufferable self-satisfaction, 'we know it wasn't the flasher, Malcolm and me cleared that one up.'

'Weary Willie Fraser?' The voice of his questioner was full of disgust. 'Nobody ever thought he was a runner, right from the start. Except you,' he added with at touch of that camaraderie so typical among friends and colleagues in the CID.

'I never—' began Pat indignantly.

'OK, that's enough; settle down.' George was doing his martinet. 'This is an update, we're not here to quarrel amongst ourselves.' The meeting shuffled and stirred; why not? A touch of aggro might introduce a spot of variety to lives which were settling into an all too predictable rut of questions, paper, more paper and dull routine.

'It doesn't look as if either of our so-called stalkers are in the frame, either.' The remark was not addressed to me, Roger Prentice was targeting his potential rival for power.

The ninth day of the enquiry, and frustration was setting in. Activity, suspects aplenty during the first few days, but the enquiry appeared to be going nowhere. Suspect after suspect was being shot down, or, more accurately, sinking slowly to earth, emitting long, derisive raspberries like so many leaking balloons.

Nobody believed in Alan Pykett anymore; he almost certainly

wasn't, and probably never had been, in town. And as for Maureen, not much wonder she'd been so blasé about her so-called stalker, she was just keeping one jump ahead and refusing to talk to her illegitimate son.

Nigel Laud: two unhappy adoptive parents living some forty miles away, and him commuting glumly between them, Paulie's hired boat and a straight-haired, gungy girlfriend in a scruffy Eddathorpe flat. Something of an obsessive, Nigel; ever since he'd obtained his birth certificate and a spot of Social Services counselling at the age of eighteen.

He'd chased after Maureen Sullivan, and spent something like twelve months turning her into Maureen Pykett, complete with a wedding photo from an ancient copy of the *Manchester Evening News*. After the tale of her divorce and departure from Salford, however, he'd come to a full stop. Until, that is, by a thousand-to-one coincidence, while playing second-fiddle to Colin on an Eddathorpe pub crawl, he'd dropped on his more than reluctant birth-mother in a back street seaside pub.

Nice for him, if she'd only wanted to know. She hadn't, so once he's established her identity it was obsession time, and he'd trailed around after her like an abandoned pup. Until, that is, she'd got either fed up or nervous, and taken the opportunity to skip town.

He'd even gone to the inquest on the off-chance that she'd turn up as a witness or friend of the deceased. Enquiries were still continuing to trace her, just in case, but that, from a common-sense point of view, was almost certainly the bottom line.

'OK, pay attention,' George treated Roger Prentice to his watch-it-sunshine look. 'People still in the frame; male associates and contacts of the victim, at least.

'Firstly,' he uncovered a section of plastic film on the Overhead Projector, 'Paulie Parkes.

'He's an aging womaniser,' a few hidden grins, and once again his audience stirred. 'He has a background which suggests that he's not averse to using force when he doesn't get his own way.

Shirley, alias Davinia West, had reached the quarter-finals of the beauty contest he was running in conjunction with *Eddathorpe Rocks!* and according to her former boyfriend, Colin Critchley, he caught Parkes trying to get stuck across her in his office a few weeks ago.'

'To use a technical phrase.' Roger, far from intimidated, was still prepared to have a go. 'And Critchley says in his statement,' he interrupted, 'that the girl subsequently claimed to be an unwilling participant with Parkes in whatever fun and games were going on.'

'Why don't we nick him, then,' muttered one of our civil libertarians coarsely, 'and screw him to the deck?'

'Evidence,' I said. Time to gather this lot together before the meeting degenerated into farce. 'He's already been interviewed twice. There's little or no forensic evidence whatsoever in this case. Signs of forcible sexual interference with the victim, but no hair transfer on the body, no semen, and consequently, no DNA; just the bare evidence of a screwed-up tinfoil contraceptive packet on the floor of her room.

'The killer may have ripped a pair of earrings out of her ears, there's blood in one of her lobes, but she had acquaintances rather than friends, and nobody can give us an idea of the pattern. Apart from that, we know she was a cannabis user; there's traces of the active constituent in her blood, and forensic have come up with a grain or two of resin in her handbag, and that's our lot.'

'Did SOCO unscrew the plumbing in search of the used Johnny?' asked Pat. Somebody started a derisive snigger, swallowed it, choked, and finally closed his stupid mouth. Not the delicate type, but signs of basic intelligence stir within Patrick Goodall from time to time.

'Yes, Pat, we tried it, but the odds were about a million to one.' He nodded sombrely, no dissent, no inappropriate wisecracks just for once.

'Is there anything on the packet at all?' Determined; I could write something nice on his staff appraisal, after all. Or stubborn, perhaps.

'No trace of fingerprints, if that's what you mean. There is a packing code, though. Minute spaced nicks down one side of the foil. Packed on the foruth of February, if that's any good.'

'They don't,' continued Pat eagerly, 'marry up packing codes with deliveries, by any chance? We could make enquiries and find out—'

'Exactly how many people have been having it off since February the fourth,' suggested the inevitable humourist at the back.

'If you can't help, don't hinder,' I snapped. 'And the manufacturers are only interested in quality control and expiry dates, Pat, so I'm afraid they don't.'

'What about Critchley himself?' asked Roy Lamb, a burly, stoop-shouldered man, usually one of the quietest of the Eddathorpe DCs. 'It must have come as a bit of a shock when he found his girlfriend wrapped round an elderly man. Perhaps he was jealous, and went in for a spot of revenge!'

George exposed the second name on his list, and Colin Critchley's name appeared on the screen.

'Aged twenty-three; lead guitarist in the *Immortal Sins*. Contracted to Parkes and his theatre for the season, his group's financially dependent on him, too. Met the victim at the pub where she worked at the beginning of the season, fancied her and went around with her until he discovered she was associating with Parkes.'

'Willingly or unwillingly, as the case may be.' Roger Prentice was still plugging away.

'Critchley,' George continued, his voice expressionless, 'has no reason to like Parkes; in fact he probably hates his guts. Nevertheless, he hasn't overplayed the story Davinia told him; in fact he's a bit dismissive of the unwilling maiden tale, reckons she was lying to him, and Parkes denies it, of course.

'As for a revenge killing, it's a possibility; he's been questioned, he's not been eliminated. To be fair, he'd dumped her well before the crime; plenty of time for his feelings to cool, and there's absolutely nothing forensically to link him to her flat.'

Conscientiously, George presented the third contact on list: Ralph Sheppard, boat owner and slightly dodgy businessman, followed by his Disco Manager at Bloaters, the landlord Danny Smith, and finally by the policeman's friend, Davinia's Dad.

'You're not serious?' The inevitable voice at the back.

George sounded relaxed, 'No. He's just one more male contact, that's all. The same with the ex-boyfriend who gave her the knife. Both back home around the relevant times of the killing, according to enquiries made by their hometown police; for all I know, they were probably getting plenty of Yorkshire ale down their necks.'

'The South Yorks police?' It wasn't much of a joke, but at least it raised the semblance of a laugh. Entertainment was pretty thin on the ground.

'What about his alibi?'

'Who?'

'Parkes.' Pat, the man with the single-minded approach.

'It's not exactly an alibi, is it?' George sounded as if he was encouraging him, 'Anyway, it was you and your partner took his girlfriend's statement, so you tell us.'

'Her name's Lindsey Preston, and she's a dancer, or so she says. Chorus line, that is.' He paused for the inevitable leer, but it was a half-hearted gesture. Pat sounded serious for once.

'The house wasn't exactly full on the Monday night, and they finished bang on time. One curtain call, change and away. There was a group, including Colin Critchley, but not his mate Laud, he went off on his own. Parkes invited Lindsey along for a meal.'

'Why not Nigel Laud?'

'Parkes doesn't like him, and anyway, he said he had a date.'

I interrupted, 'Chasing after the woman who didn't want anything to do with him, his mum.'

'Yeah, probably. Anyway, they went for the meal, Paulie cut

her out from the rest of the herd, and they went for a nightcap at his apartment. Usual thing: usual for Paulie Parkes, that is.'

'She was ready, willing and able, huh?' Roger again.

'She's not Miss Goodie Two-shoes, if that's what you mean.' Not exactly insubordinate, but no respecter of persons, isn't Pat. 'Anyway, no row, no trouble, she had a couple of drinks and he called her a taxi just before half-one.'

'So what's your point, Pat?'

'Not an alibi, just like George said.' He ignored the daggers directed at him from a status-conscious sergeant. 'It only tells us that she left early, and he couldn't get it up.'

'Yes, we already knew it: her statement doesn't cover him for the rest of the night. We've got the same problem with Critchley and Sheppard, come to that. And bloody Danny Smith sleeps in a separate room from his wife.' George fixed him with a far from sympathetic stare.

'And come to think of it, *Patrick*,' he said, presumably in revenge for the George, 'that's not in the statement, young man.'

'What isn't?'

'The fact, as you so charmingly put it, that he couldn't get it up.'

'Obvious, in'it? That's why she left.'

'Did she say so?'

'Well, no, not exactly.' Two out of ten for the half-embarrassed look. 'Stands to reason, though.'

'It's never obvious and it doesn't stand to anything, Pat.' Clocking the double entendre, he paused and looked around, daring the troops to titter. It never came.

Satisfied, he continued his blitz on Pat, 'It's worthless if she hasn't specifically said it, and equally useless if you don't write it down. But it is relevant, and you can go and get an additional statement to cover it.'

Lecture over, he turned to me, 'It doesn't help our cause, though, does it, boss?'

'No.'

Not when you're investigating a sex crime which took place in the middle of the night, and your main, if not your only halfway credible, suspect, wasn't even feeling like it as late as half past one.

Gloomily, I stared at names reflected on the screen of the OHP. One possibility missing; Edward Wilson, not eliminated but under surveillance in hospital, anyway. My mood lightened; a quick police interview tomorrow, and maybe I could lay all my troubles at the door of the proverbial passing tramp.

Fairfield in a new tweed suit. Vast and greenish, the creases in the trousers, the general air of prosperity, signalled top-flight gamekeeper rather than somewhat seedy poacher, for once. He prowled around my office, ignoring the visitor's chair and positively refusing to settle down.

'Somebody else you want to caution,' he moaned. 'Just like that Gordon Whatsit feller; the one you insist on calling Davinia's Dad.'

'Gordon West,' I said brightly, 'cautioned by a senior police officer and warned as to his future conduct for Criminal Damage and Breach of the Peace.' No prosecution; Gordon instructed to look contrite: *very sorry, Chief Inspector Paget, for breaking the window and causing trouble at the DSS.*

'Why the caution?'

'Because he's a grieving relative, and he compensated the management of the Pavilion Theatre for the broken glass.'

'Grieving relative, my arse!'

'It wouldn't have looked good, taking him to Court.'

'Bob, I worry about you, sometimes; I reckon you're going soft.'

'The letters may be nasty,' I said, ignoring Fairfield's deadliest cop on copper insult, and reverting to the original subject of our conversation, 'but think about the contents; apart from a couple of run-of-the-mill obscenities, they're barely an offence under the Post Office Act. Besides,' I added in a pale imitation of the Fairfield idiom, 'Ginny Cartwright is nuts.'

'She's a vicious cow, and you're her major victim. You ought to be thanking your lucky stars that she kept it in the family. She *did* keep it in the police family, huh?'

'Apart from Albert Flaxman, yes. And,' I said cunningly, 'if we take it to court you can forget any chance of the Mr X and Miss Y nonsense; the identities of all the police personnel involved will almost certainly come out.'

'Not forgetting Mrs G,' he muttered maliciously half to himself in tones I was obviously meant to overhear.

'Thea, and, er, Peter,' I countered. Never give a sucker an even break.

'Fair enough!' he remained unoffended. 'She's definitely a candidate for the booby hatch, you reckon? Not just fooling around?'

'Malcolm's wife,' I said, just to remind the more insensitive among us, 'is in St John's Psychiatric Unit. She's been there before. So long as she takes her medicine, she's perfectly OK. Sometimes she forgets, once she does that she gets bloody-minded and deliberately leaves it out. She suffers from some sort of chemical imbalance, and they'll keep her until they restore it, according to her GP.'

'She's sectioned?' In other words, subjected to a compulsory detention order. Nobody could go around accusing Peter of being a softie; he definitely wanted his pound of flesh.

'Not necessary; it's the one bright spot. She still has a lot of confidence in her own GP, so she was prepared to go voluntarily.'

'OK, OK, your decision; do what you like,' Pontius Pilate was rinsing his hands. 'God knows what Superintendent Spinks is going to say.' He was, I gathered, carefully distancing himself from the possibility of flak from Thea. Whatever their previous relationship, she still had the power to scare him half to death.

'I'll tell you this, Bob,' he said unexpectedly. 'I still think you're too full of the milk of human kindness to, ah, *clutch the nearest way*, so to speak.'

Grandiloquence now: Shakespeare, even. This time he was offended; he totally misinterpreted the expression on my face.

'I did go to school,' he murmured reproachfully. 'University material, as a matter of fact, but I never took it up.'

'Never doubted it, sir.' Own back time, 'It's only a silly superstition, anyway: just thinking about the sort of things that happen when you quote from that play.'

*Catch*, not *clutch*, but I kept the thought to myself, superstitious demi-Celt that I am. Definitely *Catch*, but I'd got too many problems of my own to risk quoting it aloud. Not the Scottish play, unlucky *Macbeth*.

# Chapter Twenty-One

'Nice of you,' said Thea, 'to find the time.'

The Aylfleet Detective Inspector glanced at me warily across the width of Thea's office, then he crossed his legs, studied the toe of a well-polished shoe and looked sad. Not a difficult thing for Harry Wake to do, with his long, pale face and drooping under-lip, he nearly always looked as if he was going to either sulk or cry. A good, dependable policeman on his last posting before retirement, nevertheless, and more Dorothea Spinks's age and temperament than mine.

Since his arrival at Aylfleet, he'd kept his divisional super-intendent reasonably sweet, which is a lot more than his predecessor had ever managed from either a professional or a personal point of view. I was mildly grateful to him; a happy Dorothea, in theory at least, equalled an unstressed me.

I did my best to look like a man upon whom irony is lost, while the two representatives from Customs and Excise stared politely into the distance. No business of theirs.

Both were in their early forties, tall, slim, with slightly receding hair, and each discreetly sported the crown and chained portcullis above the red and gold stripes running diagonally across the face of their navy blue departmental ties.

Tweedledum and Tweedledee: fortunately, for identification purposes if nothing else, one was in double-breasted blue, and the other in a three-button, single-breasted brown. Somewhat meanly, I decided, the tie did not altogether go with the latter's suit.

Blue suit opened the batting for Customs Investigations by clearing his throat; concentrating on the latest manifestations of the Spinks versus Graham feud, I hadn't quite caught his name during the introductory round.

'We're very interested in the activities of this man Ralph Sheppard,' he said abruptly, 'as I explained to you on the phone.'

Thea, diverted from her resentment at what had almost become a Grahamless fortnight at Aylfleet, scowled.

'Something to do with VAT, I suppose,' she said.

'That was some time ago,' Pattison, the one in the brown suit, stirred. 'Supplying false invoices to a purchaser for what he claimed to be non-vattable goods.'

'It was our colleagues,' said blue suit, emphasising the last word slightly, 'who imposed a mitigated penalty for the evasion of VAT. We are from the Investigations Division,' he added with a touch of asperity, 'I thought I'd made that clear.'

'How much did they collect?' I asked, interested. I'd met HM Customs, and what they laughingly regarded as a mitigated penalty, before.

Pattison consulted his file, 'Three times the value of the VAT in question,' he murmured with satisfaction. 'That would be, er, sixty-three thousand, three hundred and thirty three pounds, and thirty three pence.'

I was happy on behalf of the Treasury. No prosecution, as usual, but never mind. Maybe the nation had purchased a few extra parts for a Tornado, and we could now afford to fight somebody really important, especially with the odd thirty-three pence.

Blue suit read my mind, 'Our primary concern in these cases, is to recover the revenue. Our emphasis is different; prosecution is a primary function of the police.'

'Quite!' I had enough on my plate with Thea; catch me fighting a war on two fronts. Both visitors looked mildly surprised, perhaps a little relieved; they probably weren't going to have to struggle with some uncooperative red-necked thief-taker, after all.

'You've, er, interviewed this man Sheppard in connection with your own murder enquiry, haven't you, Chief Inspector?' Pattison was doing the amiable straight away. 'What's your impression of him?'

'Would chase sixpence down a rat hole,' I admitted. 'The wheeler-dealer type. He openly admitted negotiating the importation of soft porn on behalf of one of his mates. That's the information we passed on.'

'Yes, Frank had a look at some of that, didn't you Frank?'

Frank, alias blue suit, lowered his eyes modestly and looked sour, 'Very close to the line,' he said. 'Imported on behalf of a distributor named Harrison in Leeds. Nasty, some of it; bondage and . . .' He stole a glance at Dorothea Spinks, and stopped.

'Don't mind me,' said Thea, 'we are, after all, adults.'

'Well, ah, *Spanking!* He almost blushed.

'Sadomasochism.' Thea, point-scoring as usual, was all for calling a spade a spade.

'But not hard-core enough for seizure?' Bob to the rescue of an embarrassed male.

He looked grateful for the interruption, 'No.'

Thea began to look bored, 'Importing pornography; is that what it's all about? Another little spin-off from your murder enquiry, Bob?'

'I'm sorry, Superintendent,' Pattison reached into his briefcase, 'from our point of view, it's rather more serious than that.' I looked at him sharply, an almost imperceptible emphasis again. Important to all right-thinking people, perhaps, if not to her. Almost as if he'd been awaiting the opportunity to put Thea in her place.

'We always,' he continued, 'have difficulty on these occasions.

It's a matter of timing, of maintaining confidentiality for as long as we can.'

Catching the none-too-subtle implications, Harry Wake stirred. 'Bigmouth coppers; corruption, that sort of thing?' Interdepartmental rivalry climbed into the saddle and rode again.

'Like yourselves,' said Pattison, 'we try to secure our operations as tightly as we can.'

I sighed; I'd been there before. In other words, if anything went wrong, we would all end up indulging in a long round of mutual recriminations and slander in an effort to apportion the blame.

'Then if it's not the importation of pornography,' murmured Harry wisely, 'it's got to be drugs.'

'You've heard something yourself?'

'No.'

Pattison looked satisfied; for a moment I thought he was going to say, 'Good!' Instead he launched into a long, diplomatic spiel about the quality of their information, the importance of maintaining its integrity until the time was ripe, and their willingness to launch a joint operation with their valued colleagues within the police.

Reading between the lines, recent Government policy had left them short of men, they might need lots of bodies to assist them with searches, they feared that a drugs operation might conceivably bugger-up our murder enquiry, and somebody at higher level had warned them not to tread on our toes.

'Why Sheppard?' I said.

Frank Who-ever-he-was smiled thinly, 'We can't keep an eye on the owners of every tinpot boat,' he said. 'But lately, Sheppard has been drawing attention to himself. He's gone backwards and forwards five or six times; mostly by air. Last week, however, he used the boat; he's an amateur, nervous; we think it was a dummy run.'

'A mixture of business and pleasure, according to him.'

Pattison turned down his lips in an apparent pastiche of the Teddy Baring style, and I remembered what Ralph Sheppard had said to me: almost the exact words.

'You've spoken to him already?' I asked.

'Not personally; when he last docked his boat he was a willing volunteer; he cleared Customs in the normal way.'

'The business part consists of the importation of girly magazines on behalf of this Harrison chap,' continued his partner. 'Every trip he made is followed by a legitimate importation of a consignment of videos and mags.'

'Sounds reasonable,' said Harry Wake.

He was awarded a glance of superior disgust, 'You think so? Trip after trip, allegedly on somebody else's behalf. And all for the sake of the importation of a few thousand quid's-worth of gear for this character in Leeds? Nah, he'd be wasting his time; it's all a blind.' He nodded towards the telephone on Thea's desk, 'If he was genuine, after the initial business contact, he'd have let his fingers do the walking, mate.'

'Or sailing or flying, as the case may be.'

'Yeah,' he muttered ungratefully; by this time he was in full spate. 'Think about it; the latest, a trip to Zeebrugge, then on to Amsterdam, the drugs capital of the world.'

I thought about it; amateur dramatics time. The Dutch authorities would have really loved to hear him saying that.

'Anyway,' he added hastily, seeing that his audience remained unimpressed. 'Cannabis resin, we've confirmed it, we know he's back there at the moment and if he follows the pattern he'll almost certainly be back here by the end of the week. It's all down to contacts,' he said proudly, 'excellent intelligence from the other side.'

Psychic phenomena now; I glanced across at Harry, the Aylfleet detective inspector's face bore the trace of a sardonic smile. Still, bells rang at the back of my mind: THC in the body; traces of cannabis resin in Davinia's bag. Nothing to get too excited about in itself, of course; just one small possibility among many along the way.

'You've, er, been supplied with details of his contacts on this side of the water?' I asked.

'Well,' for the first time Pattison sounded doubtful, 'there's his employee, the disco manager here in town.'

I glanced at Harry, 'Gavin Westcott,' he muttered.

'But that's not exactly a worldwide network, is it?' I said.

It was Thea's turn to stir uneasily, 'You're not telling me that he smuggles cannabis simply to stock a disco in a small provincial town? A place this size,' she added nastily, 'would hardly merit a cargo of drugs in a rowing boat once every ten years, let alone extended negotiations, and two trips across the North Sea within a couple of weeks.'

Pattison looked superior, 'We're not suggesting this enterprise is as amateur as all that. This is a convenient place to bring it in and transport it onwards. Despite its size, Aylfleet is, after all, a port.'

Well, more or less. Situated at the head of a long, muddy estuary, and possessing nothing more than an ageing dock served by a run-down ferry service, and visited by the occasional grain-carrier and the odd timber ship, the locals, still proud of their seagoing connections, would probably have kissed him for that.

'There's the Leeds connection, and then there are his business associates in Humberside,' said Frankie, 'we'd like police cooperation when we start looking into them.

'Anyway, Sheppard may be making money, but he's strictly DIY league. He's nobody's Mr Big.' He was still in there plugging for his team, but however good their basic information, it was fairly obvious that, putting it politely, they were still doing a spot of whistling in the dark.

'Are you going to let it run?' Harry perked up at the very thought.

'Let you follow it to its destination? Well, no, my superiors are hardly in a position to allow—'

'There's not a lot of point in chatting to his associates if you've got nothing of substance to chat about.' Harry, with the bit firmly between his teeth.

'Surely,' I said, sniping away in support, 'we can set up a joint surveillance operation, find out where he's dropping it off and bag the lot.'

'Can't see the point otherwise,' said Thea loyally. 'Not unless you're only wanting to make use of police cells.' Was there the tiniest hint of cynicism in her voice?

The two Customs Officers exchanged uneasy glances; the natives were over-restless, this interview was not turning out the way they'd planned.

'We thought—' said Frank.

'That you might like to interrogate the other guy as well.' Pattison doing his best to save the day.

'The other guy?'

He cleared his throat, 'There is one other local connection,' he conceded.

'And this local; has he got a name?' They wouldn't be holding out on us, would they? Only saving the best till last, so perish the thought!

'We understand,' said Pattison, glancing hurriedly at Harry Wake, 'that this man may have a connection with your enquiry, too.'

'Yes?'

'A man named Parkes?'

'Sheppard claims to have met him casually at the Marina,' I conceded, 'but Paulie Parkes says he doesn't remember Sheppard at all.'

'Parkes, the ex-TV entertainer,' reiterated Frankie, with evident satisfaction, rolling the name lusciously around his mouth, and I braced myself for news from a customs colleague. Whatever it was, he obviously wasn't averse to rubbing it in.

'That's right.'

'A much-married man.'

'Three times,' I admitted. 'I'd heard: alimony, and so on. That's why he's supposed to be in debt.'

'Know the maiden name of Cynthia, his second wife?'

I didn't, but I could guess.


'So the hospital wants to keep Pykett's unfortunate double,' said George with relish. 'Fancy that.'

I settled myself in the only visitor's chair in the glass and hardboard cubby hole that passed for the Eddathorpe detective inspector's office, and grimaced ruefully.

'And Derek Paget is going on as if he has to pay the salaries of his escorts himself. Just because that bloody Staff Nurse loves scruffs,' I said unreasonably. 'She's convinced the hospital authorities that they shouldn't let Wilson out until tomorrow, at least.'

'Why not?'

'Just like he said: broken cheekbone, broken ribs, bang on the head. That'll do for a start.'

'That doesn't usually bother them; I thought they needed the beds?'

'Another parallel with Pykett,' I admitted. 'Poor bastard is pretty debilitated; another one who's led a pretty hard life.'

'Not as hard as yours,' said George unfeelingly, 'if the overtime bill keeps on going up. Personally, I think you've got more chance of winning the lottery than charging Wilson with Davinia's death.'

'So do I,' I admitted, 'but if you don't buy a ticket you don't get to play the game.'

'What's that supposed to mean?'

'If I withdraw the watch and he walks out of hospital without my interviewing him thoroughly, I won't be absolutely sure, anyway, and Fairfield will probably have my guts.'

'True, but what happens if the hospital don't release him by tomorrow? Keeping coppers idle is not going to endear you to the boss.'

'He'll be out by morning,' I said with spurious confidence. 'Just you wait and see.'

'What about Paulie Parkes?' There was no stopping the catalogue of doom and gloom, once George had got the bit between his teeth. 'What about fetching him in again; try the drugs angle, and give him a bit of a trot.'

'Not until his ex-brother-in-law returns.'

George looked pensive, 'You're taking a bit of a risk, aren't you? If word gets out, Wilson isn't the only suspect who could clear off. Just for the sake of keeping faith with Tweedledum and Tweedledee?'

'Their names,' I said briefly, 'Are John Pattison and Frank Dawes.'

'Frankie and Johnnie, huh? Are they—'

'Don't even ask,' I warned him. George can be very childish at times.

'What are you going to do, then?'

'No record on the computer, and keep everything strictly to ourselves, for a start.'

'Ah,' said George, 'I thought you'd soon be getting around to that.' He reached into his desk drawer and produced a concertina of printed computer roll. 'A print-out of the audit log,' he said.

With no enthusiasm whatsoever, I stared at the concertina of paper he'd dumped on top of his desk. A record of every transaction on the system since the enquiry began. Times on; times off; officer user codes; file interrogation codes, the lot.

'Well?'

'No unauthorised transactions on the computer, so far as I can see.'

'Well somebody,' I said vengefully, 'has been leaking information like a sieve.'

George was being reasonable, 'It doesn't mean they're members of our murder enquiry team, boss. There's plenty of bits of paper, and plenty of careless bobbies, come to that.'

'You reckon that somebody just left a copy of Pykett's descriptive form lying around?'

'It's quite likely, isn't it? And *somebody* made a few extra photocopies and passed them on to Buchanan's vigilante yobs. They went looking, and beat up an innocent man.'

'So, you're thinking of going back to Buchanan, eh?'

'Not to worry, boss; it's already in hand.'

'Oh, yes?'

'I thought,' said George dreamily, 'that we ought to send somebody to talk to him again. Explain to him how dangerous grasses are, and ask him, politely of course, to drop a hint about his duff informant's name. Send people of subtlety, I thought, men of outstanding tact.'

'Patrick Goodall, for example?'

'Pat and his partner,' George admitted smugly. 'He's back, and he feels hard-done-by and irritable at the moment, does Big Malc.'

# Chapter Twenty-Two

I was pleased to see it, the old firm back together, Pat and
Malc. A combination of work and his partner's talent for
trouble would take Malc's mind off his domestic difficulties;
give him something else to worry about at the very least. Only
one problem, however; it was the custody sergeant rather than
Detective Constable Cartwright who was looking uneasy, even a
trifle harassed and straight-faced.

'Thanks for coming down, sir.' The sergeant said.

Of the four of them, only Patrick looked totally happy;
Malcolm awarded me a cool, marginally hostile look, while Ian
Buchanan immediately opened his mouth to complain.

'It's absolutely ridiculous, dragging me here. An example of
petty, officious spite.'

'Yes?'

'They stormed into my premises,' started Buchanan, without
so much as a by your lea—'

'No,' I said, 'not you; not yet. I want to hear what the arresting
officers have got to say.'

Malcolm relaxed a little; not quite so hostile now, and Pat
gave me a sample of his usual over-confident grin.

'At approximately one-forty-five this afternoon,' he chanted,
'in company with Detective Constable Cartwright, I visited Mr
Buchanan's shop in the High Street in connection with enquiries

we were making into an offence of Grievous Bodily Harm With Intent, contrary to Section Eighteen of the Offences Against The Person Act, committed in Victoria Park on one Edward Wilson in the early hours of yesterday.'

I glared at him warningly. An imitation of the clockwork policeman; a deliberate attempt to upset Buchanan, and Pat at his irritating best.

'Anyway,' he continued hastily, 'we asked Mr Buchanan about the list of people participating in his, er, citizen patrol scheme; the one he gave you and Sergeant Caunt the other day. We also asked him whether he'd provided them with any information or a description of a man who'd previously been convicted of rape.'

'And he said he didn't know what we were talking about,' interjected Malc, 'so we asked him to check the names we had against the original names on his list.'

'And when he opened his office drawer ...'

'He practically snatched my own file out of my hand!' yelled Buchanan.

'Not at all; I saw part of what appeared to be a confidential police document in his folder, so took possession of it,' said Pat.

'No search warrant!'

'No need!'

'Be quiet!' The custody sergeant slapped one hand down on his desk. 'Now then,' he turned to Pat, 'you say this document belongs to the police?'

'These documents, more like. He had four photocopies of a CRO 74, complete with photo, so I arrested this man,' he finished triumphantly, 'for handling stolen goods.'

'Four bits of paper,' jeered our prisoner, 'worth about forty pence altogether, which I photocopied myself.'

'You haven't got a machine.'

'Charity shop in the High Street,' snapped Buchanan, 'ten pence a time; you can check.'

The custody sergeant began to look doubtful; it still begged the question about the origins of the document he'd copied, but not a bad story, that.

Patrick didn't hesitate; he picked up one of the copy forms from the desk and held it up to the light, 'Care to bet on it?' he said. 'On the charity shop having the same watermark on its paper as the packs in Eddathorpe CID?'

It was barely possible, but there could be a Chief Constable's baton lurking somewhere in Pat Goodall's knapsack; rude and reckless though he was. Providing, of course, that the disciplinary enquiry didn't get him first.

Teddy called me up to his office just before five o'clock. In the driving seat, as usual, behind his opulent desk, he was wearing his solemn, enigmatic look, which meant that I wasn't supposed to know whether he was annoyed about something, or amused.

'I assume,' he said dryly, 'that you know what Goodall and Cartwright are up to, Bob?'

'Yes, sir. They've arrested Buchanan; I think they're OK, although I must admit it's a bit thin.'

He nodded slowly, 'That wasn't what I had in mind; if that man has been poking his nose into police business and receiving stolen documents, it's a reasonable arrest and it seems all right to me.'

'Fine.'

'You haven't heard any more from the custody sergeant, eh?'

I shook my head.

'About your delinquents going backwards and forwards, and cluttering up his cells?'

'Not a word; he was looking a bit harassed, though, when he called me downstairs a couple of hours ago. He was worried about Buchanan then, I think.'

'He's got a lot more to worry about now, apparently. Five more in the cells, and they've gone out again to search for a sixth.'

'Handling stolen paper?' I kept my voice even, but I was uneasy all the same. Persecuting Buchanan's heroes was alright in principle, but it sounded as if I'd got two detective constables who were busy pushing their luck.

'And GBH, and they're thinking about conspiracy, too. He's accepted their prisoners, so far, but nobody's been questioned yet, and he's far from happy about what young Goodall said as they went out again just now.'

'And what was that?'

'Something along the lines of *another one for the skylark! Tell the boss!*'

Detective Constable Goodall and his flip and cocky mouth. Just the sort of thing to say to a serious-minded sergeant, burdened by PACE and the *Home Office Administrative Directions*, and with a cell block bulging with a crowd of slightly dodgy suspects provided by a reckless CID. I did a rapid revision of my recent opinion of Patrick: he had a ninety percent chance of achieving unemployment, and in any case I was beginning to wish that he'd damn well go and be a Chief Constable somewhere else.

'I think they meant me, sir.'

'I'm sure they did, but I must confess to a little curiosity as to what's going on. After all,' he murmured silkily, 'when push comes to shove it's my responsibility, and *I'm* the boss around here.'

Gloom descended; Teddy mounting his high horse. A combination of inquest and bone-picking session was on the cards, scheduled to start at any moment now.

A thud of elephantine feet on the corridor outside, a murmured conversation with his secretary, and after the most cursory of knocks, Pat and Malc burst in. Malcolm was still preserving an air of gravity, but his colleague had the air of a man whose efforts were to be rewarded with a bottle of whisky and a well-deserved OBE.

'You wanted to see us, sir?'

'Sit down, both of you. I assume the vessel is now full?'

'What vessel?'

'*The Skylark?*'

There was a pregnant pause, 'Oh,' said Patrick. 'That. It was just a joke.'

'Just.' Teddy waited long enough to make any normal person feel uncomfortable, but it wasn't the kind of ploy to worry Pat. 'Would you like to tell me,' he continued mildly, 'precisely why you've, ah, accumulated all these victims of your bow and spear? Playing Nimrod, are you?'

'Eh?' Both detective constables looked blank.

'Nimrod,' I said by way of explanation. 'In Genesis. A mighty hunter before the Lord.'

'If you say so, boss.' It's an unjust world: Teddy makes the eccentric Biblical allusions, I end up winning the reputation as an unreconstructed nut.

'Why all the prisoners,' I said, enunciating slowly and clearly, 'in the cells?'

'Ian Buchanan for Handling; five members of his so-called Citizen's Patrol for Handling, and one more for GBH.'

'Hopefully,' said Teddy, 'there is some kind of logic behind all this?'

'Yessir.' Spokesman Pat. 'Ian Buchanan folded as soon as we told him what we wanted to know. He admits receiving the copies of Pykett's descriptive form; he admits handing them out to his yobs. He was, he also says, only trying to effect an arrest of a wanted man on behalf of the police.

'Any rough stuff, naturally, was never part of the plan. All something to do with the flawed human material that fell into his hands.' He gave us a moment to assimilate this sample of the Buchanan phraseology before he added with a touch of pride, 'He's definitely scared to death.'

'He told you, did he, the names of the men who attacked this tramp?'

'Not exactly, sir; He reckons he doesn't know, but he told us who received copies of our Pykett form. We went to see 'em; anybody who'd still got his copy was nicked for handling, and the guy who hadn't got one was nicked on suspicion of GBH for being the clever-clogs who stuffed his copy into Ted Wilson's pocket in the park.'

'I see,' Teddy stared at him narrowly, 'and I take it that the object of this exercise is to discover the identity of the second man involved in the assault?'

'Yessir.'

'And don't you think that you could be said to be going about it in a very heavy-handed way?'

'We're not oppressing anybody, boss. Just arresting genuine suspects,' injured innocence was now the name of the game. 'We'll question them all in due course.'

'Especially,' muttered Malc, 'the one who hasn't gotta bitta paper to his name. He obviously knows the identity of his moronic pal.'

'Very well,' Teddy looked at his watch. 'You've arrested seven; you can keep Buchanan until you're satisfied as to his role in this. You can keep the men *reasonably* suspected of the GBH. As for the rest with their bits of police paper, talk to them and release them on police bail before the first review.'

'Six hours? Is that all we've got?'

'Six hours from the time they arrived,' Teddy was quoting the *Police And Criminal Evidence Act*, 'and I think I'm being generous, so you'd better get your skates on, hadn't you?'

'What about conspiracy, sir? To commit GBH.' Pat sounded like a small boy whose favourite toy was about to be snatched from his hand.

'Did Buchanan specifically agree with all of them, and did they agree with each other to beat this man up?'

'Buchanan admits going around to see 'em individually and briefing them about their so-called patrols,' said Malc, getting the point. 'There was no general agreement. In any case, Buchanan denies any violent intent on his part.'

'Sensible man,' Teddy employed his sour, down-turned smile. 'So that appears to be your answer, DC Goodall. And besides, you don't have much chance with conspiracy charges with the Crown Prosecution Service these days, they fight very shy!'

'Sir!' But Patrick hadn't given up; there was still a gleam in his eye. It was his turn to look at his watch, 'It's almost five.'

'Just as I said; it's time you got on.'

I could see it coming; there was a flicker of an exchange between Pat and Malc before he struck.

'Yessir.' A Goodall special: apparent acquiescence, followed by a carefully timed pause. 'Can we go and arrest Eric Forster straight away, then?' he asked, deadpan. 'Forster drinks with Buchanan; he stole the photocopies in the first place, and the civvies go home at five.'

Teddy was deadly serious; full uniform, wrath-of-God expression, and he was even wearing his hat. Reflecting his mood the cell-block staff looked equally stiff and serious as they brought in Buchanan and his pals, lining them up in front of the custody sergeant's desk while the rest of us, including Teddy, stepped back. Only the duty solicitor, counting eight separate fees in one evening and no hassle, didn't seem to care. It wasn't a cheerful spectacle; the ragged line, the screwed-down, sloping desk, neon strip lights, and flaking, cream painted brick walls of the custody suite.

'Francis Galton, Ronald Turner; step forward.' The custody sergeant was out to impress. 'You Galton and you Turner are jointly charged that on or about the 14th of July, at Eddathorpe in this county, you did unlawfuly assault one Edward Wilson, thereby inflicting upon him Grievous . . .'

Buchanan, his face set, glanced uneasily to his right; I was the one in range. 'Look,' he muttered uneasily, 'it was nothing to do with the rest of us, don't you think—'

'Be quiet while the officer reads the charge!' Teddy, with news of our interview with Eric Forster, civilian clerk, behind him, was suffering from an acute attack of puritan morality. He was, in the words of Patrick Goodall, feeling thoroughly pissed off.

The words of the joint charge under Section 18 of the Offences Against the Person Act and the caution rumbled on, 'You, Galton, have you anything to say?'

'No, sir!' The sergeant's lips might have twitched.

'You, Turner?'

'Yeah; if he wasn't Pykett, he was still a lousy thief,' The words were delivered with chilling assurance.

How very nice; I could hear the argument. If we did it, then we were absolutely right! One fractured cheekbone, concussion, a couple of broken ribs, and left unconscious all night: said to have taken a purse and a twenty pound note; a thief.

'You will both be remanded in custody for court at 10a.m.' The custody sergeant glanced at the duty solicitor; he knew the score; he shrugged.

'Cells five and six.'

The jailers' keys rattled: two men on their way.

Imperturbably, the custody sergeant turned to the rest. Buchanan, our important local businessman, wasn't even first. Police bail under Section 83 of PACE: no sureties, return here for a decision as to prosecution in a month's time. Another set of police documents handed over: one bail notice each.

'Listen,' said Buchanan, his eyes shifting back and forth. Baring or Graham, who was running it; who to address? 'Surely you can caution the rest of us? After all, it's a minor matter; it was all a mistake!'

Teddy glanced towards me, lowered his eyes and almost imperceptibly, he inclined his head. Buchanan was stale news; Teddy's erstwhile civilian clerk was still in custody, and, with the duty solicitor preparing his spiel, the boss was getting ready to disappoint him; no release. Our superintendent, dressed up for the big review, was awaiting what he clearly regarded as the main event.

As his four companions shuffled and fiddled with their returned property, I placed a companionable arm around Ian

Buchanan's shoulders and urged him out. He took it as an omen; he even seemed pleased.

'D'you know what sickens me, Ian?' Christian name terms with the prisoner; a typical hypocritical cop.

'I'm sorry?' Not what he'd expected, and with freedom in front of him, Buchanan reared up.

'Edward Wilson is still in hospital,' I murmured, ignoring his original question, 'and you never once asked me how he was.'

# Chapter Twenty-Three

———————◆———————

'You rotten bastards,' said Wilson, 'you took my suit while I was in hospital the other day.'

'Come on, now, you're helping yourself; you volunteered.'

He looked across at me with a slow, yellow-toothed grin that said it all. *I know, you know, I know that you know that I*... It was all part of the old, stately, semi-ritualistic CID waltz. And he also knew that I – Never mind!

'Do I get to keep this?' He fingered the lapel of an elderly but still-respectable jacket which had once belonged to George. George had, as he freely admitted, grown out of it some time ago; about 1985, at a guess. Still, it wasn't too bad across the chest. The trousers were another matter; the waistband was hidden beneath the coat, but it must have been well on its way up to his armpits, tightly braced or belted to make any kind of fit. God knows what would happen if the custody sergeant insisted on removing the means of committing suicide, if we ended up placing him in the cells.

'Yes,' said the generous donor, 'you can keep that.'

'And the shirt and tie, socks and shoes?'

'Yes.'

'OK, then; I probably won't sue yer for wrongful arrest.'

'Thank you,' I replied gravely. 'It's not new from Savile Row, but it's a big improvement on the usual Forensic paper suit.'

'It's a big improvement,' said George promptly, 'on that ragman's reject you had on before.'

Wilson ignored that.

'You won't find anythin' on it,' said Wilson confidently, 'I'm not a psychopath, ya know.'

'No? You just like the occasional gleg through other people's windows,' suggested George.

'All right, I admit it, I was wrong. But I *was* sorta looking for somewhere to kip at the same time.'

'From the beginning, please.'

'Right; I came to town, I gotta room, an' I got slung out.'

'We know,' said George, 'for non-payment of rent; but you got this mate of yours to safeguard your Giro from the DSS.'

'And then you started sleeping in the allotment sheds at the back of Cranbourne Avenue.'

'Yeah.'

'And you used to drink at the Standard, where Danny-boy Smith bullied you, and Davinia West used to pull you a pint now and again. We've got all that too,' said George.

'Well, it's lonely out there on the street when the pubs have shut, that's all.'

'Ah!'

'It's all right for you; houses and families and stuff. You've no idea what it's like.'

'Looking, were you,' said George heavily, 'for a spot of affection and human warmth?'

You catch more flies with sugar than you do with vinegar; I handed out a warning glare.

Wilson was oblivious to sarcasm, 'S'right!'

'So now you're telling me that you peeked through other windows, as well?' I was determined to cut this short.

'I suppose so.'

'Many?'

'Quite a few, I suppose.'

'Over what period of time?'

'A week or two.'

'And you hung around Cranbourne Avenue?' asked George

'And Howlett Street,' I offered.

'And probably Alma Street, as well? All the Standard's barmaids; Davinia, Beryl and Maureen, yes?'

'Among others,' I said.

'You,' said George severely, 'have been a very busy boy.'

'That's all I've done, look. I've never touched anybody, on my mother's life.'

'I wish you hadn't said that,' said George cynically, 'you almost had me believing you for a moment there.'

'You not only looked through windows,' I continued, 'you followed these women in the street, didn't you?'

'I didn't do that all the time, once or twice p'raps to sort of find out where they lived.'

'To do what?'

'Nothing.'

'I don't call that nothing; you're a Peeping Tom for a start. What did you do when you got inside Davinia West's flat?'

'I didn't; I didn't! I only took a bit of a look, an' anyway the curtains were always drawn after that.'

And there he stuck: he was lonely, he was drawn to women who'd been nice to him, unlike some people he could mention. And anyway, in Beryl's case, he knew where she lived but that hadn't got him very far because her rooms were upstairs. She was skinny, too.

Davinia was a bit of a magnet; she lived downstairs. The house where she lived was also a bit of a magnet because of the empty flat. So far and no further, but no vandalised doll, no earrings, no rape, no murder, not ever, and not at all.

'I suppose,' I said conversationally, 'Davinia was a bit of a soft touch in some ways; sorry for you, eh?'

'What makes you think that?'

'Well, she wasn't nasty to you at the Standard; didn't relegate you to the pub doorway, for a start.'

'Yeah; see what yer mean.'

'Always pleasant, huh?'

'I've said.'

'Nice to you; talked to you when she pulled your pint. Spot of empathy, eh? Somebody who'd had a rough deal, just like herself?'

'I suppose.'

'No suppose about it, Ted. Mother dead, deserted by her stepfather; sad. Did she ever tell you how she'd been in care?'

'No; don't think I ever heard her saying that.' He was doubtful, more than doubtful, downright suspicious as to what was going on. He hadn't worked this one out yet; he was puzzled, wary of a new line of attack.

'Rough, though, wouldn't you say? Not much of a start in life for a youngster like that?'

'Right.' Still doubtful, but he was perking up; he was beginning to think that he recognised an old police ploy.

'Pretty, too.'

'You trying to make me feel guilty or something?'

A bright light was finally shining at the end of the Wilson tunnel; he thought he knew the game. A stupid one, too: a naive copper making an appeal to a suspect's better nature equals a constabulary prat. He stirred himself and stretched; tentatively, he even smiled.

'Not at all, Ted; I was just explaining why she kept her mouth shut.'

'About what?' He couldn't resist it, but the smile froze.

'Oh, about a purse,' I said airily, watching his face, 'or seeing a pathetic old man, for example, being caught back-stage at a beauty contest a week last Saturday night?'

Malcolm came into the office, slowly, reluctantly, as if he was wearing lead boots. He closed the door and sprawled rather than sat in the seat opposite my desk, staring at me sullenly.

I tried to look at things from his point of view; it was fairly obvious that I wasn't his favourite DCI.

'Malc,' I said, 'you know as well as I do, it couldn't go on.'

'No.' He studied me from under half-lowered lids, the injured party making no concessions, giving nothing away. I wanted to clear the air, but if he was expecting an apology he was out of luck.

'Let's try to be objective for a minute; putting you in touch with the Welfare Officer and the Benevolent Fund Committee was a good move, right?'

'Yeah.' The admission was little more than a sigh; as depressed as he was resentful, I gathered.

'Ginny just took it the wrong way.'

He placed both hands on the arms, and levered himself up in his chair, 'I'll tell you straight; it's caused as many problems as it solved.'

'Once Mr Fairfield discovered—'

'Mr Fairfield,' he mimicked. 'Is that why you did it, because you're scared of him?'

'Listen, Malcolm, this is a disciplined service, not Fred Karno's army, and any of your creditors, at any time they fancied, could have gone straight to the Chief.'

He wanted to blame somebody, I supposed; he wanted to make the most of his resentment, and he certainly didn't want to face up to a remark like that. He didn't reply, but the glower on his face said more than enough.

'We are talking about your job, you know,' I tried to keep the irritation out of my own voice. 'I can't prejudge the result, but putting it at its lowest, a disciplinary hearing for failing to settle your debts wouldn't have done you any good.'

'It was my family and my business, and nobody invited either you or Mr bloody Fairfield to stick his nose where it wasn't wanted!'

'At the time,' I said, annoyance overriding discretion, 'I seem to recall that you were pretty relieved that we had.'

'Why didn't you see me, and tell me about it?' he asked, changing tack. 'The letters and all?'

'I didn't know.'

'Only at first.'

'Right; then it involved Paula Spriggs and Peter Fairfield, as well as Superintendent Spinks. It was an official enquiry by that time. It's not even as if we knew she was behind the letters from the beginning; what did you expect people to do?'

'She always called her Theodora, not Dorothea,' he said reflectively, the light of scandal kindling behind his eyes. 'I could have told you that.'

'And I suppose,' I replied, 'it was you who told her the Peter and Thea story in the first place. What was it, a bit of Romeo and Juliet; tales of long ago?' It wasn't the only story he'd told her either, but I was determined to keep him off my own particular strip of blighted grass.

'We were just talking,' he said uncomfortably, 'you know how it is.'

'I know,' I said unthinkingly, 'how it ended up.' And then I saw the change in his face. 'Look,' I added hurriedly, 'it's not a total disaster, she'll soon be back on an even keel, and nobody's going to take a thing like this to court.'

He looked at me incredulously, 'You mean you haven't heard? That's why I came to see you. For Chrissake, boss!' My eyes flickered guiltily towards the pile of unread messages in my basket, 'Heard what? I've been busy all morning.' It sounded a lame excuse.

'Ginny's missing from hospital,' he snarled, 'and you're wasting my time. I just thought you were playing it crafty, and beating about the bush!'

'Galton and Turner?' asked Teddy.

'Custody; a seven day remand.'

'And Eric Forster?' His lip crinkled with distaste.

'Court bail.'

'Couldn't expect anything else, I suppose. Never mind, he's done his last shift here!' Suspended, pending legal proceedings, then the sack. The civvy Trade Union might turn bolshie from time to time, but no official in his right mind would waste time and effort on a cause like that.

'And your man Wilson is down in the cells?'

'Yes, sir.'

'Just a theft?'

'And a bind over order for the Peeping Tom. I'm almost tempted to bail him, boss, but he's nowhere to go.'

'Bail him,' said Teddy dryly, 'and he can go anywhere, providing he travels west.' I smiled agreeably at the totally unexpected, something approaching a Baring joke.

'We do seem,' he murmured gently, 'to be ankle-deep in relatively minor crime.' He awaited the reluctant nod, and continued, 'And now we've got another female missing from home.'

'Missing from hospital,' I amended, 'and strictly speaking, Virginia Cartwright didn't go missing from our patch.'

'But every local effort,' a touch of Arctic weather entered his voice, 'will be made to trace—'

'Goes without saying,' I said. Momentarily, our eyes locked. Mutual irritation. He'd thought I was trying to slide out from under, I blamed him for thinking that I was evading my responsibilities towards Malc.

'But you're sure about Wilson,' he said abruptly, 'and Davinia West?'

'Quite sure.'

'I trust you, Bob.' While thousands wouldn't? As a testimonial to my intelligence and skill, I wasn't entirely convinced.

'But,' here it came, 'time's getting on, and murder enquiries . . .'

'Go stale?'

'Have this tendency to devolve into side issues, I would have said.'

Another one climbing on to the bandwagon; oh dear.

It didn't please him, but I told him about the latest super-secret Aylfleet enquiry. It reinforced his existing prejudices, but whatever he thought of side issues, he'd have been even more displeased if he'd discovered that Thea Spinks was one ahead of him on the need-to-know.

# Chapter Twenty-Four

A sluggish grey dawn, and the tide in the estuary crawling reluctantly back along the channel and over the sleek, greyish mud. We'd kept the CID car out of sight beyond the rise which overlooked the New Age Traveller's camp; a dozen assorted vehicles laagered around a laboriously assembled patch of sand and gravel to protect the residents from the all-encroaching mud. Twenty-five past four; Bernice and all the brothers and sisters were safely tucked up in bed.

Cold, depressing, and totally unproductive, so far. No signs of the *Blue Marlin* making its illicit way up the estuary, and my end of the reception committee was thoroughly fed up. Even Pat, the proud possessor of a very expensive image intensifier abstracted from the Technical Support Unit stores, had tired of his new toy. The distant assortment of silent caravans, buses and converted ambulances, together with a totem pole and an amateurishly constructed teepee, held what was left of his attention for a while.

'That Red Indian thing; it's a sweat lodge, right?'

Roger Prentice, recruited for the Aylthorpe end of the surveillance operation, sighed. 'Yes, I told you; they sit round and promote health and a sense of community solidarity in there. They reckon they're a tribe.'

'Men and women together?'

'I should think so.'

'In the nude?'

'Don't ask me,' he spared me a brief, lascivious wink. 'Why don't you ask the boss? He knows Bernice; he could probably get you a free ticket, if you like.'

'If we ever have to do observations out here in winter,' I muttered, 'you, Roger, are going straight to the top of my list.'

'I hear she's very sweet-natured,' said Roger innocently. 'Just the girl for Pat.'

In the background, Frank Dawes, the fourth, silent member of our party, huddled disapprovingly into his coat.

The conversation flagged, it was almost high tide. The distant thud of engines brought us to life briefly. Frank Dawes, in his role of expert, looked at his watch. 'It's only the ferry,' he said, and sure enough the less-than-elegant bulk of Aylfleet's very own *North Sea Trader* soon loomed out of the early morning mist, chugging its clumsy way up the fairway towards its berth.

'It's a miracle the way a few coats of paint hold that rust bucket together,' said Pat, hoping to initiate another round in the long-running Aylfleet versus Eddathorpe feud featuring the attractions and counter-attractions of an ancient port and a cheap-and-cheerful seaside town. Dawes, a non-native was indifferent; Roger Prentice, unsuited to the role of local patriot, grinned.

'Look!'

A couple of hundred yards behind the ferry the white motor yacht followed cautiously, its white trim imperfectly etched against the still-uncertain light. Almost unconsciously there was a surge forward to get a better look.

'Hey! don't break the skyline!' I hissed warningly, as if the occupant of the boat could hear me from several hundred yards away.

Pat eased himself back, the image intensifier still to his eye, '*Blue Marlin*,' he confirmed. Then, almost with the pride of an inventor, 'This thing is bloody good!'

I began the retreat down the slope towards the car, 'Going straight back, now?' asked Pat doubtfully.

'To Aylfleet? Yes. DI Wake will be at the Marina with his party; he's got a couple of his lads at Sheppard's disco, and George has things covered at the Eddathorpe end. What else?'

'He could have a buoy or something; drop the gear in the channel, mark it and—'

'*Cornish Smugglers of the Eighteenth Century,*' said Dawes derisively. 'You been reading a book?'

'No, I only thought ...' Pat Goodall flushed and his voice trailed away, while Roger Prentice and I exchanged a silent thought: if the boat, not to mention Sheppard, turned out to be clean we could always blame HM Customs for deriding our lad.

'Go on,' I said, nodding encouragingly towards the waiting car and its UHF radio, 'you can give 'em the good news, Pat.'

'Well?' said Dorothea Spinks.

'He's docked; he's still hanging around on his boat. All he's done is be a good boy and report his arrival, so far. Customs have finally agreed to let it run. The surveillance team is in position, and we've covered the likely delivery points at this end.'

'And his property in Humberside, just in case?'

'Yes ...'

She picked it up straight away, 'But they didn't want to tell the Humberside police? They don't trust us, do they? Heads down, mouths shut; ruddy Customs and their need-to-know?'

'They're very cautious people,' I said.

'I'm a very cautious person, too.'

Smugly, she produced a file from her locked drawer and handed it over. Magistrates' Warrants to search for drugs.

'But this is a joint operation,' I protested, 'and they've got independent powers of search. Once they show a thing called a Writ of Assistance, they're straight in. Customs officers are entitled to break down doors, search any premises, the lot.'

'I've heard.' She looked at me almost coquettishly across the width of her desk. 'Keep these in reserve in case of, er, accidents, shall we say, and keep your own counsel, Bob.'

'Thank you, ma'am,' I accepted the warrants. 'D'you know something that I don't?'

'I've been here before,' she said simply, 'a long time ago. Customs and Excise are a bit like bank managers; they're reluctant to do anything unless they've got a belt and braces *and* a piece of string to hold up their professional trousers.'

I raised my eyebrows, awaiting confidences, 'Oh?'

'Nothing too heavy,' she assured me. 'But I went on one of these so-called joint operations, once. All very professional, until we failed to spot the delivery in one particular case. Fairly solid suspicion, but they weren't absolutely sure, so they refused to use their ruddy Writ to search. By the time we'd gone and obtained a magistrates warrant . . .'

'No gear?'

'Not a smell. Be nice to 'em, Bob; it's their show and it's their information we're using, after all. But if they start behaving too much like civil servants, you've got your own little bits of paper to back you up, OK?'

'OK.' I shuffled through the addresses, folded them carefully and pocketed the lot. Who was I to argue if Dorothea wanted to play the prophetess of doom? I could, if all went well, keep the evidence of departmental distrust and treachery firmly out of sight.

'Oh, and Bob!'

'Yes?' I was already on my way to the door.

'There's Harry; Harry Wake, you know?'

'Yes?'

'Don't forget this is an Aylfleet job, and he's the Aylfleet DI. Let him deal with it, once you've done your stuff. I know you're the supervisor, but don't be greedy. After all, you do seem to have an undetected *Eddathorpe* murder on your hands.'

I thought about it, but discretion being the better part of

valour, I didn't speak: a crude, pithy, extremely unfair, totally sexist remark.

'Having a fine time?' There was a pregnant silence at the other end of the phone.

'If,' said Harry Wake finally, 'you call sitting around a scruffy Marina with a pair of binoculars, a few sandwiches and a flask of tea, fine. Why don't you come and join us, boss?'

'Not a lot doing, eh?'

'Pattison's getting restless; so are the other teams. Sheppard has been docked for nearly five hours now, and he hasn't made his move.'

'Well,' I said cheerfully from the comfort of my own office, 'you know what they say about police work, Harry; ninety-five percent boredom and five percent stark terror.'

'I think,' said Detective Inspector Wake a trifle stiffly, 'that you're talking about war.'

'You're probably right,' I admitted sadistically; no long waits for me. 'Nothing happening at all?'

'He walked out for some groceries, earlier,' muttered the Aylfleet DI enviously. 'And a few cans.'

'Contact anybody?'

'Not so far as we know.'

'And that's it?'

'Well; he did speak to that scruffy odd-job type that hangs around. He's buggered off now; Sheppard's back on board and Pattison's all for rummaging the boat unless something happens soon.'

'Discourage him for as long as you can. If Sheppard's got contraband on the *Marlin*, it's doing no harm where it is. Besides, we've got our own enquiry to consider; remind him of what we agreed.'

'He's talking about consulting his mate, Dawes.'

'And where's he now?'

'With George Caunt and his lads in Eddathorpe; they're parked down the road from Paulie Parkes's flat.'

'Good,' I grunted. 'Dawes is the senior man. I think I'll go down and see.'

Harry switched off his mobile, but not before I overheard his less-than-complimentary valediction, 'And stuff your luck!'

'It's running, boss!' Pat's voice was exultant, 'And DI Wake and DS Prescott are giving that Bloaters place a spin.'

Round the corner from Paulie Parkes's apartment, half in, half out of my elderly, radioless vehicle, and I was being treated to a sample of telly-bobby verbiage with words like 'spin.'

'I take it,' I said sourly, 'that Sheppard has moved, and they're now searching that disco-cum-club?'

'Yeah,' he wasn't in the least abashed. 'They tried to raise you, sir. They couldn't even get you on your mobile phone.'

'Damn!' One of my many failings; much to the amusement of my junior colleagues I was not always right there at the cutting edge of technology. I frequently forgot to switch it on.

'About twenty minutes ago,' Goodall was gloating; a mixture of the man with the news, and the happy subordinate more than willing to rub it in. 'Some scruffy labourer turned up with a van. He went on board and came back with something that looked like a great big can of gash. Rubbish,' he added hastily, 'the, er, Navy are inclined to say gash.'

'Just get on.'

'Anyway, this labouring type drove off; he tipped some rubbish at the wheelie-bins near the gate, but then he just kept on coming, he must be nearly at Retton by now.

'Sheppard followed on about five minutes after; he popped in to see his man at the disco, so the majority of the Aylfleet team have gone in after him with the Customs guy and his Writ of Assistance, and they're, er—'

'Giving the place a *spin?*'

'Yessir.' The irony was lost on Pat.

'And we've definitely got somebody trailing this labouring feller North out of Aylfleet town?'

'Yes. George, sorry, Sergeant Caunt, has instructed 'em to keep well back if he does a right at Retton. Once the van's beyond the crossroads, other than Eddathorpe, there's nowhere else to go.'

'Where's George now?'

'Hanging around in that newsagent's opposite the apartments, boss; first floor. That other Customs nerd is moaning his head off, and he wanted you to know the story first, before you went in there and started mixing it with him.'

Dawes, as Pat had said, was moaning. I could hear him all the way up the stairs in the newsagent's shop. The shop-keeper himself had given me so many nods and winks on my arrival that I thought his head could have been in danger of falling off. In any case, it didn't take a genius to realise that another Eddathorpe legend of gossip, innuendo and downright misrepresentation was in the process of being formed.

George looked at me wearily from across the small, neat sitting room as I went in. He remained by the curtains looking out, while Frank Dawes was sprawled in an over-stuffed armchair by the unlit gas fire.

''Lo, George,' I nodded to the other half of the joint operation, 'well?'

'He's definitely on his way; he's the disco manager's brother, and he'll be well past Retton by now.'

'Anything else from Aylfleet?'

'Not yet.'

Dawes stirred uncomfortably in his armchair, 'Mr Graham, I've got a very bad feeling about all this.'

'I don't see why; there's a search in progress at Bloaters, and our other man is on his way.'

'That's just the point. We've heard nothing positive from the Aylfleet end of the operation, and this man is just some sort of dogsbody at the Marina. He might be nothing to do with the drugs.'

'Well, we'll soon know, won't we, once he turns up here?'

'If he visits Parkes? The man is Sheppard's ex-brother-in-law; he could have a thousand and one legitimate reasons for sending a workman to see him.'

I looked at him incredulously, 'But this was all your information in the first place, Mr Dawes.'

'There's nothing to link this other man; I would very much prefer to go back and rummage the boat before we go making fools of ourselves here. Parkes is, after all, quite a well-known man.'

'While the delivery is made here, and the stuff, whatever it is, vanishes into thin air? We need to search!'

'Well, I do not wish to be, ah, offensive, or indeed uncooperative, but . . .'

'Yes?'

'I do have to pay proper regard to the interests of the public as a whole, and my superiors are extremely wary of complaints.'

'You're refusing to use your Writ?'

'I'm sorry, but I've been thinking very seriously about this. I really feel we ought to go back to the boat before we impinge on Mr Parke's privacy and his, er, civil rights.'

George looked thunderstruck; at the risk of sounding racist, the bugger had welshed. Never mind: I simply fingered the warrant in my inside pocket, and conferred a series of heartfelt blessings on the perspicuity and foresight of Dorothea Spinks.

# Chapter Twenty-Five

Paulie Parkes had made it so easy I felt almost sorry for him, but not quite. One ring on the doorbell, a sight of the warrant, one copy dumped into his reluctant fist and straight in. Paulie had cried. The man who'd made his living by sticking verbal pins in other people had finally run out of wisecracks and wept. Then he'd wanted to know what was going to happen, and he'd begged for bail, and that was before we'd even left the flat. Like taking sweets from a baby, and I don't know who looked the worst when we found the contraband drugs, still covered in their shiny polythene wraps: we had a straight choice between him and fearless Frankie Dawes.

Our labourer was more phlegmatic; there was, admittedly, thirty kilos of cannabis resin in Paulie's living room, and we, cunning buggers, had obviously seen him pick it up. And drop it off too: another semi-amateur in a panic. He must have thought we'd got X-ray eyes.

What about a deal, therefore? He was, to coin a phrase, only the gofer; we could take a nice long statement from him if we liked: all about Paulie, all about Ralph. He was, when all was said and done, only the mule.

'What's your name?'

'John Westcott.'

'Your brother runs Bloaters Disco, right?'

'Yes.' Suddenly the deal wasn't quite so easy after all; a cloud passed over his face.

'Keeping it in the family, eh?'

Pat and Malc took our bearded gofer. George and I drove Paulie and Frank. It was a long, silent drive back to Aylfleet. What with our overwrought ex-TV personality on the one hand and a bruised Civil Service ego on the other, some would say that our journey was pretty emotionally charged.

'A promise is a promise,' I explained to George.

'You're handing all this over to Harry Wake?'

'I as good as said I would when I spoke to Thea.'

Excuses, excuses: George sniffed.

Harry Wake, on the other hand, was more than pleased. He went backwards and forwards from interview to interview like a sniffer dog with two tails. Parkes, Westcott and Westcott coughed. Cannabis delivered by John to Paulie at Eddathorpe; and from Gavin Westcott there was an admission that he'd received five hundred tablets of E. A spot of personal, private enterprise involving the boss and his manager to increase the profitability of a small-town Club.

Sheppard denied everything; no importations whatsoever. Never, not so far as he personally, was concerned. *Ecstasy? No! you're absolutely wrong: Gavin Westcott says so? You must be joking, chaps!*

Part two of the interview was worse. It made the men from Customs wish they'd opted for the simple solution and searched the boat. *So that's cannabis?* Sheppard sounded so genuinely incredulous, I'd smiled. *Who'd have thought it? I've never seen the stuff before. Well, yeah, all right, I've seen it, but never in bulk. Looks just like strips of hardboard, eh? Just the stuff for a spot of Do-It-Yourself!* He's stuck to his story, too; I'd especially enjoyed the crack about the DIY.

After that, he'd looked down his nose at Aylfleet: there were bound to be such piddling little solicitors in such a piddling little town. He'd wanted to see his very own big city brief, all the way from *Grimsby*, no less. We had to sit around for something like two and a half hours before this paragon turned up; funny or not, we found that waiting had some tendency to coagulate the constabulary smile.

Not that it did Sheppard all that much good in the end: shiny plastic, covering flat planks of the best quality Syrian Gold carry fingerprints, don'tcha know? And Ralph, aided by his bemused solicitor, more familiar with conveyancing than crime, was finally, after a private discussion, inclined to see sense.

'OK, I'll tell you. What happens now?'

'Her Majesty's Customs,' announced fearless Frankie grandly, 'are going to seize your boat.'

'But it's worth double what I paid for it. Maybe seventy, eighty grand!"

Harry Wake stared at Sheppard balefully. 'You imported the stuff. Thirty kilos and five hundred tabs.' Then he turned on Dawes in pursuit of the usual cops versus customs spat. 'And I would have thought that the price of a boat was the least of his current problems, Frank.'

The customs officer flushed, then, taking his turn, he went through the story of the importation, the handing over of the cargo to John Wescott for onward transmission to Paulie Parkes, as well as the story of lucrative sideline in seagull-stamped tablets of E. It was there, however, that the story stuck; Ralph was prepared to admit what he had to, but he was saying zero about his source of supply.

'You're so clever,' he said flatly, 'your information must have come from somewhere, so you can work it out for yourself,' and eventually Dawes and Harry Wake retired, and I was joined by George.

'Really, this is getting like a relay race, Chief Inspector,' claimed the solicitor from the bigger town. 'This continual questioning appears to be a deliberate, oppressive ploy.'

'We're going into a totally different interview,' I admitted. 'Perhaps Mr Sheppard would care for another break?'

'No thanks,' said Sheppard with apparent calm, 'Talking of oppression, I don't think I can take any more of your lousy canteen tea.' He sat in the very bottom of his self-dug hole and bared his teeth, while his solicitor winced. A bad bugger, but admirable in his way; nothing like his former brother-in-law, soggy Paulie Parkes.

'You do not have to say anything,' I reiterated formally for the benefit of the tape, 'but it may harm your defence if you do not mention when questioned something you rely on later in court.

'Anything you do say may be given in evidence.'

'Taken down in evidence,' he said.

'I beg your pardon?'

'You say taken down, and I reply *knickers!* Right?'

'Mr Sheppard . . .'

'My client,' said the solicitor heavily, 'is under a great deal of stress.'

'Too bloody right I am,' Ralph Sheppard leaned forward and slammed both hands violently down on the table in front of him with a reverberating crash, while George tensed and, lawyer or no lawyer, he got ready for a quick counter-move as soon as things got rough.

'I know the score, gents; don't for a moment think I don't. Lock up the wicked drug dealer, and then fit him up for the murder of Davinia West, OK?'

'I intend to ask you some questions about her death; is that another way of telling me that I've got good reason for doing so?'

There are times when you're nice to 'em, and others when it's necessary to lay it on the line. Even Sheppard's lawyer looked as if he'd been slapped. As for Ralph, his head flicked up, and he looked at me for the first time with a hint of real fear.

'You believe that, don't you?'

'Believe what?'

'That I did it, and you think that I was trying to put you off just then by getting my blow in first.'

'And were you?' This was not the interview I'd planned; the carefully constructed, Home Office-inspired Principles of Investigative Interviewing were sailing straight out of the window. It was a personalised, as opposed to a formalised interview all right, but the subtle psychological approach looked as though it might already be dying the death.

'I was looking for an advantage, because I didn't think you'd believe me, yes.'

'That's honest, anyway,' I was seeking to get things back on track, 'and that's all anybody could ask.'

'Mr Sheppard,' the solicitor obviously thought it was time he started to earn his keep, 'I think we ought to talk privately again before you answer any of these questions, indeed you are not obliged to assist—'

'You weren't a lot of help over the cannabis, were you?' snapped Sheppard, not altogether unreasonably, I thought. 'One minute you're telling me that I might as well confess, and now I've got nothing to lose and everything to gain by talking, you're telling me to bloody well shut up!'

'The weight of the evidence ...'

'Yes, well, right, I've got it, OK, but I didn't do Davinia. I'm innocent, so let me handle this in my own way.'

'If you want me to remain here—' the solicitor began to draw the shreds of his dignity around him like a cloak.

'Of course I want you; otherwise it's two on to one! And anyway I wouldn't trust either of these two as far as I could spit!'

The man looked across at us; George and I stared back. Amity and friendship were unlikely to form a significant part of our professional relationship, but with a client like Sheppard in common, the merest hint of fellow-feeling began to emerge.

Slowly, step by agonising step, we went over the old, familiar ground. The first meeting between Sheppard and Davinia at the

Marina in company with Colin Critchley, what he knew about the bust-up between them, the tentative offer of the dancing job at weekends.

'Look,' he said, 'I told you, it never got off the ground; that miserable bastard of a landlord wouldn't wear it at any price.'

'You sound pretty annoyed.'

'Irritated, more like. It was no skin off his nose, he had plenty of other staff.'

'How do you know that?'

'I went to see him, didn't I? Tried to jolly him up, but he was as stubborn as hell.'

'At the Standard?'

'Why not?'

'It's hardly your sort of pub.'

'Oh, I get it,' he leaned back and gave me a sarcastic smile, 'you reckon I was getting obsessive about her, is that it? You boys certainly know how to make bricks without straw.'

'You met her, you ended up in a sexual relationship, you admit that. Then you tried to set her up in a part-time job, and you also, er, helped things along a bit, didn't you, with Paulie Parkes?'

'The beauty contest? So what? It's not what you know, it's who you know in this life that gets you what you want.'

'And you wanted Davinia West?'

'And that's abnormal or something? Do me a favour, pal.' He shook his head wonderingly; the sheer stupidity of cops.

'Talking of abnormalities,' I said, 'I'd like to show you this. For the tape, I am showing Mr Sheppard exhibit DW 2, a damaged doll, with string around its neck and a metal skewer piercing the lower body. Do you recognise this?'

'Christ!' He watched me place the bucketed, yoked, blonde-haired miniature milkmaid down upon the interview-room desk between us, his lips compressed and he stared across at me with what looked like an air of genuine shock.

'Dutch?' I asked.

'Belgian; what sort of fucker would do a thing like that? I bought it for her in Bruges.'

'Ah, the five-day holiday,' I said. 'The unauthorised absence from work.'

'That's right, you're beginning to sound like that creepy landlord. He raised Cain when she wanted a few days off.'

'And what about this? I am showing Mr Sheppard exhibit DW 19, a ladies handbag, accompanied by DW 20, a packaged specimen of approximately 0.2 grammes of cannabis resin recovered from it. Is this the remains of another of your gifts?'

'You're a real Mother Grundy, aren't you? Moaning on about a few grains of puff when you've got a crazy bastard out there who does things like that!' He tapped the plastic packaging covering the doll.

'Did you supply the resin?'

'For Chrissake, it was a bit of a sample; she was curious, yes.'

'Any more gifts, Ralph?'

'What sort of gifts?'

'Jewellery, for example?'

'No.'

No score there, but maybe it was time to gamble; have a go at piling it on.

'But she knew you had access to drugs? A middle-aged obsessive with a young woman half his age, he wines and dines her, beds her, tries to get her a job, fixes a beauty contest for her, takes her abroad on holiday, and even involves her in his drug-dealing activities. Then, maybe she tries to break it off with him? Not too bad, is it, for bricks without straw?'

'Mr Graham!' The lawyer was on his feet, indignation etched on every line on his face. 'You have gone far enough. You have piled speculation on top of speculation; you have given my client absolutely no opportunity to answer your individual points, and you have no evidence to link him with murder at all. I insist that this interview terminate, and that

I have an opportunity to consult with Mr Sheppard privately at once.'

'That,' said Ralph Sheppard going very red in the face, 'sounds like a good idea, and it goes for me, too.'

Outside, George stared at me sadly; his more-in-sorrow-than in-anger look. 'I think,' he murmured, 'we bolloxed that one slightly. We might have said a bit too much in there.'

A bit rich, I thought pettishly, coming from a detective sergeant to a DCI. Then again, in terms of his personal contribution to this particular fiasco, he was being more than generous to me, George.

# Chapter Twenty-Six

We didn't get back to Eddathorpe until nearly half-past eight when the evening was closing down, and on the way George and I bickered like an old married couple.

'Don't worry, he didn't do it,' I said.

'And if he did you're well out of it now; you shot that interview right up the arse.' It's difficult when they're so much older than you are; some people have little or no respect.

'The problem with old CID cynics,' I pontificated, 'is that they're unwilling to leave ill alone. Once they've interviewed a suspect they never seem to make their minds up to pack it in. They always go harping on about how he *might* have done it, just in case they were wrong.'

'We don't like getting caught out by devious bastards, that's all. Anyway, a good detective goes by the evidence, an' if the evidence won't stand it, he walks away and gets on with something else.'

'Without a backward glance?'

'Yes.'

'In your dreams, matey; ha, bloody ha.'

'You're not telling me everything, are you?'

'No.'

'So Ralph Sheppard was just a paper exercise, just in case, and so was having another go at Paulie Parkes?'

'Not really, no. I've got a feeling about this one, just a touch more than that to tell the truth. But I haven't got anywhere solid where I can hang my hat, and chatting to those two about Davinia might have been of some help.'

'Reasonable suspicion, boss?'

I shrugged.

'We could always go out and do a Hacker,' he said.

I shuddered; Detective Superintendent Ronald Hacker (Retired), my former boss, a far-famed bully and thicko, and a man who'd have locked up St Francis for animal cruelty on the merest whim.

'Who do you fancy, anyway?'

I told him.

'Why?'

'Oh,' I replied airily, wilfully misconstruing the question, 'the usual reasons for rape: a perverted drive for dominance, power; jealousy and frustration, maybe. Then there's the question of suppressed male violence, not to mention the sex.'

'OK, don't tell me,' grunted my subordinate rudely, 'and you can save all that guff for an article in the British Association of Social Workers' magazine.'

It was a trifle on the early side for a public house three-nines, and it came just as we'd had our statutory chat with Roger Prentice, updated the action forms and were making a well-deserved exit in the general direction of a long, cool pint.

'Fight,' said the control room sergeant, 'in the Royal Standard,' just as we were on our way out.

'Can't hear you,' said George.

'Aw, cummon; we're short of staff.'

'Aren't we all?'

'Are your lads attending?' I asked, doing a quick body count of the CID strength; one DCI, one potential acting inspector, a detective sergeant and two detective constables, and all in search of a watering hole. Conscience struck.

'Yes, sir. We've only got two men on the streets,' pleaded the uniform man pathetically, 'and two more in the area car.'

'We were going for a drink, anyway.' Pat Goodall feeling macho, always ready for a scrap.

'But not in that dump!' protested George, making a grab for the hook containing the CID car keys, nevertheless.

Once out in the yard I was glad to occupy the boss's spot in the front passenger seat, while, amidst much muttering and moaning, three not inconsiderable figures squeezed into the back. Five coppers in an aging Ford Escort is, tell 'em at Dagenham, rather more than enough, even for the two-minute journey inclusive of traffic lights which is all it took George to get to the scene.

The expensively etched front window of the Royal Standard emblazoned with leopards and lilies came to the end of its useful life as we drew up outside. Accompanied by a small Britannia table, it disintegrated into a shower of lethal shards upon the fortunately-deserted pavement just as Pat was about to step out.

'Lively!' said Patrick approvingly, wrenching himself free of the over-familiar embrace of his colleagues, and making for the door, closely followed by Big Malc.

Roger Prentice alighted more slowly, as befitted his age and rank. He eyed the lone, unoccupied area car, it's blue light flashing, parked amidst a small group of junior would-be vandals a few yards up the street.

'Hey!'

Three or four heads jerked, and an equal number of hitherto happy faces set in a collective scowl.

'I know every one of yer, and I'll make it my business to kick yer backsides purple if anybody touches that car!' George and I, uncertain of either the truth, wisdom or even the legality of this declaration, nevertheless glowered in support prior to piling into the pub.

It was, as Pat described it later, a pretty good fight. The uniforms from the area car had got more than enough on their hands. A mass of struggling bodies occupied the area immediately in front of the bar, while Danny-boy Smith, complete with a rounders bat, and with one knee up on the counter and the other leg trailing, was whacking out indiscriminately.

One of the bodies, a partially applied set of handcuffs swinging from one wrist and a youngish constable attached to his waist, was attempting to climb the bar. Pat and the other uniformed man from the area car had already managed to wrestle a double-chinned, pendulous-gutted giant to the floor, where, incredibly, the PC was yelling snatches of the caution into his ear.

It was, however, the far corner of the bar counter, next to the flap, where the real excitement was taking place. Two women, hands to mutual hair, were screaming and dragging each other backwards and forwards, legs lashing out in all directions in attempts to land kicks, while a couple of male would-be peacemakers danced tentatively around them, as if the combatants were too hot to touch. In the background, a yelling harpy, her mouth stretched grotesquely as she screamed advice to her favourite, appeared to be the leader of an appreciative all-male claque.

George, I noticed a trifle bitterly, made a beeline for the young PC, making a grab for the unhandcuffed wrist of his victim in order to complete the arrest. Roger Prentice reached across the bar and seized Danny by the scruff of the neck, twisting with the other hand and clamping the falling rounders bat in one meaty fist. Malcolm, too, was seriously engaged, and I had, I realised, been left with the other outstanding priority. I truly hated Wild West cat-fights, and I'd definitely been handed the very dirtiest end of the stick.

'Gawon! gawon! gawon!' screamed the harpy. 'She started it! Show 'er she can't do that to you!'

Choosing the softest target first, I swung her round, and, for the first time recognised my facially-distorted opponent. 'Beryl, shut up!'

'She did, she did! She started it,' yelled an over-excited Beryl. 'And all she wanted was her P 45!' Sense, at least so far as I was concerned, was not being spoken yet.

I pushed forward while one of the peacemakers, seizing his own opportunity to grasp the lesser of two evils, made for Beryl, tentatively reaching out. 'Come on, now, love; leave it to the police.'

'You,' snarled Beryl untruthfully, lashing out, 'get your sodding hand off me left tit!'

By this time I had troubles of my own. The nearest combatant, whose smudged make-up, draggled hair and torn dress hardly qualified her for the role of Danny's immaculate, if over-enamelled wife, now held her opponent by the lower jaw and was attempting to batter the back of her head against the wall, while the latter was still kicking out and and pummelling away at the landlady's ribs. My first attempt at separating them was rewarded by a well-planted knee in the groin.

'Tart!' screamed Mary Smith, ignoring the injured male, still concentrating on the job in hand. 'Barmaids, I've shit 'em! Tarts, every one of you. Tarts! Think I don't know what's been going on?'

'You've the mind of a sewer rat, Missus!' The voice was muffled; a long way from home, but in the stress of combat, the original, unmistakable accent was coming out. 'If I ever touched such a creature as that, sure I'd need to be as mad as yourself!'

'Alright, alright, that's enough!' This time, keeping well out of the way of the flailing legs and knees, I manoeuvred my way behind the landlady, threw both arms over her shoulders, and wrenched hard, separating her from her victim. Unfortunately, in stepping back, I became entangled with a bar stool, tripped, and in a flurry of legs, tights and knickers, we both ended up on the floor.

The audience cheered.

'The laundry's back!' shrieked Maureen Pykett, raising one

hand to check her bleeding face, 'an' there's a Peeler as loves yeh, after all!'

'It was all getting too much,' admitted Maureen, 'what with one thing and another, wouldn't you think?'

'Nigel, especially?' I prompted.

'What was I supposed to do? I was eighteen when I fell pregnant, and a village of three hundred people was an unforgiving sort of place twenty years ago.' She looked older, bleaker, at the memory, lines of pain etched across her face.

'In County Mayo,' I said.

She looked up at me sharply, 'You reckon Ireland's so special, mister? You'll find bigots and gossips anywhere you care to look.'

In Eddathorpe for example; I held my peace.

'Anyway, I came to England, and whatever he might think now, it wasn't easy to give him up, but I did it and I cried for him and then I put it behind me and got on with dealing with what was sent.'

A fatalist then, and a nice turn of phrase to cover it all.

'Like Alan Alfred Pykett,' I said.

She shrugged, 'Like Alan,' she began, 'now there's a thorough-going bastard, to be sure.' Then she pulled up short. 'Dear God,' she said, 'I get it, you've been wasting your time looking for him!'

'Not unreasonable, is it? A woman is raped and murdered, and a second woman who used to be married to a violent sexual offender disappears.'

'Believe me, mister, I am sorry and sorry for that. I have never set eyes on the devil for years.' The soft, formal voice trailed away, and she looked at me firmly with genuine regret in her eyes.

'The, er, stalking . . .' I said.

'Now there's a man I'd shop tomorrow if ever I thought it was him! I'd never stand back for that one; not on your life!'

'What about Ted Wilson?'

'Ah,' she said evasively, 'the lonely, harmless man.' Unwilling to drop him in it, and still sticking to the original party line. I remembered our first conversation, the chopped barroom philosophy, and, looking back on it, the hints.

'But it was Nigel hanging on that I couldn't stand,' she continued. 'It was all dead and done with, and he was after having a fine family of his own. Why did he have to come and worry me?'

It was, I supposed, one way of putting it. 'And that was it, you disappeared?'

'I'd outstayed my welcome, anyway. It was time I moved on. What had I got in a place like this? A ratty little job, and a rented, furnished house.'

'And Danny-boy Smith?'

'Aaach!' She made a sound of pure disgust. 'Rubbing his belly past us while we were serving, now and again. I wouldn't take him free with a packet of cornflakes. That was just jealousy, her with eyes like a pair of mortal sins, watching us like a cat. A fine pair they make, her mad-jealous and him bone-mean.'

'Us?'

'Your woman, Davinia, too.'

'But not Beryl?'

'I'm soft, but Beryl can turn nasty, mister.' Tell me about it. 'Besides, she's not his type.'

'Which is?'

She glanced significantly downwards at the still-spectacular chest.

'I see.' At the unintentional *double entendre*, and for the first time during the interview, she smiled.

'OK, so you were upset because your son reappeared and opened up the past; you were fed up with Danny-boy harassing you, and you're now hinting that he was after Davinia as well?'

'I don't know how far that went, do I? We weren't close, and she was — well — a bit sly. So I'm saying nothing about that, right?'

'But there might have been something in it with her?'

She shrugged.

'You're not being exactly helpful, are you?'

'I've worked in pubs for years; I like a bit of a jaw, but I'm not one to flap me mouth and put a man in jail, if that's what you want.'

'I want to know about Danny-boy Smith and his ways.'

'Personally, if it was murders you was looking for, I'd have thought that *she* was more your mark. She doles it out in teaspoons to him, poor feller. You have to laugh; d'ye know she has her door locked half the time, and him in a separate room? Then she wonders why she practically has him climbing out of his tree!'

I grinned across at Maureen, the lady who didn't gossip, the lass who just liked a little bit of a harmless jaw.

'Tell me why you came back,' I said.

'Well, for one thing there's the personal stuff in me house, an' for another I've already written and phoned for me P45.'

'Your tax record? I take it, then, that you've got another job?' At last, Beryl's one-liner, delivered in the stress of battle, was now beginning to make sense.

'In Bridlington; I'm staying out of here.'

'And Smith and his wife have known about this for some time?'

'*She* knew. She tore my letter up, and I could never get hold of him; she told me where she was going to hang my employment record, with a little hole for the nail, when I phoned.'

'Great!' I said, 'so you weren't really missing for long. I suppose,' I added sourly, 'it never occurred to you that you were a witness in a murder enquiry, and you might be required to help the police?'

'With what?' she said opening her eyes wide at the very suggestion. 'I've told you, I know nothing; I've said nothing, nothing whatsoever, at all.'

# Chapter Twenty-Seven

'I wouldn't call it an unauthorised search,' said an unrepentant Pat.

'I would,' replied George. I couldn't make up my mind whether he was flaunting his authority, or merely trying to stir up a bumptious junior for fun. 'What would you call it then?'

'A legitimate purchase from the machine in the bog. I hope they're going to reimburse my quid.'

'Two for a pound, eh? From the Royal Standard pub?' I stared at the green cardboard package on the table between us, the brand name etched in a flowing script across the front, *Glees!* Semi-frivolously, I wondered how the Finance Department was going to take it, detective constables purchasing condoms at the expense of the job.

I picked up the package, green cardboard covered in a plastic wrap. Disappointed, I examined the date on the back, DEC 2001.

'Not a lot of use, is it? Wrong date.'

'Why don't you open the package? That's the expiry date, boss.'

Pat, the rubber products expert; I sighed. George went to fetch our exhibit while I opened the box, and stared uncomprehendingly at the row of carefully spaced dots forming the packing code impressed into the edges of the foils until his return.

'Well?

He pressed an unused foil-covered package against our torn, flattened, carefully preserved exhibit.

'Bingo! The 4th of Feb!'

'*Now* you can do his premises properly,' I said recklessly, 'I'll give you written authority for the search.'

All the same I was uneasy; cast-iron evidence it was not. Precisely how many packets of *Glees!* now nestling in how many vending machines nationwide, had been packed on the fourth of ruddy Feb?

The search team left; I looked at my watch and brooded. I was going to have to talk to Danny-boy tonight, and prisoners were entitled to their beauty sleep according to the rules. George was reluctant, I was gambling, but time was getting on.

He was as friendly and cooperative as we had expected from the start, 'You're living in fantasy land,' he said, head down, staring determinedly at the interview-room desk.

'Your wife—'

'My wife is a crazy jealous cow; she reckons I was slipping that old slapper a length and that's what started the fight.' I paused for a moment, lost in admiration for his delicate turn of phrase.

'Slapper?'

'Slang for tart.'

'Not round here, it isn't; fancy yourself as a big city boy, do you? You've been watching too much TV.'

'You two are wasting your time; are you going to charge me or not?'

'With what?'

'Having a go with the rounders bat. Then we can all go home.'

'You don't seem very worried about Davinia West.'

'That's because I've got nothing to be worried about.'

'When did you last see her?'

'I told you; the Friday night.'

'When on Friday night?'

'Just before midnight; she came in late, so Mary made her stay and wash up.'

'You never saw her on Saturday?'

'I told you that, too.'

'Tell us again.'

'I – did – not – see – her – on – Saturday – because – she took – part – in – the – beauty – contest.'

'And,' said George, 'You – did – not – see – her – again – at – all?'

'No.' He tired of the game immediately. He looked up at George and scowled.

'So you definitely didn't see her on Sunday or Monday, either?'

'No, Sunday was her day off.'

'You didn't go round to her flat?'

'I'd better things to do.'

'You didn't fancy her, then?'

'She was just a girl who worked in the bar. She was all right.'

'A quarter-finalist in the local contest, and she was just all right?'

'OK, she was a looker, so what?'

'And you fancied her?'

No reply.

'Like you fancied Maureen?'

Silence.

'You know, like when you used to rub up against her behind the bar.'

'Bitch,' he muttered. 'Sticking her tits and her arse out all over the place.'

'Davinia?'

'The Irish cow. Know something? She used to work there topless a year or two ago!'

'Before your time,' said George. 'But you fancied a grope and a squeeze now and again, nevertheless?'

'And that was what made Mary jealous, huh?'

'It's no business of yours.'

'Oh, but it is. You made it our business, Danny. What happened on Monday night?'

'When?'

'When you saw Davinia West.'

'Shirley; her proper name was Shirley.'

'Please yourself.'

'Pretending to be something she wasn't; common little piece.'

'Another, er, slapper, perhaps?'

'You needn't play the high and mighty with me, pal; you know very well what I mean.'

'I'm not quite with you, Dan.'

'She was hardly inside the pub door before she was at it. Men!'

'Oh, yes?'

'It sold a few pints for us, though,' he grinned at me salaciously, 'I must admit.'

'These men; tell me who they were.'

'That kid Colin Critchley, for one. She boasted that he was a big rock star: pretending again!'

'Oh, yeah. And then there was his mate?'

'Mate, what mate? Oh, you mean the pretty boy who hung around with him. Bit of a pouf, if you ask me. No, she didn't go after him.'

'Ah, so you're of the same opinion as Paulie Parkes?'

'What?'

'That Nigel was a bit of a pouf?'

'Well, I don't really know. But that was another one after her, Parkes.'

'How do you know that?'

'Stands to reason, dunn'it? Letting her win the contest an' all. She chased anything in trousers to help her get on.'

'And you were the boss, and you were in that position, at least for a time, eh?'

Silence.

'Did she ditch you when something better came along?'

His eyes flickered back and forth, but he made no reply.

'Who else?'

'Well, what about that boat owner? The one she reckoned was a millionaire. Some millionaire; you've got him locked up, so I hear. So why don't you question him?'

'He took her abroad for a bit of how's-your-father, didn't he?'

'Right!'

'And you were pretty upset?'

'I wouldn't say that.'

'Not when she cleared off with him for five days?'

'Oh, that; the business. I see what you mean.'

'Not just the business, Danny; you were after her, too.'

'No.'

'She just waltzed off to Belgium with him, didn't she? Never considered your feelings at all. He gave her presents too. What about the doll?'

'What doll?'

'This one: the one she told you about, from Bruges?' I placed it on the desk in front of him, the skewer through its belly glinting in the cold neon light.

'I don't know what you're talking about.' He stared determinedly in another direction, and suddenly his face looked old.

'OK; but she was playing fast and loose with you, wasn't she? And you went to see her didn't you, on the Monday night?'

'And what was my wife supposed to be doing? You must be cracked.'

'She's not exactly an alibi, is she? It's in both your statements, Danny; you sleep in separate rooms.'

He shrugged.

'Must be a bit frustrating for you . . .' started George, but the landlord was expecting that one, and simply stared.

'You knew about Davinia winning the contest, though?'

'Oh, sure.' His face filled with relief, 'of course I knew. See what you're getting at, now. The girls told me about that.'

'About her winning the contest?'

'Yes.'

'So you didn't go out after closing time on Monday night to have a chat?'

'With Davinia?'

'Shirley,' I said vengefully, 'or Davinia; please yourself.'

'No.'

'I'd now like to show you this exhibit, Danny, DW 1; it's a foil from an empty contraceptive packet we found beside her bed.

'And these; one of my officers recovered this packet from the machine in your pub. They match.'

'So what, there must be thousand of them around.'

'Of course there are. But what would you say if I told you that the packing code shows that they were both packed on exactly the same date?'

'That somebody might or might not have bought them from my machine.' Not happy, but not especially shocked.

'You don't pack them into the vending machine yourself?'

'No, they're a franchise, the agent does it.'

'So you even had to buy your own packets from the machine?'

'You're not getting at me that way!'

'But I am getting *to* you, Danny, eh?'

His lips tightened, and he looked at me through hot, venomous eyes, but you can't use a facial expression as evidence in court.

'Tell me about Wilson.'

'Who?'

'The tramp, the one you used to bully; you took his money but you used to practically make him drink his pint outside.'

'By the door, anyway; he stank.'

'And?'

'And nothing; that's it.'

'They thought he was Pykett, didn't they, Galton and Turner,

Buchanan's little mates? And when they spoke to you, you put two and two together, and jumped to the conclusion that Wilson might be Maureen's ex. That's why they beat him up.'

'So?'

'So they did have a chat with you, beforehand?'

'You trying to pin that on me as well?'

'We've interviewed them, you know. Did they or did they not have a chat with you?'

'Yes, alright they did; but I'd no idea what they were going to do.'

'Of course not, but they pumped you about Ted Wilson, who he was, what he was; right?'

He visibly relaxed, 'As long as you know that what they did was nothing to do with me.'

'Perish the thought!'

'No need for sarcasm; they asked me, I told 'em he was using the name 'Ted', and that he hadn't been around for long: he could have been anybody, OK?'

'And because he could have been anybody, he could have been a rapist called Alan Pykett, 'cos he resembled the photograph they showed you, eh?'

'Yeah,' he was looking even more confident by this time, 'Fancy 'em having a thing like that. Police confidentiality, pah! The coppers really blundered there.' He was openly jeering now.

'Yes,' I admitted, 'we really made a nause-up of that, they even knew about Wilson being a thief.'

'No, not until I told—' He'd fallen, and he knew it. A crude, old-fashioned CID trap.

'That's right,' I said encouragingly, 'you told 'em all right. You told 'em about the stolen purse and the £20 note from the Pavilion Theatre, Danny.

'There's only one thing we can say for you, old son. You didn't walk in cold and rape her, did you? She told you all about Saturday night first, so you must have had quite a chat.'

'I don't know what you're on about, I think you're mad.'

'And you're a liar, remember? You said you'd not seen her at all since the Friday night. She saw Ted Wilson being slung out of the Pavilion on Saturday. She was the only one there who knew him at the theatre, and she didn't tell, so how and when did you find out, Danny? A little stroll round to Cranbourne Avenue, well after closing time on Monday night?'

'You're making this up.'

'She'd been your girlfriend, eh? Wanted her to be a bit more exclusive in her ways? Or did she say no to you on that particular night?'

White face, white at the lips; silence. And he was still in there batting; trying to retrieve whatever he could.

'Maybe I'm wrong; maybe she wasn't your girlfriend at all. Try to persuade her, did you? Pushed it too far, and then . . . ?'

'No.' Employing his wife's trick by this time; his lips scarcely moved.

'Why skewer the doll, Danny? Jealousy? Did you know it was a present from Sheppard on the trip to Bruges? Or were you trying to tell us something; that you'd cracked up temporarily? Or are you really insane?'

'Right at the beginning,' said Danny-boy Smith with icy control, 'you said I could see a solicitor if I wanted. I want one now, and I'm not talking to you any more.'

It was well after midnight before we finished and we were both more than ready to go home. The rest of the CID, or so I thought, had already gone; until Paula came into the room, that is. She walked heavily, almost flat-footed, holding one hand behind her in the hollow of her left hip. In the other she was carrying a drawing pin and an envelope, both of which she dropped on my desk.

I took one look at her tired face, at the make-up in urgent need of renewal, and sat her down.

'I thought you'd gone home hours ago,' I said with contrition, 'sorry, love.'

'I'm not made of eggshells, you know,' she raised a bit of a grin. 'I was still upstairs when you lot went out and did your seventh cavalry stuff; who d'you think has been running the computer system all this time?'

'What about a drink?'

'A drink-type drink? I'm not supposed . . .'

'This isn't the Met, duckey, we've only got coffee – or tea.'

'No thanks; I was on my way home, anyway, when I found this pinned to the back door; it's addressed to you.'

A grubby white envelope this time, and a rusty pin. We all stared at it for a few seconds, and then we did a collective double-take.

'Oh, no; not again!'

'Funny way to deliver it,' said George.

'Funny time of night, too.'

'Could have been there for hours, and nobody noticed until I came along.' She sounded as if she wished she'd missed it herself. 'Go on, open it,' she said.

Even before I opened it, I knew it was nothing pleasant; it's not my sort of luck, and nobody pins messages of love and affection to a police station door. No access to a typewriter, this time; it was written in manuscript today. A semi-decipherable scrawl on a crumpled notelet incongruously decorated with a bunch of flowers.

*'When she's dead,'* she wrote, *'you'll all be able to laugh. She's mad, she's bad, she's sad, isn't she? You'll all be able say that, especially you, Mr Graham, why did you have to send your bullies; why did you hate her so?*

*'Malcolm is an idiot, isn't he? He hasn't got a clue what was going on. All of you pretending, pretending to be nice, and all the time you dragging him down into your own dirty ways. Think I don't know about you all? Filth and Sex, that's all there ever is in the end.'*

There was no signature; no need. Guiltily, midnight or not, tired or not, we stayed and launched some sort of a search. Uselessly trying to live up to the caring police image, you understand, while all the time, unknown to us until days later, Ginny Cartwright was out there somewhere, sucking and rolling, rolling and sucking in the sea at the edge of the retreating tide.

# Chapter Twenty-Eight

Home at three-thirty, back at eight a.m., and in the meantime I was subjected to a degree of domestic flak of the *Where have you been? What have you done? What time do you call this? And all out on the booze, I suppose?* Until I gave her the news, and Angie cried.

With the day in front of me, and a broken night behind, I was not therefore in the mood for Peter Fairfield when he arrived at at eight twenty-five a.m., complete with his usual parcel of fun and games.

'Found her yet?' he grunted by way of greeting.

'No.'

'I don't suppose it's a hoax?'

'I doubt that very much.' I didn't feel like sirring anybody, not after talking to Malcolm, not after our failure to find her last night.

'Saw details of your prisoner,' he continued, not even a change of tone, 'when they sent the divisional bulletin across to Headquarters at seven o'clock.'

Oh good, but I kept the thought to myself: heads of CID have been known to get up early, too. He sprawled out in the visitors' chair and treated me to a sample of his more-in-sorrow-than-in-anger look. There was a tuft of unshorn hair on his cheek parallel with the tip of his left ear lobe; Chief Superintendents can be imperfect too.

'Smith's still in the cells, I take it?' he said.

'Yes, for further enquiries. We don't need to charge him until the full twenty-four hours are over. Thirty-six, if Mr Baring will back us up.'

'He will.'

'I think so, too.'

'Then you can take him before the magistrates for further detention, after that.'

'Yes.'

'And then, when they finally get fed up, you'll have to let him go.'

I kept quiet: thank you for all your sympathy and constructive criticism, Peter. There are times when senior officers get right on your wick.

'The lawyers will never wear it. Far too thin; it'll never get off the ground.'

'You think so?'

'I know so, Bob. The contraceptives were a bit of a coincidence, I grant you, but all you've got is one good lie, a choked-off verbal and a string of chopped-logic on your side.'

'Lousy interview, I'm afraid you ballsed it up.' And all this with that hint of self-satisfaction that commanders employ when it's only a junior, lone and unsupported, whose career prospects look likely to be shot.

'No chance, huh?'

For a flicker of a millisecond, doubt stirred behind his eyes. 'You're looking to further enquiries to save your case?'

'Something like that.' I opened my desk drawer and withdrew the plastic bag. Carefully, employing tweezers and taking infinite care, I teased the earrings from the package and placed them side by side on a clean piece of blotting paper on the desk surface.

'Gold and amethyst; London hallmark, nine carat, with the manufacturer's imprint. Goodall found them wrapped in tissue, behind the soap in a shaving tube in his chest of drawers. Pretty well hidden,' I said.

He pushed one hand forward to touch.

'No!'

I handed him a magnifying glass instead, and pointed. It was one of the few occasions I'd ever used one; I felt just like Sherlock Holmes.

'Blood, I reckon, on that one; a tiny bead, and damage to the victim's ear lobe. It's in the pathologist's report.'

'DNA?'

'Hopefully, yes.'

'Sending it to the laboratory at Huntingdon?'

'Straight away, and we're checking the local jewellers where he must have bought it. Present for the girlfriend at some stage, and then she wouldn't come across. A careful man, Danny, recovering his earrings. Pity he kept them; and not so much careful, I suppose, as mean.'

'You're a jammy bugger,' muttered Detective Chief Superintendent Fairfield staring at me, reluctantly lifting his eye from my glass. Momentarily, he paused, then, memory stirring, he gathered his forces and resumed his role as the man who could never be wrong.

'It's not copper-bottomed until you get the report from the Home Office Lab, of course. And another thing, you haven't found Alan Alfred Pykett yet,' he added reproachfully.